AFRICAN LITERATURE TODAY

12 New Writing, New Approaches

A review
Editor: ELDRED DUROSIMI JONES
Associate Editor: EUSTACE PALMER

Incorporating Cumulative Index
Volumes 1–12

 JAMES CURREY

First published by Heinemann Educational Books 1982

First published in the United States of America 1982
by Africana Publishing Corporation

James Currey, Woodbridge, Suffolk

ISBN 978 1 84701 123 7

Transferred to digital printing

James Currey is an imprint of Boydell & Brewer Ltd
PO Box 9, Woodbridge, Suffolk IP12 3DF, UK
and of Boydell & Brewer Inc.
668 Mt. Hope Avenue, Rochester NY 14620, USA
website: www.boydellandbrewer.com

This publication is printed on acid-free paper

Contents

Editorial

This number is largely devoted to the work of writers whose works have not received much critical attention either because they are relatively new, or because not being what might be described as mainstream they may unintentionally, perhaps, have been damned with faint praise or neglect.

Just as this editorial was about to be drafted Camara Laye, the Guinean novelist and scholar died in Senegal. Tribute is due to him as one of the pioneers of modern African fiction. Each of Camara Laye's three fictional works had a character and atmosphere of its own. *L'Enfant noir* (*The African Child*), the idyll of childhood in Tindican remembered in French surroundings far removed from those earlier scenes of tranquillity, was bathed in a nostalgia which was unlikely to survive the shock of a subsequent encounter. It was not strident enough for some in denouncing colonialism — it was not strident at all — it was quietly assertive of a way of life whose validity within its context needed no defence, but whose vulnerability to threatening forces of change cried out for protection. Ironically only the forlorn weeping matriarch saw any danger. Her tears for a departing son were tears for a doomed way of life.

Le Regard du roi (*The Radiance of the King*) for all — or whatever — its debt to Kafka, was a very original and full working-out of an idea whose germ appeared in various forms in the work of Senghor to the effect that Africa had something to teach Europe:

> For who else would teach rhythm
> to a world that has died of machines
> and cannons?

> or

> Africa is the leaven which the
> white flour needs.

Clarence, the white man in the novel, gradually and painfully finds that the old condescending offer of service or the cosmetic brush against the exotic pleasures of Africa would no longer suffice as commitment. Unless he surrenders himself totally to the will of the king, he is really an irrelevance, even something of a nuisance in Africa. How, one wonders, was this interpreted by the makers of French overseas policy if they read it at all? It is gentle in tone but its meaning is clear. In *Dramouss* (*A Dream of Africa*), the hero looked for grandfather's gold ornaments wrought at the forge only after ritual steps, sacred incantations, the mystical appearances of totemic figures, but found only cheap tinsel. Yet the dream of the black lioness of Africa represented hope for the return of a lost integrity.

Camara Laye was a member of the early wave to whom form was as important as content, though even the brief description above shows how significant the content of his writing was. The silence of his last fifteen years as far as fiction was concerned, was sad for African writing.

Gabriel Okara is no new voice, but while his small body of poetry is very well-known, his novel has had indifferent success. If *The Voice* is ever to make the impact that its social content deserves, it has to overcome the obstacle of the boldly experimental prose which Okara devised for it, which has left it in something of a backwater. Iyasere's vigorous attempt in this issue to 'examine the rhetorical techniques of composition in order to set forth the dialect of the novel's vision' may revive interest in the prose work of a writer who only needs to beat the mystic drum of his poetry to draw dancers into the ring even before the interpreters come in to further instruct their steps. The matter is basically linguistic — lexical and syntactical — and once a quaintness is overcome at that level Okara's serious purpose is by no means remote.

In the vanguard of the new wave of Nigerian playwrights is Femi Osofisan who is a complete man of the theatre. An actor, he appeared in the Nigerian premiere of Soyinka's *Madmen and Specialists*, and he plays Mokan in his own play *The Chattering and the Song* which is discussed in Obafemi's article on 'Revolutionary Aesthetics in Recent Nigerian Theatre'. What is striking in the play is Osofisan's mastery of theatrical art as well as his social message. His use of the play-within-a-play subtly suggests meaningful ironies in the change of rôles assumed by some of the characters. Osofisan's *Once Upon Four Robbers* is apparently not yet available in print but it is a matter of great satisfaction that

The Chattering and the Song has been published in Nigeria. Another growing theatrical voice in Nigeria, Bode Sowande, is also introduced in this issue probing the contemporary social scene.

On the eastern side of the continent, a spate of anti-hero novels has caught the popular attention in a way that Okot P'Bitek's *Songs* created an appetite for popular poetry. The African language play performed at village level may also indicate a way to provide the missing link whose absence Juliet Okonkwo mentioned in *ALT* 10.

An editor feels most inadequate in dealing with South African writing where many worthwhile works are unknown outside the country; there is a general lack of access to the works and a consequent lack of the basis for sound literary judgement. Articles on South African literature thus have to be specially written by 'insiders', having in mind a readership which is unlikely to have had any background knowledge and therefore requiring more help than usual. This requires unusual skill; but we have had, and have been grateful for, such articles in the past.

Sembène Ousmane, whose fame as a film-maker is so well deserved but who is relatively unknown within Africa, has for years seriously portrayed the position of women in a Moslem society which is fast becoming commercially western orientated. Recently, he has reiterated this theme in the novel and the film *Xala*. In this issue a new femininist voice, Mariama Bâ, is introduced in what should be a fruitful new theme in African Literature.

The earlier 'man of two worlds' and imperial themes are beginning to look somewhat distant as African writers continue looking about them, but since human nature seems to alter very little in its essentials it is not in the basic themes that we may expect to see changes; rather it is in the responses to these themes, in the metaphors of their presentation in changing times. Ironically we may often take refuge in history.

The Next Two Numbers

Number 13 will focus once again on the Novel. Articles are invited which will show trends and developments in technique, preoccupation, attitudes etc., of African novelists in general or of particular writers. Regional developments particularly in new or less frequently treated areas will be especially welcome.

Number 14 will be *Africans and Non-Africans Looking at Africa.*
How have the outsiders and the insiders seen Africa? What differences of portrayal have there been between them? What similarities — in structures, theme and sympathetic stance? The starting points for comparative studies are endless. The deadline for the submission of actual articles will be December 1981.

Proposals for articles should be sent with a brief summary to the Editor, Professor Eldred Durosimi Jones:
Principal's Office
Fourah Bay College
University of Sierra Leone
P.O. Box 87
Freetown
Sierra Leone
All articles should be well typed preferably on A4 paper and double spaced. References to books should include the author or editor, place, publisher, date and the relevant pages.

Narrative Techniques in Okara's *The Voice*

Solomon Iyasere

> I think we have spent too much time renovating the shrines of our ancestors. It is time we stepped out into the present to seek the painful truth and meaning buried underneath its bloated surface. Thus our literature must move hurriedly from that of élan vital to that of exploring the anguished state of our present human condition.[1]

It appears there exists a form of conspiracy among critics of modern African literature against the Nigerian writer Gabriel Okara. In spite of the fact that he has distinguished himself as an able poet and novelist, critics still pay little attention to his fiction. Ironically, his poetic 'novel' *The Voice*, one of the finest African novels of social analysis, has received less critical attention than several deodorized, tourist-oriented African novels.

Perhaps the reason for this benign neglect can be traced to the unique character of the novel and the critic's initial response to it. *The Voice* departs from the norm of modern African Literature: it does not deal with the usual externally-directed, anti-colonial theme and the narcissistic glorification of an African past that most African novels indulge in — a theme that attracts critics and publishers of the literature like bees to a hive. It is engaged in extreme experimentation with the English language (its Ijawization), which seems to offend several of the critics' puritan sensibilities. Furthermore, several of the critics who commented on the novel when it first appeared were more visceral in their remarks than cerebral, and unfortunately, a few who attempted to deal with the novel on its own terms were more interested in stressing the literary influences that shaped the work and placing it in the European tradition, than in exploring the unique habitat and vision the novel presents.

What seems baffling in all this is that the unique features of the novel which should strongly recommend it for more vigorous critical attention seem ironically to dissuade critics from attending to it. Is it that we are numbed by creative works of 'self-apprehension' in which the harsh, if nihilistic, *active* social realities are presented?

The Voice is a significant novel in the corpus of African literature which should receive more intense critical attention, especially at this time when African literature is gradually, if grudgingly, moving away from the externally-directed creative works in which the assertion of the African presence is inordinately pursued, to the internally-directed work charged with serious socio-political analysis. *The Voice* belongs to this emerging form of African fiction. The novel forcefully apprehends and explores the lurid, paradoxical state of the Nigerian situation in particular — a society where the vital human values are fast perishing — 'where nothing has any more meaning but the shadow-devouring trinity of gold, iron and concrete', and the amoral human condition in general.

Yet the value of the novel does not lie only in its vision, but also importantly in the various narrative techniques such as its scenic mode of presentation, its sophisticated use of images and symbols, its anthological descriptions, employed by the author to order and give life and vitality to this vision. Thus, my aim here is to examine these rhetorical techniques of composition in order to set forth the dialect of the novel's vision.

The Voice in the Vacuum

The dominant socio-philosophical theme of *The Voice* arises out of Okolo's search for *it*. This search shapes the entire novel and reveals the terrible truth about the empty, meaningless existence of the people of Amatu and Sologa. These peoples' failure to commit themselves to or believe in anything with conviction turns their lives into an absurd charade. Refusing to accept this hollow existence, Okolo determines to resurrect and reassert belief, faith and commitment:

> 'All I want to do in my search,' Okolo spoke out at last, 'is to revitalize my flagging faith, faith, in man, belief in something,' he said with all his inside and his shadow. 'Belief and faith in that something we looked up to in times of sorrow and joy have all been taken away and in its stead what do we have? Nothing but a dried pool with only dead wood and skeleton leaves. And when you question they fear a tornado is going to blow down the houses they have built without foundations.'[2]

As dramatized throughout the novel, the positive-existential view of life directs and shapes Okolo's actions and his relationship to the meaningless outer reality. In the traditional village of Amatu, 'Man has no more shadow, trees have no more shadow. Nothing has any more meaning but the shadow-devouring trinity of gold, iron, concrete. . . . ' (p. 89). Traditional human values are vanishing; the great majority of the people have become content with their private, desperate lives; they no longer have the moral courage and vision to fight for the restoration of these perishing values. With few exceptions, these people have not only divorced and alienated themselves from their true selves but also have come to accept and even celebrate the meaninglessness of their present existence. Out of fear, the people refuse to fight injustice, even those injustices which directly affect their lives; in their moral dissolution they refuse to believe firmly in anything. As a result, they accept the transitory for the external, the mediocre for the excellent.

These are the uncomfortable facts about Amatu that Okolo recognizes upon his return. Unlike these people, Okolo is not satisfied with this futile existence but determines to restore the disintegrating human values — honesty, compassion, and commitment:

> If the masses haven't got *it*, he will create *it* in their insides. He will plant *it*, make *it* grow in spite of Izongo's destroying words. He will uproot the fear in their insides, kill the fear in their insides and plant *it*. He will all these do, if only. . . . (p. 90)

In seeking to achieve this end, Okolo clashes head-on with the corrupt elders of Amatu and Sologa. This contrast sharpens and intensifies the differences between Okolo and the other villagers. In delineating these scenes, Okara will often employ similar but contrasting images and patterns of speech to dramatize and distinguish Okolo's attitude from the others'. Importantly, Okara allows these images and the characters' speech to present and define the essential differences and does not make connections or point contrasts overtly. Character is set against character and scene against scene as if in a play. Okara cues in the reader to this effacement of the authorial voice by deliberately casting the first scene in the dramatic mode. When the first three of Izongo's messengers are sent out to Okolo to deliver the decree of the elders of Amatu concerning his presence and search, Okara subtly presents without comment their groping, stumbling journey through the twilight:

> So the messengers, three messengers, set forth on their timid road for Okolo's house. They walked slowly and then faster, and soon one of them hit his foot against a stone.

First messenger: 'My right foot has hit against a stone.'
Second messenger: 'Is it good or bad?'
First messenger (*Solemnly*): 'It's bad.'
Second messenger: 'Bad? My right foot is good to me.'
Third messenger: 'Your nonsense words stop. These things have meaning no more. So stop talking words that create nothing.'
First messenger: 'To me there is meaning. My right foot always warns me.'
Second messenger: 'To me too there is meaning. If my left foot against something hits as I walk, it's a warning be.'
Third messenger (*With contempt*): 'Nonsense.' (p. 24)

First messenger (*Also angrily*): 'Me know nothing? Me know nothing? Because I went not to school I have no bile, I have no head? Me know nothing? Then answer me this. Your hair was black black be, then it became white like a white cloth and now it is black black be more than blackness. The root, what is it? You keep quiet. Answer me. I know nothing, you say.'
　Second messenger (*Throws his eyes back and front, left and right and speaks with lowered voice*): 'Speak of this thing no more. The ears of Amatu are open. If this the ears of Izongo enters, we will fall from our jobs. You know this yourselves. As for me (*shrugs his shoulders*), if the world turns this way I take it; if it turns another way I take it. Any way the world turns I take it with my hands. I like sleep and my wife and my one son, so I do not think.' (p. 25)

Second messenger (*Lowering his voice to the ground*): 'Talk not like this, hold yourself. I tell you, yourself hold before this thing a big thing turns.'
　These teaching words their ears entered and their insides entered. So they locked every word carefully in their insides as they silently walked towards Okolo's house without their mouths opening. (pp. 25–6)

In this crucial episode, the physical act of striking one's foot against a stone is, for the first and second messengers, a symbolic event pregnant with meaning. To them this incident is an omen presaging bad luck. The insistence of the third messenger on the absurdity of believing in omens reflects the denial of imaginative meaning in this society. Not yet persuaded that all language is nonsense, is meaningless, the first messenger affirms through dramatic metaphor the superficiality of the third messenger. Just as the roots of his hair, where the colour should be determined, have nothing to do with the actual colour of his hair, so the roots of language, the basic meaning of words, have nothing to do with the words he speaks. The essence of his hair, like the essence of his language, should shape the outer form. But for the third messenger, so deeply steeped in but afraid of Izongo's ways, appearance is all. Disregarding the root, he can modulate reality to suit whatever the occasion demands, so that the superficial and external becomes the real. Interestingly, it is the second messenger, the one for whom the stubbing of his toe has meaning, who understands the metaphor and applies it to himself, although he too leads a chameleon existence.

At this point, the second messenger recalls the omnipresence of Amatu's ears. If they insist on exploring the reality behind the façade and attribute significance and meaning to words and events, they will lose the material benefits provided by Izongo and his corrupt regime. In Amatu, the appearance of value and of meaning is the only value there is, for the reality is consistently suppressed and denied. What is real is what is tangible and perceivable by the senses. Any other level of meaning or of reality, any symbol-making, cannot be. The idols of 'gold, iron, concrete' persuade even the first messenger so that he too abandons meaning for money, just as 'the whiteman' in Sologa will do. The potential is in Amatu, as the initial responses of the first and second messengers testify, but this is buried beneath the burden of 'gold, iron, concrete'.

In this way, the scene progresses from the assertion and discussion of meaning, to the denial of meaning, and finally to silence. To the same fate, Izongo and the elders of Amatu will subject Okolo, literally 'the voice'. They will discuss Okolo's fate, deny him a place among them, and ultimately commit him to the silence of the river, just as the three messengers have buried 'the voice' within themselves. The movement of this first scene dramatically encapsulates the movement of the entire novel. Though the stubbing of the toe is a meaningful event to the first two messengers, they are urged and finally persuade themselves to go on as if nothing had happened. In a similar fashion, the river, at once an image of life and of death, the source and end of all things, will roll over the 'debris' of Okolo and Tuere tied together in the canoe, falter momentarily, and then flow smoothly on 'as if nothing had happened' (p. 127).

In the opening scene the author does not substitute personal appearances for artistic rendering. He allows us to see the messengers, to see the people of Amatu, in action, confining themselves and the values of their past in the empty materialism of the present. Because we see these messengers lock themselves up just as they lock up the meaning of their 'teaching words' within themselves, we are allowed to see them and the other people of Amatu as Okolo sees them. The presentational, dramatic mode sets up this 'symbolic scene' for the reader and allows him to perceive the function and significance of the scene for himself. The author does not intrude to guide his audience but lets his images and symbols do the task.

Set against this physical journey of the three messengers who deny meaning, Okara depicts the metaphorical journey of Okolo who seeks meaning and affirms the continuity and vitality of life:

> It was the day's ending and Okolo by a window stood. Okolo stood looking at the sun behind the tree tops falling. The river was flowing, reflecting the finishing sun, like a dying away memory. It was like an idol's face, no one knowing what is behind. Okolo at the palm trees looked. They were like women with hair hanging down, dancing, possessed. Egrets, like white flower petals strung slackly across the river, swaying up and down, were returning home. And, on the river, canoes were crawling home with bent backs and tired hands, paddling. A girl with only a cloth tied around her waist and the half-ripe mango breasts, paddled, driving her paddle into the river with a sweet inside. (p. 26)[3]

Characteristically, to Okolo the face of the sun is 'like an idol's face' and though no one knows what is behind, he believes that there is something behind; that the face, the appearance, is not everything but that the larger reality is hidden, submerged and enigmatic. Okolo views the entire scene before him in terms of metaphor: the palm trees are like women with hair hanging down; the egrets are like white flower petals; the canoes are human; the girl's breasts are half-ripe mangoes. These metaphors suggest the interconnectedness, the continuity of life which is also imaged in the flowing river, implying a greater reality behind the surface of things. This way of seeing is akin to the first and second messengers' notion that stubbing one's toe means something, but is more sensitive, more refined and fully developed. Rather than suppress and deny the meaning behind things, Okolo seeks it out. Appropriately, Okara depicts what Okolo sees in terms of metaphor, in direct contrast to the materialism of the messengers and of the other people of Amatu. The contrast between the two ways of seeing is accented by Okara's juxtaposition of contrasting scenes and characters, a technique of imagist presentation which effectively dramatizes Okolo's search, his alienation from his people, and the terrible emptiness of those who are unlike him.

Okara consistently portrays the inhabitants of Amatu as hollow, faceless masses. They are people without 'a strong inside', without 'shadow or chest', and people whose lives are devoid of any moral value. In portraying their facelessness, Okara again employs the technique of juxtaposition we have seen him use in shifting from the depiction of the three messengers to the description of Okolo. Having set scene against scene, he now sets character against character, defining the peoples' sameness as played off against the individuality of Okolo and Tuere. Like the 'larger and darker clouds, some to frowning faces, grimacing faces changing, were skulking past without the moon's ring, suffocating the stars until they too lost themselves in the threatening conformity of the dark cloud beyond' (p. 26), the messengers and the other people of Amatu gather near Okolo's home. Again and again Okara refers to them using terms which reiterate their facelessness; they are 'the people', or 'a crowd, a crowd of men, women and children talking, whispering, and three men talking and gesticulating in front' (p. 27). Unlike Okolo, they remain nameless; any one of them who does act alone is 'a man', or 'somebody'. And when they attack Okolo, they remain a nameless, anonymous mass, constantly referred to as 'they' in contrast to Okolo whose name is often reiterated:

> The four of them put their heads together while with their eyes they looked at Okolo. They put their heads together for awhile and walked towards Okolo, as if stalking an animal. And Okolo stood looking. They moved nearer. Okolo stood. They moved nearer and suddenly, pounced on Okolo. Okolo and the men fell to the ground. Hands clawed at him, a thousand hands, the hands of the world. Okolo twisted, struggled and kicked with all his shadow, with all his life and, to his astonishment, he saw himself standing free. He ran. Running feet followed. He ran. A million pursuing feet thundered after him. He ran past his house without knowing and ran into another. A woman giving suck to her baby screamed. Out Okolo sprang and ran. The running feet came nearer, the caring-nothing feet of the world. Okolo turned a corner and nearly ran into a boy and girl standing with hands holding each other. They did not look at him. He turned a corner. A dog barked at him. Okolo ran. (pp. 27–8)

The effectiveness of this description of the flight and pursuit of Okolo derives largely from the cinematic effect achieved through the juxtaposition and alternation of descriptions of the pursuers and the pursued. Okara shifts from describing Okolo to describing the mass following him without using connectives. The simple, often stark sentences which describe the action are strung together without transition from one to the next, just as the scenes in the novel are set against one another without overt connections between them.

This amorphous mass of inhumanity pursuing Okolo is further set apart by their silence. Having denied 'the voice' within, the meaningfulness of self, they cannot speak, they 'opened not their mouths. The remaining crowd hushed. The silence passed silence. The three messengers faced Okolo, opening not their mouths' (p. 27). After their abortive pursuit of Okolo, they huddle together, 'talking and arguing', but the sound they generate is indistinct, inhuman, a drone like the buzzing of flies, in contrast to the voice of Tuere:

> Faces, a mass of faces glistening with sweat in the moonlight stood, talking, arguing. Grim faces like the dark mysterious forest afire with flies. Then a shadow blocked his view, then silence. And a voice clear and cool like a glass of water, from the standing shadow sallied forth. (p. 28).

The people's fear of themselves, their lack of moral courage and commitment to any positive value, enables Chief Izongo, the embodiment of moral decadence and political corruption, to manipulate and coerce the people into accepting his corrupt, hypocritical mode of existence; they have become 'a mass of grim faces'. What makes the whole absurd situation more tragic is that some members of Amatu, much as Okolo, are able to perceive and acknowledge their valueless existence, Chief Izongo's moral bankruptcy, and his vicious schemes to deny the inhabitants of Amatu their individuality and humanity, but they do nothing to change the situation. In contrast to Okolo's view of life, Tebeowei's attitude is characteristic: 'Everything in this world has changed. The world is no longer straight. So if a person turns his palms down I also turn mine down. If he turns them up, opens them and shows them to the eye of the sky, I also turn mine up and show them to the eye of the sky' (p. 49). Unlike Tebeowei, Okolo's inside 'is not filled with money, cars and concrete houses'; he is committed to seeking the truth, and to the restoration of those vanishing traditional human values which once gave life in Amatu meaning and vitality:

> 'If you put a black paint over a white paint, does it mean there is no white paint? Under the black paint the white paint is still there and it will show when the black paint is rubbed off. That's the thing I am doing — trying to rub off the black paint. Our fathers' insides always contained things straight . . . Our insides were also clean and we did the straight things until the new time came. We can still sweep the dirt out of our houses every morning.' (p. 50)

The conformity and facelessness revealed in the first messenger's metaphor (affirmed in Tebeowei's and the second messenger's confessions) is pointedly dramatized in the automatic, conditioned responses of the villagers of Amatu to Izongo's commands, as during the 'trial' of Okolo:

> On seeing Okolo standing in his front, Chief Izongo with a jug of palm-wine in his hand, laughed loud and long and then suddenly stopped. The Elders around him all looked at him.
> 'Laugh!' he commanded, and the Elders opened their mouths showing their teeth like grinning masks and made a noise that could hardly pass for laughter. (p. 41)

> 'And to show that there is nothing else in your insides you will your hands raise when I ask the question again. Anyone who raises not his hand I know is not one of us. Now this is my questioning word: Did I say I was going to answer Okolo's question by deed?'
> Hands flew up with the precision of drilling soldiers even before Chief Izongo went half-way through his questioning words. Some both hands raised and, one who thought his hands went up before any other waved them so as to catch Chief Izongo's eyes. (p. 46)

The only one who will not conform to Chief Izongo's demands is Okolo:

> But Chief Izongo's eyes were not for those he had put into his bag. Who, he thought in his inside, was his last obstacle was in his front standing and the way he looked at Okolo seemed as if he wanted to look him to death. With his eyes still on Okolo he sat slowly down and ordered the palmwine to be passed round. (p. 46)

Unlike the Elders, Okolo does not laugh on command but smiles his own smile when he wants to, a smile which raises fear in Chief Izongo: 'With a smile in his mouth, Okolo looked at Izongo and fear snaked towards Izongo's inside and he gulped down a mouthful of palmwine. So when Okolo said with smile smile in his mouth that he would keep his thoughts in his inside if his hands were untied Chief Izongo's jug stopped at his lips' (p. 46). Because his hands are tied, Okolo's hands do not shoot up in response to Chief Izongo's question, but Izongo knows well that even if untied, Okolo's hands would not respond. He will not untie them until Okolo agrees to be one of them, an agreement Okolo will never make:

> 'Keeping your thoughts in your inside alone will not do,' Chief Izongo said grinning. 'Your hands will only be untied if you agree to be one of us.'
> 'No!' Okolo said. 'No, never!' (p. 47)

This dramatic conflict between Okolo and Chief Izongo, between

Okolo and the land of his forefathers, necessitates Okolo's imposed exile, his ostracism by his people. The gulf between Okolo and the others of Amatu is made a physical reality, the only kind of reality these people can comprehend.

The effectiveness of this dramatic mode of presentation cannot be over-emphasized. The event itself, rather than the overt attitude of the narrator, dominates. The reader listens to no one but the characters themselves, who move as if upon a stage. For these reasons, this technique creates and sustains an immediacy of effect. In allowing us to see Izongo directly and the other members of Amatu society in action, the author compels us to experience the people's moral decadence and the absurdity of the master-slave relationship that exists between Izongo and the villagers. At the same time, we can respond immediately to Okolo's struggle and his moral commitment to releasing the villagers from their moral and political bondage. Here, as throughout the novel, Okara dramatizes rather than explicates the political hypocrisy and moral bankruptcy of Izongo and the Elders of Amatu, who exploit the weakness of the masses for their own political and economic advantage. But this disease and the absurdity it makes of human existence is not limited to Izongo and Amatu; it also infects Sologa which is ruled by another embodiment of corruption, 'Big Man'. We learn, with Okolo, that the terrible reduction of life to material concerns has spread far beyond the confines of Amatu to become a general infection.

In presenting Okolo's symbolic journey to an exile in Sologa, Okara continues to employ the dramatic technique that has worked so well in the first part of the novel. Without any explicit narrative transition, Okara turns directly to the depiction of the scene aboard the boat taking Okolo to Sologa:

> The outboard engine-canoe laboured against the strong water of the river. It was the rain's time . . . Slowly, slowly the canoe moved like the walk of an old man.
> Okolo opened his eyes and looked in front of him. The people were sleeping. He looked towards his left. The people were sleeping. He looked towards his right. The people were sleeping. A man was snoring, and saliva flowing like an okra soup out of his mouth's corner. A woman, wearing an accra suit, though sleeping, held firmly her playing child sitting astride her lap . . . A fat man with a belly like an oil puncheon, was breathing like a man blowing a fire, with his mouth open wide. He wore a dark singlet reaching down to only his navel and the sides were bursting. . . .
> And next to Okolo on his left hand side, a girl sat. She rested her head

on his shoulder, sleeping. She must have killed sixteen years. If not, she must have less or little more years killed. But she had reached a woman. Her breasts were standing and were not fallen. They were standing and were calabash breasts. She was dressed in an accra suit. A new one. Okolo had not heard a word coming out of her mouth, even when she had not slept. Silence, she was, itself. No, she was silent more than silence. She rested her head on Okolo's shoulder, sleeping. Next to her a woman sat, sleeping. She was sleeping and yet talking. Okolo looked at her. She must have killed forty to fifty years, for her hair was dark-brown instead of black. She must have dyed her hair which was now fading. But she was sleeping and yet talking. Okolo looked at her. Then she coughed and opened her eyes. Okolo quickly removed his eyes. (pp. 58–9)

In his analysis of this episode, Eustace Palmer is correct when he writes: 'The canoe is a microcosm of Amatu and Sologa society, and the sleeping passengers symbolically demonstrate the spiritual lethargy and complacency of that society. Okara sketches in their qualities, presenting the unattractive, unpleasant people as braggarts with hard, loud voices, and honest ones — Okolo and the sixteen-year-old girl — as silent.'[4] The sleep of the people, their torpor, is a spiritual sleep, a moral torpor.

Like the people of Amatu, their concern is only with material acquisition. The 'philosophy' they espouse is philistine. So dedicated are they to the gods of 'gold, iron, concrete' that they exploit even their own children as a means of obtaining wealth. The grotesque fat man, whose body is a testament to his over-indulgence and laxity, 'had told everybody loudly that he had, with his cooking, sent his son to college. His son would soon finish and join the Council and then money "like water flow" he had said, rubbing his hands, and laughed a laugh which made the groaning engine sound like the feeble buzz of a mosquito' (pp. 58–9). Like this man's hollow, raucous laughter which reduces the roar of the canoe's engine to the feeble buzz of a mosquito, the voice of the woman with the dyed hair had 'torn to pieces the engine's sound' (p. 59). Like the fat man, this woman has passed on to her son a legacy of cupidity, and taught him to use formal education not to advance his mind or to liberate him from the abysmal corruption of society, but to fatten his pocketbook, 'her son having passed standard six the previous year was now a clerk. A heap of money he was earning and the girl was his wife' (p. 59). The relationship of children to parents is not one of love and respect, but a legal contract of financial indebtedness. Because the fat man paid for his son to go to college, his son will now repay him when money 'like water flow';

because the woman paid for her son's training and his job and his wife: 'Her son to whatever she said must listen' (p. 60). The same enslavement to 'gold, iron, concrete' is shared by the man with the saliva flowing from his mouth. A policeman, he has through bribery 'taken home bags of money and was now returning to Sologa' (p. 60). With the exception of the young girl who keeps silent, and of Okolo through whose eyes we see this mercenary baggage, the people aboard this canoe substitute money for meaning.

This abuse of what is meaningful and valuable in life extends also to the abuse of language: the fat man talks loudly and endlessly; the policeman 'seemed not to have tired of talking'; and the lady with the dyed hair talks even in her sleep. All of their words, like themselves, are dedicated to the concerns of money. The abuse of language in all its forms, so well demonstrated in the empty rhetoric of Izongo's adviser with his MA and PhD degrees, is repeated here by the people aboard the canoe in their cacophonous declarations of gain. Though Okolo had naïvely hoped to find in Sologa people whose insides were like his own (p. 51), he only finds empty people who are the same as those of Amatu:

> Okolo did not move from his bed. There he remained talking with his inside until sun down. Nobody sees what he sees. His talking seems to him throwing words away like one who throws money into the river. That's what they think. But they do not see it in their insides that words and money are not the same thing. Money may be lost forever but words, teaching words, are the same in any age . . . He will continue to speak the straight thing at all times, though Woyengi knows, it is the hardest thing to do in these new times. But continue he will, so long as they do not sew his mouth up with needle and thread. . . . (pp. 51–2).

These new times that Okolo determines to conquer are so lost to money that even those who have none can talk of nothing else, as the man with the black suit aboard the boat testifies. For the people of Amatu and Sologa, for the entire world which has any relevance to Okolo, money has replaced meaning and metaphorical language is, as the third messenger insists, 'nonsense'.

In this absurd, meaningless world of Amatu and Sologa, Okolo is not only alienated from the people, as is Tuere, but also denied the smallest vestiges of human contact. In the society Okara consistently portrays, flesh does not touch flesh; genuine human relationships no longer exist. Okolo is vigorously repudiated and accused of committing an act of defilement for his compassion in protecting the sixteen-year-old girl from the violent storm.

Okolo's castigation for this innocent action dramatizes the depth of the moral corruption of the people. They have become so rotten that they cannot see anything but defilement and evil in any act, no matter how innocent. Though the young girl, like Okolo and Tuere, speaks the 'straight thing', her words do not convince her mother-in-law (pp. 102–4), not even when supported by Okolo's oath sworn to by Amadosu, the things of the ground, and the dead (p. 109). While it may at first seem encouraging to find in this warped world the sixteen-year-old girl who does speak 'the straight thing', the infectious evil of her mother-in-law affects everything, even Okolo, causing him to change his actions and question himself. On his return journey to Amatu, Okolo is careful not to touch anyone again (pp. 110–12).

Okolo's ostracism in Sologa, to which this event with the girl contributes, is apparent from the first day of his arrival there. As in the scene on the boat, Okolo, and through him the reader, come to a full realization of the degeneracy of the hollow world of Sologa and his alienation from that world, with Okolo's imprisonment in the dark room:

> The voice chuckled and said: 'We are taking you to a place where you can find *it.*' At this two chunks of darkness detached themselves from the darkness and gripped Okolo's hands and pushed him through the black black night like the back of a cooking pot. . . .
> Okolo for years and years lay on the cold cold floor at the rock-like darkness staring. Then suddenly he saw a light. He drew his feet with all his soul and his feet came. He drew his hands and his hands came. He stood up with his eyes on the light and walked towards the light. As he moved towards the light the light also moved back. He moved faster and the light also moved faster back. Okolo ran and the light also ran. Okolo ran, the light ran. Okolo ran and hit a wall with his head. Okolo looked and the light was no more. He then stretched his hands forth and touched the wall. His fingers felt dents and holes. Okolo walked sideways like a crab with his fingers on the wall, feeling dents and holes, dents and holes in the rock-like darkness until his feet struck an object. As Okolo stopped and felt the object his body became cold. His heart-beat echoed in the rock-like darkness and his head expanded. Still, he felt along the object until his fingers went into two holes. As his fingers went into the holes he quickly withdrew them and ran. He ran and fell, ran and fell over other objects. He ran and knocked against the wall and fell. Still he ran, then suddenly stopped. He saw a light in front of him. He moved gently crouching forward like a hunter stalking game. Then when he nearly reached the light, he rushed forward. (pp. 76–7)

Okolo's imprisonment in the dark room, the thematic and structural centre of Okara's novel, symbolically dramatizes Okara's pessimistic vision of the society in which Okolo lives. By imprisoning Okolo in Sologa, Izongo's messengers reveal their familiarity with and acceptance by Sologa; both cities reject the quest for meaning and the restoration of the traditional values. In this prison the people of Sologa and Amatu have made by themselves for themselves, the discarded skeletons represent the remains of what used to be real. They are all that is left of those values that once invested life with meaning and significance, all that remains of the people who held those values. In a sense, the people of Amatu and Sologa come to regard the quest for meaning as the quest for death.

The fact that there is, for Okolo, a way out of this dark tomb seems to suggest that there is some hope of resurrecting meaning and values. But that hope will flicker and disappear — like the light Okolo follows — unless kept alive by the stubborn effort of the truly alive, such as Okolo and Tuere, or even the carver, whose 'sweetness of his inside is in finding it' (p. 85). But the hope the light promises is faint and dies, just before Okolo comes upon the skull; he cannot see what is before him but he can touch it; the fact of his own death, in a sense, becomes a tangible reality just as his metaphoric search takes on a physical reality in this scene. The death of vitality and of meaningful existence, suggested by the skull, presages Okolo's own death, particularly since the flickering light recalls the ominous fire in Tuere's hut. The single flame which flickers and dies and then shoots up and burns passionately as twin flames, dramatizes imagistically the union in love and death of Okolo and Tuere:

> Then suddenly Okolo heard walking feet. Feet walking towards the dying embers at the hearth. Then he saw the embers move and glow like a new-appearing sun or a going-down sun. Then he saw splinters of firewood drop on the embers. And then he heard her trying to blow the embers to living flames. She blew, blew, blew and blew, but the embers only glowed not responding like a god more sacrifice demanding. They only glowed showing a face intent in supplication. She continued to blow, her breath continuing in soft gusts. Then a token flame shot up momentarily and died. . . .
> Then there were more blowings. Then suddenly a twin flame shot up. The twin flame going into one another and becoming one, grew long and short, spread, twisted and danced, devouring the essence of the firewood like passion. (p. 33)

The interlocking of these episodes, the meeting and union of Okolo and Tuere, Okolo's imprisonment, and the death of the two are also imagistically linked to the opening and closing parts of the novel. When we first see Okolo it is sunset; when we last see him it is sunrise, represented in this scene by the embers which 'Move and glow like a new-appearing sun or a going-down sun'. From the outset of his quest, then, Okolo's fate seems inevitable, a fate symbolically and tangibly realized in the imprisonment of Okolo in the dark room.

With Okolo's escape from the room, Okara reinforces what his symbolic scene has intimated. The frustration of Okolo's effort by the policeman and the policeman's denial that there are any human bones in the Big Man's house reaffirm the destruction and denial of values and truth which the 'burial' of Okolo with the skeletons portrayed:

> 'And the people dragged you away?'
> 'Yes, people dragged me away and put me in the dark room with bones like. . . . '
> 'Not so fast. People dragged you away and put you in the dark room. Yes?'
> 'With bones like human. . . . '
> 'Ssh! This is not a true thing. So do not say it. People will believe not. Did you with your eyes see the bones?'
> 'No, I felt one.'
> 'Aha.'
> 'It's true!'
> 'Aha, it's true, but with your eyes you saw it? This man a big man be.'
> 'Let's go to the house and — '
> 'My Jesus! I have a family, man! — a wife and two children and one is in college. My Jesus, go to the big man's house and look for human bones? You are an intelligent man be.' (p. 79)

The policeman finally ignores Okolo and leaves him talking to himself. Determined to believe and act as if nothing had happened, the policeman eliminates all traces of his encounter with Okolo:

> With this the constable this way and that way looked and walked towards the direction of the house. And when he saw Okolo no more, entered a telephone booth. He brought out the piece of paper on which he had written Okolo's statement and putting it into his mouth, chewed it. Then he came out and went to a bar and washed it down with a beer! (p. 80)

The policeman physically internalizes and eliminates the truth Okolo brings to light. In a similar way, the people of Amatu and Sologa have internalized, buried and will finally eliminate the truth about themselves that Okolo represents. What is metaphorically true will be made literally true; Okolo has already been 'internalized' by being buried in the dark room; it only remains for his inevitable fate to be fulfilled. Like the policeman, the people of Sologa and Amatu ultimately deny Okolo's very existence. The people of Sologa ostrasize him and send him 'home' to Amatu where his journey brings him to the death which the imprisonment in Sologa foreshadowed:

> When day broke the following day it broke on a canoe aimlessly floating down the river. And in the canoe tied together back to back with their feet tied to the seats of the canoe, were Okolo and Tuere. Down they floated from one bank of the river to the other like debris, carried by the current. Then the canoe was drawn into a whirlpool. It spun round and round and was slowly drawn into the core and finally disappeared. And the water rolled over the top and the river flowed smoothly over it as if nothing had happened. (p. 127)

There are a few who will refuse to act as if nothing had happened. There rests the faint chance that in the efforts of the cripple, Ukule, Okolo's teaching words will not die. Ukule has spoken of Tiri who claims that he, like Okolo, will speak out. After the return of Okolo to Amatu, Izongo's celebration is brought to an end:

> But the drums, the singers and the dancers were lifeless like soup without pepper and after a small time Izongo raised his hand to stop the celebrations. When everything stopped he stood up from his seat and without a word he left, followed by the Elders to their meeting place. And the people began to move away silent. The dancers and singers, their bodies became cold and they moved away, silent; and the drummers their fingers became fingers of a shadow on a wall and they moved away and the drums lay silent, dumb. (p. 122)

The people are lifeless and silent because their life, their 'voice' is gone. Izongo stops the celebration to plan the death of Okolo; with that act, Izongo has finally deprived the people of Amatu of the one who stood for vitality and strength and meaning. That Okolo's teaching words will not die remains only a promise on the lips of an old cripple. The young, strong, wise Tiri of whom Ukule spoke has not yet raised his voice. We have heard the promise but have not seen in action the change Tiri spoke of. With the deaths of Okolo and Tuere there is only a faint hope, like that flickering flame, that the vanishing human values which they embodied will ever be restored.

The success of *The Voice* lies in Okara's ability to employ the various rhetorical devices of fiction to apprehend, explore, and concretize Okolo's desperate quest for meaning in the tragically empty worlds of Amatu and Sologa. Okolo's world, dominated as it is by social injustice, corruption and spiritual emptiness, presents a lurid, anguished reality analogous to the quotidian reality of Nigeria today. No other Nigerian novel, so far, has captured this reality with greater depth, freshness and sensitivity.

NOTES

1. Solomon O. Iyasere, 'Lecture Notes on African and World Literature', unpublished paper.
2. Gabriel Okara, *The Voice*, London, Heinemann, (AWS 68), New York, Africana Publishing Corporation, 1970, pp. 88–9. All further references, which are incorporated into the text, are to this edition.
3. For a detailed analysis of this passage see my article 'Oral Tradition in the Criticism of African Literature', *The Journal of Modern African Studies* XIV, 2, Cambridge, 1976, pp. 112–13.
4. Eustace Palmer, *An Introduction to the African Novel*, London, Heinemann, 1972, New York, Africana Publishing Corporation, 1972, p. 163.

Individualism and Community in the Theatre of Serumaga

Andrew Horn

After several well-received international tours of his plays by his own Theatre Limited — Abafumi Company,[1] Robert Serumaga has probably become the best-known East African dramatist to audiences outside the region. This is a result not only of his dedication to the theatre but of his extraordinary entrepreneurial ability, a commercial and publicity sense at least comparable to his acting, directorial and writing talents.[2] But while his skills as a theatre craftsman have been generously acknowledged, and his ambitions as a political figure have been widely noted, Serumaga has often been bitterly criticized for an apparent lack of social commitment and political concern in his plays,[3] quite contrary to most of his contemporaries in East African theatre. This apartness is the inevitable consequence of a radical individualism, tending distinctly towards solipsism, which characterizes all his central characters. It is not that the social and political are absent, for they form the necessary back-drop to each of his five plays and his novel. But however social and political issues may precipitate crises in Serumaga's work, they are never closely examined, receding quickly into the middle distance. For Serumaga's Olympian protagonists are always men apart, what Herman Melville called *isolatoes*,[4] cut off not only from nation and community but from friends, family and, in the final exigency of alienation, from self, by madness, hallucination and self-deception.

However self-indulgent they may be, these artists and intellectuals live in a terrifying loneliness. The sensitive individual of heightened, if distorted, perception must face alone the horrors of failure, public exposure and painful self-knowledge. He inevitably bears, in the pattern of romantic individualism, a deep wound, a secret sin, an unrevealed weakness which he tries to conceal behind an elaborate performance. For Serumaga's main protagonist is always an actor: a player, a compulsive raconteur with a slick music-hall patter, whose extravagant rationalizations are woven out of ironic quips and baroque fictions. In the end, however, this central figure — essentially the same character throughout Serumaga's work despite variations of circumstance — is forced to acknowledge that beneath his histrionics, cynicism and cavalier postures of self-confidence, he is a failure.

Serumaga is concerned with both the agony of self-discovery and the tragic collapse of the gifted deceiver. But it is never the character's failure alone. Society is always shown to have betrayed him and forced him into compromise, deceit and degradation; it is, therefore, civil community and its directive polities which Serumaga most condemns. It is this particular attack, not on specific social structures but on human community itself, which goes so abrasively against the grain of East African writing and theatre. For while John Ruganda may call for a moral renewal in *Black Mamba*,[5] Ngugi wa Thiong'o for economic and political reconstruction in *The Trial of Dedan Kimathi*[6] and *Ngaahika Ndeenda*,[7] Elvania Zirimu for the revision of traditional social codes in *Family Spear*,[8] Byron Kawadwa for the humanization of administrative authority in *Oluyimba lwa Wankoko*,[9] Chris Mukiimbi for a reassessment of Buganda's feudal past in *Kikwambaga*,[10] and Nuwa Sentongo for the revaluation of perception and inter-personal obligations in *The Invisible Bond*,[11] only Serumaga rejects the very possibility of progress in confederation. In Serumaga, Hell is not only within oneself but, as for the closeted travellers in Sartre's *Huis clos*, 'other people'.[12]

Serumaga's formative theatre experiences were, unlike most of his East African contemporaries, in Europe where as an undergraduate in Dublin and later as a radio producer in London,[13] he not only saw a good deal of professional theatre but acted on stage and television. Perhaps of greater significance, however, to his development both as actor and playwright (and an influence neglected by other critics) was Serumaga's work in variety and revue as a 'stand-up' comedian. No one in the theatre is more isolated and exposed than the solitary 'stand-up comic', precariously negotiating the shifting moods and disparate interests of an often vocally critical audience, without the support of elaborate staging and, above all, without other actors.[14] This unique loneliness seems to have been for Serumaga emblematic of the isolation of the artist-intellectual. For each of his main characters is a solo showman and each of the plots pivots on this single self-dramatizing figure — one deeply defined introspective Consciousness — around whom other, flatter characters are used merely as foils.

Nihilism and Foreclosure: A Play (1967)

Serumaga's first staged play was Elizabeth Keeble's Theatre Limited production at Kampala's National Theatre of A Play, in October 1967.[15] Performed, like several of his subsequent pieces, without act, scene or interval divisions, A Play was written for a conventional box set, proscenium arch and an essentially naturalistic *mise en scène*, although overlaid by an expressionist dream-play. He was later to move farther and farther away from these conservative stage conventions: towards the spareness of absurdist theatre in *Majangwa* (1971); the explosive staging of Grotowski and African ritual in *Renga Moi* (1972); and *Amanyakiriti* (1977).

On the anniversary of his wife's mysterious death, Mutimukulu, the main protagonist of A Play, is haunted by an unfocused sense of guilt, precipitating the long central dream sequence in which several vaguely threatening characters remind Mutimukulu of his moral culpability and his human vulnerability. These figures include a distinctly Beckettian pair called John and Peter who, strongly reminiscent of Vladimir and Estragon in *Waiting for Godot*,[16] spend most of their stage time at 'play' (hence the title): 'Let's play a game about death' (p. 93). The action is largely made up of these games: the game of the wife's re-murder (pp. 80–2); the game of 'Heavensgate' (pp. 93–4); and the game of the hanging (p. 95).

In what is the most direct statement of the play's theme, the Head of Mukasa, the Kiganda[17] thunder god,[18] speaks of a guilt that must eventually reveal itself, of lies that must return to harry the liar like a horned leopard:

> Mutimukulu, what have you done? . . .
> I am Mukasa, God of thunder and lightning.
> I am crime-is-dry-meat-that-never-rots.
> I am poison, which once eaten will show up sometime.
> Death holds no secrets for me, and I dig guilt out of the darkness of men's souls. . . .

There is an anthill where I am sitting,
And you and the truth have parted, and gone your different ways.
When you meet on the other side of the raised ground,
The truth will have become a leopard with horns on its head.
Will you let it eat you, or will you speak out in its face? (p. 57)

It is significant that this moral foreclosure is pronounced by Mukasa, whom John Roscoe identifies as 'the god of plenty', 'a benign god . . . sought to heal the bodies and minds of men',[19] and whom Sir Apolo Kagwa describes as:

> . . . very good and kind . . . consider[ing] everybody his child, never killing anyone. Whenever he came around all the prisoners on his estates were set free. Whenever a priest committed an offence for which he was to be killed Mukasa offered a bull in his stead. . . . [20]

Here even the forces of increase and renewal are turned against the *isolato* and become the agents of reduction, slaughter and dissolution.

But if Mutimukulu's torment is guilt, Serumaga never clarifies the reason for it. The wife, Rose, seems to have been shot accidentally by her lovers — perhaps John and Peter (p. 80, p. 100) — who meant to kill Mutimukulu in a chieftaincy struggle (p. 79). Her adultery makes suggestions of her husband's complicity in her death even more obscure.

Also unresolved are the ideological contradictions suggested in Mutimukulu's philosophical exchanges with the Old Man. At first Mutimukulu, once a 'man of principles and convictions' (p. 59), seems to be arguing for social co-operation and communality:

> Mutimukulu: Egoism, greed, self-perpetuation, dominance, that's what competition is about.
> Old Man: On the contrary: there is no better way of fostering human co-operation and self-improvement. (p. 75)

But later he turns passionately on the democratic institution of voting in an assertion of autocratic individualism:

> Mutimukulu: Vote? The vote! That's what's wrong with this whole place. Every cretin, every putrifying mass of human refuse thinks they can settle all manner of issues by the simplest act of their hands being counted. What makes you think that your two miserable votes can cancel out or even balance my vote. (p. 77)

The play seems to hover between an exposition of nihilism — life as pointless 'play' between birth and death[21] — and an assertion of a para-human fate which inexorably pursues every misdeed and its perpetrator. Distinctly Roman Catholic references abound[22] — 'Jesus, Mary, Joseph, I will kill you' (p. 90) — and even the judgment of Mukasa has more the texture of Christian damnation than of Kiganda traditional cosmology. Indeed, Serumaga's only published poem, 'End of the Road', is a statement of religious doubt in orthodox trinitarian terms:

> That egg will split into a bird;
> The rainbow is drops of rain
> Seen against the sun.
>
> White hens egg-bound for the market
> The bearded kid is a goat
> A shilling a pound.
> Caterpillar into butter-fly.
> Sperm into man
> No dust, no doubt
> Mystery has left the baobab tree.
>
> My facts are straight now
> But where is the meaning?
>
> I need a symbol
> Fused with a fact
> Or I'll act
> As if
> There were three in one
> Only two remain
> The third is dead.[23]

All here is change — transmutation, division and reconstruction — but without any apparent unifying motive force. The dead limb upon which the trinity is seen to hobble is presumably God. In the end, one wonders whether the 'play' we see in Serumaga's first stage piece is not less that of Beckett's clowns in the *néant* than that of T.S. Eliot's Anglo-Catholic Furies in *The Family Reunion*. As these comments suggest, *A Play* is not particularly 'African' in the most parochial sense: its theme is universal, its dramaturgy wholly European and its language (except for Mukasa's few lines) nowhere coloured by the unique locutions and rhythms of Ugandan English. At times the 'Britishness' of the English is quite discordant, cutting across characterization: Mutimukulu calls the Maid 'love' (p. 55), and man's nature 'a ruddy crocodile' (p. 58). This stands in contrast to the conscious use of Ugandan English in the plays of, for example, Ruganda, Zirimu and Sentongo.

It should also be noted that the language of *A Play*, as well as lacking a local texture, often works against Serumaga's superb sense of the theatrical.[24] In, for example, the exchanges between Mutimukulu and the Old Man, a self-consciously gnomic manner, a derivative writing style, and the use of undramatic images more suited to print than to the stage reduce the dialogue to a disjointed series of flatly abstract statements of the 'life is . . . ' variety:

> Old Man: Escaping from the prison of your own folly. Life has a substance and a shadow. And more often than not, we chase the shadow and miss the substance. The fault lies with us, not with nature. (p. 59)

The play is also fractured by grave discontinuities of structure. When, just after mid-point the focus shifts from Mutimukulu to the extended asides of Peter and John, a wholly different play begins to grow in the belly of the text, as catalysts overshadow the reagents. This digression is all the more distracting for being theatrically far more effective than the main body of the action. Later, the use of a single actor to play both the Old Man and the Doctor (p. 100) serves only to diminish the quality of indeterminate reality which Sermumaga has laboured so hard to establish, suggesting that the play's action has been only a lunatic hallucination, a *rêve à clef*, reducing Mutimukulu's existential anguish to a clinical curiosity.

In sum, *A Play* is challenging, if gravely flawed, and clearly demonstrates the thematic dramaturgic concerns, which were to preoccupy Serumaga for several years. It is perhaps best read as an *incunabulum*, pointing towards the playwright's more mature and ambitious work in the 1970s.

Concealments and Disclosures: The Elephants (1969)

Mutimukulu was played by Serumaga in the 1967 Kampala production[25] and is a prototype of the character recurrent throughout Serumaga's writing: the tortured, isolated individualist. Such a figure is David, in *The Elephants*.[26] A research fellow in an African university not unlike Uganda's Makerere, David has become attached to Maurice Diop, a refugee painter from an adjacent Francophone country. David, whose own parents were shot during some past political disturbance (pp. 24–6, pp. 38–9), has hidden from Maurice the fact that his family also have been killed by soldiers (pp. 47–8) and has regularly written letters, posted covertly across the border, purporting to be from Maurice's father:

> Yes, I've built a life for Maurice through the written word. It's a web of existence: father, mother, brother and two sisters. Real to him. In here! (*Shows letters.*) I have written it all! (p. 49)

Into this delicately constructed relationship is thrust Jenny, a white American Peace Corps volunteer who, unknown to David, has been planning with Maurice to be married. (There is no strong dramatic reason for either Jenny or her admirer Richard to be expatriates, except to give the play a cosmopolitan patina and to allow a few tangential swipes at stereotypically depicted white liberalism.) In the final scene the various fictions and obsessions are revealed and the revelations, in turn, destroy Maurice, David and Jenny.

The background to these elaborate concealments and disclosures suggests Uganda, with its vast lake and troubled Francophone neighbours.[27] The civil disruptions in which David's family have died recall Dr Milton Obote's 1966 republican *coup d'état*, the setting for Serumaga's earlier novel *Return to the Shadows*,[28] and the description of David's home — hilly, overlooking a river, amongst coffee and banana shambas (p. 38) — is similar to the West Bugandan settings of *Majangwa* and the novel. But Serumaga has consciously distanced the action from any specific social context: unlike Makerere, his university abuts directly onto the lake shore; the political circumstances of the slaughter of David's parents are never mentioned; and Maurice Diop's surname is distinctively West African (Senegalese).[29] For *The Elephants* is not intended as a social or political statement.[30] It is, rather, an exploration of individual psyches in the process of dissolution and of the 'self-destructive pretence[s]' (p. 48) upon which human egos rely. 'Art,' says David, 'no longer deals with revelation but concealment' (p. 7), as he proceeds, like Mutimukulu, to discover the vital cost of such concealments.

The play's central metaphor, that of the pygmy and the elephant, concretizes the notion first articulated by Mukasa in *A Play*, of the lies which destroy every man from within:

David: . . . Do you know the pygmies? Well, they have a most sophisticated way of eating elephants. Poisoned darts and all that are figments of tourist imagination. When a pygmy decides to eat an elephant, he does not kill it. What he does is he gets inside it, and starts eating away. The elephant experiences only a slight discomfort, until the pygmy strikes some vital part. It could be lunch time or dinner time. That's when the elephant falls. Do you know that?

Jenny: No.

David: Well, when you see a herd of elephants eating grass and thorns, there is probably a pygmy inside every one of them. So I told Richard he was a big elephant, with a little man inside him eating away. He will weaken. In fact, elephants do weaken considerably. In the end they are no better than just big mice. (p. 32)

As Serumaga explained, when asked by a *Uganda Argus* interviewer why he had earlier intended to call the play 'The Fishnet':

We all have these holes, and if someone comes along and blocks up these psychological holes then we suffocate. The play is about a man who creates a certain kind of world around himself with the help of his friends. He is not aware of having created this world until the holes in its artificiality are blocked up by someone else. I am interested in a man living in an artificial environment which he has created, unknowingly perhaps. We might see all sorts of weaknesses in this life form, but do we stop to contemplate that if we destroy it, we might destroy the man?[31]

If *The Elephants* shares the thematic concerns of *A Play*, the Beckett/Pinter music-hall qualities of John and Peter also reappear in David, whose patter of philosophical wise-cracks probably owes a great deal to the 'stand-up comic' routines of Serumaga's student days. But now the showmen have moved to centre-stage and been consolidated into a single character: in his story of the pet-food purchaser in Westbourne Grove, David acts out both the grocer and the West Indian (pp. 16–18); in the report of his mother's murder, he is both narrator and little boy (pp. 24–6).

Mutimukulu's assertion that 'life is no more than a communal dream' (p. 9) is further elaborated in *The Elephants* in enactments and concealments, although within a plot as flawed by centrifugal distractions as that of *A Play*.[32] Indeed, in both these early stage pieces, as in *Return to the Shadows*, one has the sense of a striving for a tone of significance which is never quite achieved, of plots which have been only sketchily worked out and must be patched together and swept along by the power of the featured performer for whom the play was conceived, Serumaga himself.

The Olympian in Retreat: Return to the Shadows (1967–9)

Having examined these two early plays it might be useful to look back at the work which preceded and presaged them, Serumaga's only major non-dramatic piece,[33] his novel *Return to the Shadows*. Written while Serumaga was still living in London,[34] it strikes themes and rehearses narrative forms which deeply inform the two subsequent plays. Here, in Joe Musizi, the 'lawyer, economist and rich businessman'[35] who is the novel's narrator-protagonist, is the prototype of Serumaga's isolated egoist. A man of 'intellectual rationalizations and cynical explanations' (p. 5), Joe has begun as an idealist, full of what his friend Moses calls 'high falutin ideas about African Socialism, African Democracy and African you-name-it-we've-got-it' (p. 139), storing up arms and funds against the opportunity to mount a 'revolution' (p. 45). But he is disillusioned when the childhood friends who are his co-conspirators prove to be as venal and unprincipled as the incumbent politicians they oppose.

As the novel opens, Joe finds himself in flight from the violence of a *coup d'état*. The narrative then charts his arduous journey upcountry to his mother's home, where he finds his family raped and slaughtered, and back again to the capital, all his intellectual-izations now rendered barren: 'as they went, Joe's hand went to his thigh to take a note but he found that he had nothing to say' (p. 171). Joe's journey is set in a thinly disguised Uganda — the inverted 'Adnagu' (p. 1) — against events very similar to those of 1966, when the then prime minister Milton Obote abrogated the constitu-tion, suspended the president Sir Edward Mutesa (who was also the hereditary Kabaka of Buganda), declared a state of emergency, and ordered the army under Colonel Idi Amin Dada to storm the Kabaka's palace at Mengo.[36] Serumaga, a staunch loyalist and royalist,[37] had reacted deeply, if idiosyncratically, to these events, especially as he had been in Uganda at the time and had undergone indignities at the hands of the military. Obote's radical action had seemed to many conservatives, monarchists and Buganda sup-remacists to be, in the Kabaka's phrase, 'a desecration', eclipsing traditional feudal personalism with a resolutely populist republi-canism.

Yet much of this deeply felt political background remains back-ground, displaced by the novelist's preoccupation with Joe's indi-vidual psyche. Joe's credo — Olympian, individualist and detached — is articulated early on:

> . . . let fate run its course, get a small area of safety for yourself and hold on to it. The world beyond, its sufferings and its glories, are only the macabre orchestrations of a band of inherently imperfect men. One's duty was to seek a little comfort and not be sacrificed on the altar of an

idealism pursued by creatures so obviously unworthy of such providence. (p. 7)

As later in *Majangwa*, it is society — human community — which is identified as the ultimate source of evil. The individual's achievement is only attained despite society, but his crime is always imposed by and is the direct responsibility of society: 'Then you find when the killing has been done and the destruction complete, a soldier stands, dazed, before the society which forced his hand and warped his consciousness' (p. 22). Here, as elsewhere in his work, Serumaga seems to box himself into a self-contradictory position. Excluding both behaviourism and indeterminism, his preoccupation with the individual moves towards a romantic anarchism. As Moses says of Joe: 'Some of you African Socialists make Adam Smith look flaming red by comparison' (p. 140). Even the dashed revolutionary plans of Joe and his colleagues seem to be without any specific programme. They are to be implemented against a stolid and corrupt mediocracy of 'intellectual mercenaries' and 'assembly line civil servants' (p. 133). But there is no vision offered of what would constitute the new order.

Some years earlier, before he had begun to write seriously, Serumaga had demonstrated a profound discomfort with the options apparently presenting themselves to the newly self-governing nations of Africa:

> Which way are we going to achieve economic development faster? Can we say that with socialist methods we may achieve economic development faster than by capitalistic methods? That is one choice, but the other is whether we are going to preserve the communalistic elements in the old society and bring them into the new society. Is this a good thing or shall we split our society and become individualistic? This is an ethical choice.[38]

But it was a choice Serumaga was not then prepared to make, as the preponderance of interrogatives in his statement suggests. Even in this early novel, intimations are introduced of the impossibility of consolidation and re-integration, of resolving these tensions between the individual and the community. As his work progresses, Serumaga's voice becomes increasingly that of disillusion and disintegration, of informed and jaded despair.

In style and form, *Return to the Shadows* often seems to be a narrative pressing forcefully towards theatre. Dialogue exchanges have the rhythm and pattern of spoken conversation and could easily have been written for the stage. It is hardly surprising, therefore, that Serumaga turned next to drama. In *A Play* may be found distinct echoes of the novel: Joe's 'shadows' — the accusing dead enthroned upon lavatory seats (pp. 91–4) — become Mutimukulu's ghostly visitors; the violent role-playing of the *kondo* (criminal) 'Yakobo' Katende and his wife Rozalia (pp. 102–5) develops into the 'games' of John and Peter, and later of Majangwa and Nakirijja. Even the structure of *A Play* is similar to that of the novel, with its digressive chapters (chapters 5 and 6) which shift focus onto the catalytic characters 'Yakobo' Katende and Jeronimo, as they play-act like John and Peter, around the margins of Joe's nightmare.

The Artist Compromised: Majangwa (1971)

In *Majangwa: A Promise of Rains*,[39] a far more adventurous work than its predecessors, the personal illusions of Joe Musizi, Mutimukulu, and David are more purposefully shaped and the eponymous central character more richly realized. Majangwa was a real person: a travelling entertainer who worked the markets of towns and villages in Buganda some decades ago, achieving early honour as a royal drummer and ending as a cheap and extravagantly degraded buffoon. But this is no historical reconstruction and Serumaga's Majangwa is far more than a mere figure of popular scandal and contemporary folklore.[40] He confronts, more explicitly and vividly than anywhere else in Serumaga, the realities of the artist's role in society.

The first act opens, like so many Ugandan plays, on a stretch of rural road.[41] Majangwa, now in ravaged middle age, and his wife Nakirijja, once an inspired dancer, are preparing to rest for the night. Majangwa begins to recollect his past — selecting, embellishing, revising and inflating himself like '[t]he old frog. One day he puffed himself beyond his size, and he burst' (p. 11). It is Nakirijja, her vitality eroded by years of enervating degradation, who punctures his self-delusions by recalling bitterly what has really happened in their lives. To satisfy his audiences' limitless demands for novelty, she reminds him that he was compelled at first to vary, then to compromise, and finally to debase his performances until his art had turned into an obscene public display of the sex act:

> And I told you: don't give in to the crowds. Don't pander to their whims. Stick to the drum I said, and I to the dance. But no. You had to start. Plays you called them, funny words and actions. In between

the songs, you talked and played with me. It was all right in the beginning, but the crowds taunted us and asked for one more inch. Then your embraces became kisses, in public, till even these could not satisfy the devil in the audiences. Your speech was gone, together with the drum and song. After that it was only a matter of time before I had my back to the pavement. (p. 30)

What this erotic spectacle offers the squalid market audiences is more than just passing titillation. It is 'a promise of rains' (p. 20), a tonic for renewal and regeneration, a ritualistic act of sympathetic healing:[42]

Did you think we were cheap entertainers? No, woman. I see it all now. We were the gods' go-betweens, putting bones back into broken limbs. Yes, five shillings and they watched us, and waited and hoped that a whiff of passion would rub off on them and arouse them. The chance of a cure, woman, that's what we were to them. (p. 21)

But by transferring their own vitality to their audiences in this ceremony of carnal theatre, they themselves have been left barren,[43] impotent. In the first moments of the play Majangwa establishes his concern with the 'mysteries of the womb' (p. 7) in a rapturous panegyric to the mythical mother of Buganda's twin rivers, Mayanja Kato and Mayanja Wasswa (pp. 7–8). Later the couple discuss their failure to produce children:

Nakirijja: Do you think we will ever have a child?
              (*Silence*)
Majangwa: (*very sadly*) I don't know.
Nakirijja: My womb has been silent for too long.
Majangwa: It may not be your fault.
Nakirijja: . . . I wanted a child so much . . .
Majangwa: Oh, I don't know, woman. I have drunk from the earthen
              bowl many times, taken to the root and examined the
              cock's entrails, but nothing seems to add any edge to my
              approach. What else can I do but wait?

Like the warrior Renga Moi in Serumaga's next play, they have sacrificed the life of their flesh to preserve and regenerate the flesh of others in the community. Yet, as in *Renga Moi*, the community does not appreciate this sacrifice and even turns upon the sacrificer, destroying not only his house but the very emblem of his art, the drum:

The house. They burnt our house. How can you forget? The flames, the smoke, the ashes. They burnt our house and all our belongings. (*Heav-*

ily, after a pause) They burnt our drum too. (*Silence*) Why did they burn our drum? (*Silence*) Well, after that we had no strength against the audience. We had to beg. Do as asked. What else? Five shillings is a lot of money when all you ever possessed is a heap of ashes and no drum. Only our ingenuity saved us from becoming eternal beggars. (pp. 31–2)

Majangwa is thus seen to be only partially accountable for his personal failure. It is society, Serumaga argues, that exploits, exhausts, degrades and eventually discards the artist. In this essentially romantic notion, the artist, like the traditional spirit-medium, purges society's ills by his own suffering and is rewarded only with indifference or hostility:

Majangwa: I can look back at my life all right . . . What I can't look back at without puking my guts out is the society which paid to watch us . . . What pleasure did they get out of seeing and not doing? Little men with ten-cent coins in their palms and their hands in their pockets watching the sun and hoping for rain!

Nakirijja: (*pensively*) Yes we were the pus of a very diseased society.

Majangwa: On the contrary, we were the wound; the opening through which society got rid of its excess pus. The cure for a diseased people which has to hide behind closed doors, drawn curtains and five blankets just to sleep with their wives. (p. 15)

In this indictment, the play's own theatre audience are themselves implicated:

Nakirijja: Where are the crowds now and their five shillings?
Majangwa: Audiences are fickle, you know that.
Nakirijja: Where are they?
Majangwa: Out there. (p. 13)

In the hope of reinvigorating himself and Nakirijja, Majangwa devises a scheme for turning the tables on his parasitic voyeurs by watching them make love in the back seats of parked cars: 'Tonight, they'll be the performers and we the owners of the five shillings' (p. 23). But, during the brief second act, even this desperate plan to secure compensation from society is frustrated. The apparently arbitrary spot they have chosen on the Kampala-Mityana road is discovered to be the village of Tanda (p. 46) where, according to the Kiganda creation myth, Death descended into the earth and from which he emerges to claim the living.[44] In a terrifying mime (the Theatre Limited production used back-lighting and strobes), Death appears and shatters Majangwa's 'promise of rains', not by killing him but by frightening away the lovers (p. 51). For Majangwa, life remains, to adapt Hobbes's phrase, nasty, brutish and long — a succession of tomorrows without hope: 'It's been a long time. It'll be a long time tomorrow, too. A long way from both the beginning and the end' (p. 44). If Beckett's seminal *Waiting for Godot* posits an endlessly recurring 'now', *Majangwa*, like Athol Fugard's *Boesman and Lena*, presents life as a prolonged attenuation, a slow and painful dismantling.

Majangwa is Serumaga's first explicitly drawn artist[45] and as a theatrical performer he develops the role-playing games of Jeronimo in *Return to the Shadows*, John and Peter in *À Play*, and David in *The Elephants*. He involves Nakirijja[46] in his animated playlet of the anthill razed by a Stirling Astaldi tractor (pp. 32–4), then diverts her with the one-man routines of the 'bunch of bananas' (pp. 42–3) and the tale of Kayikuuzi and Death at Tanda (pp. 47–9). Indeed the whole play is a *tour de force* vehicle for a single actor,[47] an extended virtuoso monologue by Majangwa as he compulsively permutates his memories until he can no longer discern those which are real from those he has fabricated. This close focus on the solo performer represents a formal distillation of Serumaga's notion of the isolated individualist — the *vox clamantis in deserto* — whose spiritual gifts are perverted by a Philistine society and turn destructively inward. In form, *Majangwa* bears an arresting resemblance to Fugard's South African 'road' play *Boesman and Lena*,[48] (although without Fugard's political resonances) in its presentation of dispossessed wanderers yoked by marriage and common humanity, yet threatening each other's delicate tricks of survival. But while Serumaga sees society as a demonic assailant, Fugard sees community as the only salvation, one denied by the cynical divisiveness of an oppressive state.

When *Majangwa* was performed at the Third World Theatre Conference in Manila in December 1971, it was interestingly, Serumaga's acting rather than the play itself which brought the accolades.[49] *Majangwa* seemed too westernized for the Philippine press, which clearly entertained a rather more narrow and unadventurous idea of what African theatre should be than does Serumaga. To this line of criticism Serumaga responds convincingly:

The traditions of the past can only inspire the present. They cannot satisfy the creative urge of our generation. Between the theatrical technique of the foreign play, the symbolism of tradition and the controversy of contemporary issues, a synthesis of body and spirit must be achieved.[50]

This insoluble and often nebulous dispute over Africanness aside, the play does present several substantial problems. The dialogue, thickly aphoristic and metaphorical, sometimes demands the leisure of the book reader rather than the fixed time of a theatre listener. Structurally, Majangwa's brush with Death is less well prepared for than it seems to be in performance. Above all, the play's argument has been criticized by some in East Africa as fundamentally reactionary and suggestive of an unwelcome elitism.

The Hero Betrayed: Renga Moi (1972)

Serumaga's next project with his now renamed Abafumi Theatre Company was *Renga Moi* ('Red Warrior').[51] With dialogue in four Ugandan languages and the music and dances of several regions, it represents an attempt to broaden the ethnic base of *Majangwa*[52] and to reach into the non-verbal expressionism of African ritual, as perhaps filtered through the theatre techniques of Stanislavski, Grotowski, and The Living Theatre.

Renga Moi is based on an Acoli legend, from northern Uganda, in which the warrior-chief of the Village of the Seven Hills must choose between defending his people from armed attack and completing the ceremonies which will preserve the lives of his newly born twins, during which he is expressly prohibited from shedding blood.[53] Selflessly he decides for the common weal and leads the villagers into battle. But during his absence, grave privation strikes the village and, to propitiate the misfortune-bearing spirits, the powerful priest-diviner[54] (who frames the action with an English commentary and was played by Serumaga), decrees that Renga Moi's twins be sacrificially impaled. Upon returning home after successfully staving off the attackers, Renga Moi finds that the villagers decline all responsibility for the deaths of his twins. The warrior turns on the diviner and kills him, but this resolves nothing as the infants are already dead and their twin spirits will surely seek revenge on the father who abandoned them.

Renga Moi is Serumaga's clearest statement of the problem which has been his central concern from the beginning of his writing career. As he said in an interview during the play's London run, 'we are posing a universal question about the choices an individual has to make, between himself and his social commitment'.[55] Renga Moi's choice is to act for the community, but, like Majangwa, he discovers that the community not only undervalues his giving of himself, it ravenously demands more. Like the mob which drained Majangwa's life force and then burned his drum, the villagers of the Seven Hills accepted the warrior's self-abnegatory heroism and then destroyed his very flesh.[56] Social commitment, Serumaga seems to be arguing, is an illusory ideal. The self-sacrificer is betrayed; the brave warrior, like the intellectual and the artist, is savaged by society and remains always an *isolato* — a man alone.

The story of Renga Moi and his village is dramatized through gestural acting,[57] music and the interweaving of local languages, all orchestrated by the participant-narrator, the Diviner. In this figure Serumaga consolidates the theatricality of *Return to the Shadows* and the fictionalizing of the plays (the fabulists John and Peter, David, and Majangwa), by resolving these generic tensions in a return to the local tradition of the story-teller's enactments. As Serumaga observed some years earlier: ' . . . the practice of people getting together to watch the story-teller act out his story, or to hear a musician like the famous Sekinnoomu of Uganda relate a tale of trenchant social criticism, dramatized in voice, movement and the music of his *ndingidi*,[58] has been with us for centuries. And this is the true theatre of East Africa.'[59] It was therefore appropriate that with this production Serumaga's troupe changed its name to *Abafumi* — the story-tellers.

Although the play's array of tongues, use of total theatre and open staging techniques, inclusion of spectacular dances like *larakaraka* and *otole* and adaptation of wrenching communal rituals elicits a greater visceral than intellectual response, it is wrong to conclude, as have some, that it lacks either design or programmatic purpose. Serumaga seems to be working towards the development of a non-verbal, theatrical objective correlative. As he argued in his own controversial review of *Renga Moi*, 'The Critical Silence':

> Theatre is first and foremost a visible medium, well placed to trigger off emotions in its victims, through the presentation of concrete images. Where the novel describes, theatre exhibits the real. So that although to the critic more versed in the literary theatre, the Script (capital S please) seemed lacking, the total impact of the play drew its power from its ability to avoid the straight line story, clarify its images by its anti-naturalism and weave its pattern through a juxtaposition of images which aimed at a direct mental association rather than perception by intellectual analysis.[60]

Lewis Nkosi has presented the interesting suggestion that: 'Serumaga's stratagem of staying clear of literal language . . . may have been partly self-serving. Given the political situation in that country [Uganda], dialogue in the theatre could have been too dangerously explicit and implicating.'[61] Certainly, while *Majangwa* was written and produced during the first, relatively liberal, year of Amin's rule, by 1972 repression had begun to be far more deeply felt. The official murder in March 1977 of Luganda playwright Byron Kawadwa, whose revival of his early religious folk-opera *St Charles Lwanga* fortuitously coincided with the killing of Uganda's Archbishop Janani Luwum,[62] confirmed apprehensions about the risks attendant on spoken theatre in Uganda. On the other hand, it should be realized that most of what is spoken in *Renga Moi* is in local languages, always considered by uneasy governments to be potentially a more effective medium than the colonial tongue, as theatre is usually acknowledged to be more persuasive than the printed word. Indeed, the arrest by the Kenya Police of Ngugi wa Thiong'o in December 1977, was precipitated not by his revolutionary English novel *Petals of Blood*[63] but by the performance of his Kikuyu play *Ngaahika Ndeenda*, which propounds the same political argument.[64] And yet, if there had been anyone in Amin's State Research Bureau astute enough to contemplate on *Renga Moi*, he would quickly have identified the play's thesis — that the man of special qualities should retire from society rather than be involved in and consumed by it — as one which should be comforting to an unstable autocracy.

In Serumaga's most recent work he has continued to move away from the intellectualism of his earlier plays towards extra-verbal expressive forms. A Kenyan review of the 1978 Abafumi production *Amanyakiriti (The Flame Tree)* comments that the 'cast became living sculptures' and that the play 'appealed to the deepest emotions through mime, dance and song, leaving the audience awestruck and in some cases in tears'.[65]

Although he is often clearly derivative and prone at times to neglect both idea and form for style, and his polished and startling surfaces may sometimes conceal confused or pedestrian thought, Serumaga does remain unique in East African theatre; a man whose achievement is, admirably, more theatrical than literary and whose work shows a clear and logical development. He is, above all, sensitive to the gallops, lurches, and hiatuses of human speech, to the thrusts and hesitations of human action. The rhythms of his plays are always meticulously calibrated.

But, like his protagonists, Serumaga remains an *isolato* both professionally and ideologically.[66] While so much of contemporary East African writing has been concerned with both a perception of community and a community of perception, Serumaga has persistently argued that community can only be destructive of the individual. Each of his embattled individualists — intellectual, politician, scholar, theatrical performer, and heroic warrior — is crushed by society, turning inwards in an implosive, nihilistic solipsism. Each becomes a strafed consciousness scrutinizing itself, its thoughts centripetal and distorted. This notion of uniqueness — Georg Simmel's *Einzigheit*[67] — is romantic and fundamentally conservative, consistent with training in eighteenth-century liberal economics. But such an aggressive individualism and the solipsism consequent on its frustration have led to the rejection of Serumaga by many in East Africa who, like Peter Nazareth, feel that his 'apparent non-political approach' reveals a 'lack of sensitivity to what is going on'.[68] Be that as it may, Serumaga, unlike his vanquished protagonists, seems to thrive in his chosen isolation.

POSTSCRIPT

Since his flight into exile in 1977, Serumaga has been the subject of far more attention as a political figure than as a dramatist. In March 1979, when armed opposition to the Amin regime was gaining strength, Serumaga was briefly bruited as a 'strong candidate' for the leadership of a new Ugandan republic.[69] Some weeks earlier, he had been arrested and detained by the Kenya police at Kisumu, near the Uganda border, presumably for anti-Amin activities.[70] But, having only recently suffered the international embarrassment caused by the year-long detention without trial of Ngugi wa Thiong'o, the Kenyan government clearly wished to avoid another *cause célèbre* and released Serumaga within days.[71]

During the short tenure of Yusufu Lule as President of Uganda (11 April–20 June 1979), Serumaga was first named an assistant minister,[72] and was then reshuffled upwards to become Minister of Commerce, only to retreat again into exile and opposition when Uganda's Consultative Council replaced Lule with Godfrey Benaisa.[73] Serumaga's identification with conservative, regionalist Baganda royalists had been thus publicly confirmed. His subsequent emergence as a leader of the 'right-wing Uganda Nationalist Organization (UNO)' and his alleged control of a 'missing arms supply', led correspondent Victoria Brittain to observe that, in the future, 'Mr Serumaga and friends could cause difficulties in Uganda'.[74] There is, therefore, a profound discrepancy between the doctrine of disengagement elaborated in Serumaga's writing and the political activism into which he has thrust himself. But through it all — in both plays and politics — one may discern the figure of the Olympian romantic, the self-dramatizing individualist, the playhouse solipsist, besieged.

Robert Serumaga's death in Nairobi was announced after this article had been edited.

NOTES

1. Theatre Limited was formed as a professional acting company in 1968, jointly by Serumaga and several other Ugandan and expatriate theatre people. See Janet Johnson, 'Theatre Limited', in Serumaga and Johnson, 'Uganda's Experimental Theatre', *African Arts*, III, 3, Spring 1970, pp. 54–5. By 1971, the group had become exclusively Serumaga's project, for the production of his plays and the training of young performers. By the time of its participation in London's World Theatre Season of 1975, the troupe had changed its name to the Abafumi ('Story-tellers') Company. In 1977, it transferred its activities from Kampala to Nairobi.

2. Johnson comments that Serumaga's 'knowledge and love of the theatre and his business instincts give the company a sound basis', (op. cit., p. 54). Serumaga also helped to establish Kiyingi Productions Limited, in Kampala, for the marketing of advertising, music, and theatre and has spent several years as the Sales Manager (Motor Division) of the powerful Uganda Company. He received an MA in Economics from Trinity College, Dublin, in 1965.

3. See, for example, Peter Nazareth, 'East African Literary Supplement', *Joliso*, II, 1, Nairobi, 1974, p. 13; and Chris Wanjala, 'East and Central Africa', in 'Annual Bibliography of Commonwealth Literature', *Journal of Commonwealth Literature*, VIII, 2, December 1973, p. 14.

4. 'They were nearly all Islanders on the Pequod, *isolatoes* too, I call such, not acknowledging the common continent of men, but each *isolato* living on a separate continent of his own.' *Moby Dick*, New York, Rinehart, 1948, p. 118.

5. John Ruganda, *Black Mamba*, Nairobi, East African Publishing House, 1973.

6. Ngugi wa Thiong'o and Micere Githae Mugo, *The Trial of Dedan Kimathi*, London, Heinemann (AWS 191); Exeter, NH, Heinemann Inc., 1977.

7. Ngugi wa Thiong'o and Ngugi wa Mirii, *Ngaahika Ndeenda (I Shall*

Marry When I Choose), Heinemann East Africa, 1980 and Heinemann AWS forthcoming. It was the production of this play, as part of the community education programme of the Kamiriithu Cultural Centre in rural Limuru, which led to Ngugi's arrest and detention without trial, from 31 December 1977 to Jamhuri Day (12 December) 1978. See Karugu Gitau, 'The Play That Got Banned', *Weekly Review*, Nairobi, 9 January 1978, p. 13; Chris Wanjala, 'Where is Ngugi?' *Black Phoenix*, 2, London, Summer 1978, pp. 23–4; Margaretta wa Gacheru, 'Ngugi wa Thiong'o Still Bitter Over His Detention', *Weekly Review*, Nairobi, 5 January 1979, pp. 30–2. See also Andrew Horn, 'Theatre in Africa: Docility and Dissent', *Index on Censorship*, IX, 1, London, January–February 1980.

8. Elvania Namukwaya Zirimu, *Family Spear*, in Gwyneth Henderson (ed.). *African Theatre*, London, Heinemann (AWS 134); Exeter, NH, Heinemann Inc., 1973, pp. 109–29.

9. Byron Kawadwa and Wassanyi Serukenya, *Oluyimba lwa Wankoko*, unpublished, first performed at the Uganda National Theatre, 6 November 1971, and later presented at the Festival of Black and African Arts and Culture at Lagos, Nigeria, February 1977.

10. Chris Mukiimbi, *Kikwambaga*, unpublished, first performed Kampala, 1972.

11. Nuwa Sentongo, *The Invisible Bond*, in Michael Etherton (ed.), *African Plays for Playing 1*, London, Heinemann (AWS 165); Exeter, NH, Heinemann Inc., 1975, pp. 13–44.

12. '[L]'enfer, c'est les autres', *Huis clos*, 1944, in Sartre, *Théâtre 1* Paris, Gallimard, 1947, p. 182.

13. After completing his studies in Dublin, Serumaga worked as editorial consultant to the Transcription Centre in London and produced the BBC's programme 'Africa Abroad'. See *Transition*, 24, Kampala, January 1966, p. 2; *Transition*, 26, Kampala, 1966, p. 2; and Donald E. Herdeck, *African Authors*, Washington, D.C., Black Orpheus Press, 1973, p. 404.

14. For a particularly harrowing account of one such performer's life, see Albert Goldman, *Ladies and Gentlemen, Lenny Bruce*, London, Picador, 1976. New York, Random House, 1974.

15. *A Play*, Kampala, Uganda Publishing House, 1968; republished with *Majangwa*, Nairobi, East African Publishing House, 1974. All parenthetic page references are to the Nairobi edition. A portion of *A Play* was broadcast on the BBC's Radio 3, in April 1971.

16. See Samuel Beckett, *Waiting for Godot*, London, Faber, 1956 New York, Grove. Like Beckett's ravaged clowns, John and Peter are called 'jesters' (p. 65) and 'tramps' (p. 65, p. 66, p. 67, p. 97); their language, larded with theatrical phrases — 'a good line' (p. 65), 'his bit slightly overplayed' (p. 66), 'this is a death cell, not a theatre' (p. 92); and their interactions often in the form of music-hall turns (e.g. the story of the dog and the flag, p. 92). John's 'We must pass the

time somehow, before we die . . . tomorrow' (p. 92), recalls: Vladimir: That passed the time. Estragon: It would have passed in any case (*Godot*, p. 48); and Estragon: That wasn't such a bad little canter. Vladimir: Yes, but now we'll have to find something else (*Godot*, p. 65).

17. The people of Buganda are the 'Baganda' (singular 'Muganda'), who speak 'Luganda'. The adjectival form is 'Kiganda'.

18. John Roscoe talks of Mukasa as the 'god of the Lake' (Victoria) who 'controlled the storms', *The Baganda* (1911), second edition, reprinted Totowa, Biblio Distributors, London, Cass, 1965, p. 300. But Sir Apolo Kagwa claims that the 'god of the thunderbolt and the lightning' is Kiwanuka, in *Ekitabo Kye Mpisa za Baganda*, Kampala, Uganda Printing and Publishing, 1918, translated as *The Customs of the Baganda*, translator Ernest B. Kalibala, ed. May Mandelbaum Edel, New York, Columbia, 1934, p. 122.

19. ibid., John Roscoe, p. 290.

20. ibid., Kagwa, p. 116. This notion of Mukasa's benignity is, however, somewhat tempered by Kagwa's report that when prisoners were killed as sacrifice, the 'head captain . . . announced to all of them: "It is not I who am killing you, or who is giving you away to death, but Kibuka and Mukasa are killing you"' (p. 81).

21. Samuel Beckett, op. cit., see Pozzo's 'They give birth astride of a grave, the light gleams an instant, then it's night once more', (p. 89); and Vladimir's 'Astride of a grave and a difficult birth. Down in the hole, lingeringly, the grave-digger puts on the forceps. We have time to grow old. The air is full of our cries', pp. 90–1.

22. Similar Catholic influences are discernible in Zirimu, *When the Hunchback Made Rain and Snoring Strangers*', Nairobi, East African Publishing House, 1975, and Sentongo, *The Invisible Bond*, op.cit.

23. *Transition*, 26, VI, (1) 1966, p. 44.

24. Adrian Roscoe speaks of 'occasional linguistic ineptness' in *A Play*, 'when the wrong register is used', *Uhuru's Fire*, Cambridge, CUP, New York, CUP, 1977, p. 262.

25. The original Kampala cast of *A Play* also included Rose Mbowa as Rose and the Malawi-born Ugandan poet David Rubadiri as the Mask of Mukasa. (See *A Play*, p. 53.)

26. *The Elephants*, Nairobi, OUP, 1971. All parenthetical page references are to this edition.

27. Uganda has for years hosted thousands of refugees from Rwanda, Zaïre and Anglophone Sudan. See United Nations statistics reported in *Transition*, 39, VIII, (2) 1971, p. 56.

28. See pp. 29–32.

29. One should note, however, that specific mention is made of 'Swahili' (p. 31), 'Kiganda poetry' (p. 15), the 'heroic poetry of the Bahima' (p. 31) and a 'Kisoga flute' (p. 37).

30. Bahadur Tejani misses the point when he over stresses the promi-

nence in the play of 'criticism of the attitudes of university academi-
cians, of the greed and narrow vision of westerners who come to East
Africa for research, of the romantic vision of Africanists, of the
dynamic existence of racial tensions', in 'Robert Serumaga', *African
Arts*, III, 4, Summer 1970, p. 78.

31. *Uganda Argus*, 19 September 1969, and excerpted in *Cultural Events
in Africa*, 61, London, 1969, p. 3. Even earlier, Serumaga seems to
have provisionally entitled the play 'People Who Eat Dead People'; see
the programme notes for Theatre Limited's National Theatre production of Edward Albee's *Who's Afraid of Virginia Woolf*, in which
Serumaga played George, 28 March 1968; and *Cultural Events in
Africa*, 41, 1968, p. 2.

32. In his cursory survey, *African Theatre Today*, London, Pitman, 1976,
Martin Banham comments on *The Elephants*: 'Though some of Robert
Serumaga's prose is a little forced, the overall impact of his play is very
successful', p. 88. Adrian Roscoe (op. cit.) is rather less accommodat-
ing: '*The Elephants* . . . is a useful example of a play with a measure of
psychological power, but which, stylistically, is rather vapid. Except
in isolated cases, and despite Serumaga's claim in the introduction
that "every word matters", there is neither rhythmic energy nor
pungency of statement. . . . But *The Elephants'* warm reception in
Nairobi and elsewhere suggests how skilfully Serumaga has exploited
those areas of his craft where he knows his strengths lie', pp. 263–4.

33. A second novel, 'A Whippcot Butterfly', remains unpublished. It is
mentioned in the programme notes for the Theatre Limited production of *Who's Afraid of Virginia Woolf*. See also *Cultural Events in
Africa*, 41, 1968, p. 2, and 50, 1969, p. 3.

34. See W. Stephen Gilbert's interview with Serumaga in 'Around the
World in Thirty Days', *Plays and Players*, XXII, 7, London, April 1975,
p. 11.

35. Robert Serumaga, *Return to the Shadows*, London, Heinemann (AWS
54), 1969; Exeter NH, Heinemann Inc., p. 4. All parenthetical page
references are to this edition.

36. See, *inter alia*, Ali A. Mazrui and G. F. Engholm, 'Violent Constitu-
tionalism in Uganda', in Mazrui, *Violence and Thought*, London,
Longman, 1969; N.J., Humanities Press, pp. 147–62; Mazrui, *Soldiers and Kinsmen in Uganda*, Beverly Hills and London, Sage,
1975, pp. 14–18; Mahmood Mamdani, *Politics and Class Formation
in Uganda*, London, Heinemann, 1976; New York Monthly Review.
pp. 228–46. Obote's apologia appears as 'The Footsteps of Uganda's
Revolution', *East Africa Journal*, V, 10, October 1968. The Kabaka
presented his version of these events in his autobiography, *Desecration of My Kingdom*, London, Constable, 1967, pp. 9–26, 181–94, et
passim.

37. After the 1971 *coup d'état*, Serumaga produced a film documenting
the return from Britain of the Kabaka's body for reburial at Mengo and
lauding Amin's overthrow of Obote's government. The film, pre-

miered at Kampala's Neeta Cinema in September 1971, was broadcast several times by Uganda Television.

38. 'Talking Aloud on African Socialism', Transition, 24, V, January 1966, p. 47, the transcript of a discussion between Serumaga, Anthony Crosland, Ernest Gellner and Paul Mbayi, chaired by Margaret Roberts (Legum).

39. Majangwa: A Promise of Rains, Nairobi, East African Publishing House, 1972. All parenthetical page references are to this edition.

40. Serumaga has said of Majangwa that it is 'in many ways a synthesis of several strands in my theatrical development . . . such, for example, as its use of fact and legend, reality and myth and its exploration of the subconscious fears within a basically conscious level'. See The Sunday Post, Nairobi, 1 September 1971; and Cultural Events in Africa, 77, 1971, p. 2.

41. See John Ruganda, Covenant with Death, 1973, in Black Mamba, pp. 71–120; Zirimu, When the Hunchback Made Rain, 1970 and Snoring Strangers, 1973; Sentongo, The Invisible Bond, 1972. One might usefully compare these with Beckett's Waiting for Godot, 1955; and Athol Fugard's Boesman and Lena, 1969, in Fugard, Three Port Elizabeth Plays, London, OUP, 1974, pp. 165–221. For a discussion of this last, see below.

42. For a discussion of theatrical performance as sympathetic magic, see Andrew Horn, 'Ritual, Drama, and the Theatrical: The Case of Bori Spirit Mediumship', a paper delivered to the seminar on the Interrelationship of the Arts, Lagos, Nigeria, February 1978.

43. Cf. Lena's childlessness in Boesman and Lena: 'One, Outa, that lived. For six months. The others were born dead', p. 193.

44. Majangwa's account of the creation myth (pp. 47–9) — of the first Man, Kintu, his wife Nambi and her brother Death (Walumbe) — is quite orthodox. The myth is presented in full by John Roscoe as 'The Legend of Kintu', pp. 460–4. Roscoe's principal informant was Sir Apolo Kagwa, the Katikiro (Prime Minister) and Regent of Buganda, whose own brief comments on 'Mister Death at Tanda' appear in Kagwa, p. 113.

45. Maurice, in The Elephants, is said to have 'taken to painting' (p. 2), but his art is not central to the concerns of the play.

46. A similar device is used in the powerful central scene of John Ruganda's The Burdens, Nairobi, East African Publishing House, 1972, pp. 51–64.

47. Serumaga played Majangwa in his own 1971 Theatre Limited production. The only other speaking role was played by a talented young actress, Gladys Nakazibwe, whose performance, although somewhat overshadowed by Serumaga's, was well received by the press. See, for example, 'Insight into Real African Culture', The Sunday Nation, Nairobi, 5 March 1972, p. 25.

48. Serumaga saw Fugard's August 1971 production of Boesman and Lena at London's Young Vic theatre. But although Serumaga admits

that *Majangwa's* final scene was composed only hours before the first performance (see Bill White, 'Uganda's Olivier', *The Sunday Nation,* Nairobi, 30 January 1972, p. 28), most of the play had already been written well before Serumaga's London visit. *Majangwa* also opened in August 1971.

49. See *The Manila Chronicle,* 5 December 1971, and the *Manila Bulletin,* 5 December 1971; both quoted in *Cultural Events in Africa,* 77, 1971, p. 3.

50. Serumaga and Johnson, op. cit., p. 53.

51. *Renga Moi,* 1972, unpublished. The title has been variously translated from the Acoli: as 'A Brave Warrior' by Excalibur, in 'Robert Serumaga Shows You War-torn Village', *Uganda Argus,* Kampala, 12 July 1972, p. 2; as 'The Red Warrior' in the 1975 World Theatre Season (Aldwych Theatre, London) programme and in most articles based upon it. A.C.A. Wright, in 'Some Notes on Acoli Religious Ceremonies', *Uganda Journal,* III, 3, January 1936, explains that the '*moi* name, which is very highly prized, can be gained by killing any person, male or female, full-grown or a child' (p. 187), that the title is adopted at the '*Kwer Merok*', or 'Ceremoney for the Killing of an Enemy' (p. 186), and that the new name adopted, ending in '*moi*', is 'usually of untranslatable meaning' (p. 187). In his discussion of Acoli 'warrior titles', in *The Horn of My Love,* London, Heinemann (AWS 147); Exeter, NH, Heinemann Inc., 1974, Okot p'Bitek renders '*Arengo-Moi* . . . one who kills an enemy after hunting him out of the main body', p. 177.

52. Serumaga has been attacked as a Buganda regionalist. See, for example, Wanjala, op. cit., p. 14.

53. T. T. Steiger Hayley writes, in 'The Power Concept in Lango Religion', *Uganda Journal,* VII, 3, January 1940, that the: 'birth of twins is a happy event in so far as two individuals arrive to strengthen the Clan. But . . . the presence of *Jok* power thus manifested necessitates magical control by those affected. The twin ceremonies serve to exercise this control', p. 100. Sidney Higgins observes, in 'Acoli Birth Customs', *Uganda Journal,* XXX, 2, 1966, that the Acoli: 'recognize two distinct types of birth, the normal birth and *jok anywala,* the godly birth', p. 175, and that twins are the most common type of *jok anywala,* p. 178. In his 'Songs and Dances of the Acoli', in Denis Hills, *The White Pumpkin,* London, Allen and Unwin, 1975, Okuma Pa'lukobo notes that: 'of all *Jok* [spirit] dances, the *Rut* (twin) is the most important. *Rudi* (twins) are believed to be the special gift of *Jok anyodo* [the spirit of birth], and the wish of the ancestors. *Jok Rut* is performed before the ancestral shrine' and is 'intended to persuade *Anyodo* not to call away one or both of the twins. For twins are more vulnerable, more likely to die, than normal infants', pp. 275–6. For discussions of the meaning and nature of *Jok,* over which there is great scholarly controversy, see Okot p'Bitek, 'The Concept of Jok Among the Acoli and Langi', *Uganda Journal,*

XXVII, 1, March 1963, pp. 15–29; J. H. Driberg, *The Lango*, London, 1923, pp. 216–68; Renato Boccassino, 'The Nature and Characteristics of the Supreme Being Worshipped Among the Acoli of Uganda', *Uganda Journal*, VI, 4, April 1939, pp. 195–201; Hayley, op.cit.; A.C.A. Wright, 'The Supreme Being Among the Acoli of Uganda — Another Viewpoint', *Uganda Journal*, VII, 3, January 1940, pp. 130–7; N. Akena, 'Lango Religion', *Uganda Journal*, XXIII, 2, September 1959, pp. 188–90.

54. Okot p'Bitek says of the Acoli-Langi *ajwaka* (diviner) that he 'was a consultant psychiatrist, chemist and priest combined', Okot p'Bitek, 1963, op.cit., p. 17.

55. Serumaga quoted in Gilbert, op. cit., p. 14.

56. In another of Serumaga's Christian images, the sacrificial martyrdom of Jesus was suggested by the massive wooden cross, centre stage, before which the Diviner stood. See photographs in Gilbert, op. cit., pp. 11 and 13.

57. In this, Serumaga has been influenced strongly not only by African performance modes and contemporary *avant-garde* western theatre, but by the theatres of the East, particularly Japanese Kabuki and Nō, after the Philippine tour of *Majangwa*. See Barbara Kimenye, *Daily Nation*, Nairobi, 24 November 1972, and White, op. cit.

58. The *ndingidi* is a one-stringed bowed viol.

59. Serumaga and Johnson, op. cit., p. 52.

60. 'The Critical Silence', *Uganda Argus*, Kampala, 3 August 1972, p. 4.

61. Lewis Nkosi, 'The British Theatre and Africa', *Africa*, London, March 1976, p. 63.

62. Information based on a report from Nairobi by Victoria Brittain, 'Arts and Africa', BBC Africa Service, 13 March 1977. See also Andrew Horn, 'Uhuru to Amin: The Golden Decade of Theatre in Uganda', *The Literary Half-Yearly*, ('Africa Number'), XIX, 1, January 1978, pp. 22–49; 'Retreat from Collision', *Time*, 14 March 1977, p. 7; 'The Curtain Closes on Uganda's Theatre', *Viva*, Nairobi, March 1978, p. 93. It was later reported by Charles Harrison on 'Arts and Africa', BBC Africa Service, 12 October 1977, that Kawadwa's successor as Director of the National Theatre, Dan Kintu, had also been killed by the military, as had playwright John Male and John Sebuliba, of the Ministry of Culture. See also Andrew Horn, 'Uganda's Theatre: The Exiled and the Dead', *Index on Censorship*, VIII, 5, September–October 1979, pp. 12–15; Amnesty International, *Human Rights in Uganda*, London, Amnesty International, 1978, pp. 9–10. For further material on Ugandan theatre during the Amin years, see Andrew Horn, 'African Theatre: Docility and Dissent', *Index on Censorship*, IX, 3, May–June 1980.

63. *Petals of Blood*, London, Heinemann (AWS 188) 1977. New York, Dutton, 1978.

64. For a discussion both of the general problem of official censorship in

African theatre and of Ngugi's particular case, see Horn, 'Theatre in Africa: Docility and Dissent', 1980, op. cit.

65. 'Lively Kenyan Scene', *Viva*, Nairobi, March 1978, New York, Dutton, p. 94.
66. See, for example, the bitter comments on Zirimu, Sentongo, Ruganda, and Bob Leshoai, in 'The Critical Silence'.
67. See Simmel, *Die Probleme der Geschictsphilosophie*, Leipzig, Duncker und Humboldt, 1892, passim.
68. Nazareth, p. 13.
69. Victoria Brittain, 'Uganda Battle Leaves Amin Still Clinging to Power', *Guardian*, London, 19 March 1979, p. 5.
70. Report by Charles Harrison from Nairobi, 'Focus on Africa', BBC Africa Service, 19 February 1979.
71. For a further discussion of this episode, see Andrew Horn, 'Arts Worldwide', BBC Radio 3, 20 February 1979; and Andrew Horn, 'Arts and Africa', no. 269, BBC Africa Service, 22 February 1979, BBC Script Service, p. 5. This latter transcript also includes a general survey of Serumaga's theatre career.
72. Victoria Brittain, 'Uganda Scratches for a Start'. *Guardian*, London, 7 May 1979, p. 13.
73. Victoria Brittain, 'Lule Held Under Armed Escort', *Guardian*, London, 7 July 1979, p. 6, and other similar reports.
74. Victoria Brittain, 'Lule Denounces Nyerere's Role in New Uganda', *Guardian*, London, 18 July 1979, p. 6.

BIBLIOGRAPHY

'Talking Aloud on African Socialism', transcribed panel discussion amongst Serumaga, Anthony Crosland, Ernest Gellner and Paul Mbayi, chaired by Margaret Roberts (Legum), *Transition*, 24, V, January 1966, pp. 44–8.

'End of the Road', poem, *Transition*, 26, VI, 1966, p. 44.

A Play, Kampala, Uganda Publishing House, 1968, republished with *Majangwa*, Nairobi, East African Publishing House, 1974, pp. 53–100.

Serumaga, Rajat Neogy, Raymond Apthorpe, and Paul Theroux (interviewers), 'Achebe on Biafra' and 'Why I Am a Federalist' (interviews with Chinua Achebe and U. A. Asika in Kampala), *Transition*, 36, VII, 1968, pp. 31–8, pp. 39–44.

'A Mirror of Integration: Chinua Achebe and James Ngugi' in Cosmo Pieterse and Donald Munro (eds.), *Protest and Conflict in African Literature*, London, Heinemann, 1969, pp. 70–80. New York, Africana Publishing Corporation, 1969.

Return to the Shadows, London, Heinemann (AWS 54); Exeter NH, Heinemann Inc., 1969.

'Interview with Uganda writer Robert Serumaga soon after his first novel, *Return to the Shadows*, had been published by Heinemann' (interview by Heinz Friedberger), *Cultural Events in Africa*, 53, 1969, pp. I–II.

'Uganda's Experimental Theatre', with Janet Johnson, *African Arts*, Los Angeles, III, 3, 1970, pp. 52–5.

The Elephants, Nairobi, OUP, 1971.

Documentary film on the Amin *coup d'état* of January 1971, and the return of the Kabaka's body for reburial in the royal tombs at Mengo (unpublished filmscript and direction, premiered September 1971).

Majangwa, Nairobi, East African Publishing House, 1974.

Renga Moi, (unpublished) first produced Uganda National Theatre, July 1972.

'The Critical Silence' (article), *Uganda Argus*, Kampala, 3 August 1972, p. 4.

Amanyakiriti, (unpublished), first produced Uganda National Theatre, winter 1977.

Hamidou Kane's Hero

W. S. Shiver

At the Dakar Conference on African Literature in French, in March 1963, Mme Jeanne-Lydie Goré presented a paper titled 'The theme of Solitude in Cheikh Hamidou Kane's *Ambiguous Adventure*.'[1] This study has been widely noticed but seems, curiously, to have gone unquestioned so far; though nowhere, it appears, have the solitude and death of Samba Diallo received such concise and provocative commentary. In fact, the appreciation it offers of the author's accomplishment is hardly an appreciation of originality in this novel. The present paper shows how Mme Goré's position vitiates the nature of Kane's creation and consequently his hero's singularity and significance. We find that her position is thus misleading, although it stems from her admiration of the author as a poet.

The usefulness in calling attention to her study is evident; her understanding of Kane's hero is now regarded as authoritative. Gerald Moore said early on that 'Mme Gore [sic] succeeds in placing Cheikh Kane's "roman philosophique" within a deep perspective of Islamic thinking and thus illuminates it from a direction inaccessible to many of its readers.'[2] It is apparent that Mme Goré's view derives its authority from her uncommon knowledge of Islam. She relates the solitude of Kane's hero to Sufi mysticism and, in doing so, explains his personal death as a mystical act in a context of the 'feeling for death' among the people of his race. In effect, Samba Diallo is likened, on the one hand, to a Moslem mystic on a 'pilgrimage', and, on the other, said to exemplify the black poet's 'asceticism'. While she provides a helpful perspective on Samba's Islamic frame of reference, Mme Goré's focus on the mystical side of his life and death tends to obscure Kane's assessment of contemporary civilization. Thus, a dissent from her position seems warranted.

There are several points of contention. Certain ones can be noted straight away in passing; others deserve a full exposition. This says nothing of Mme Goré's inclusion of a whole fabric of literary and

historical allusions of doubtful relevance, as well as a good deal of
seemingly gratuitous comment and speculation about mystics and
poets — of the East and the West, white and black.

Concerning the important issue of the author's originality and
intention, she emphasizes the facet of the book that may not, after
all, be very original. She says, 'c'est une esquisse nouvelle du
pèlerinage spirituel que . . . l'auteur de *L'Aventure ambiguë* offre
à notre étude dans un contexte africain et musulman'; and the
intention of this pilgrimage, she adds, is twofold: 'mystique et
exemplairement symbolique' (p. 180). Expressed in this way (with
prominence given to the unwarranted term 'pilgrimage'), the idea
takes little notice of the problem Kane points to in a civilization
that feels no need of the sacred. The consequence of God's absence
in the world, he shows, is a great loss to westerners as well as
others, and Samba Diallo is conscious of this on a very personal
level.

The experience of his symbolic adventure is particular. In the
land of the Diallobé where his life begins, he is the chosen pupil of
the sternly devout and single-minded Thierno, Master of the
Koranic school called the 'Glowing Hearth'. The teacher imbues
this child with the permanent validity of the Word of God by insist-
ing that he learn it to perfection. By dint of some physical pain at
the hands of the Master, to whom he willingly submits, Samba
learns that 'cette parole qu'il enfantait dans la douleur, elle était
l'architecture du monde, elle était le monde même' (p. 17).[3] He
wished, however, not merely to repeat the Word but also to understand it. Hence when his elders, determined to know the secret of
the white man's triumph, decide that the young Samba should
leave the Koranic school for the European school, it is knowledge
and understanding of world order that he seeks.

Under western tutelage he soon begins to feel that outside the
order of the faith where he has grown up, there is only disorder. His
subsequent study of philosophy as a student in Paris and his meditation on the nature of western civilization lead him more and more
to think of divine order as the myth of a people whose conquest and
colonization by foreign invaders ought to be evidence enough that
world order is imposed by man whose knowledge, in contradis-
tinction to the Word, is the only recognized promise of salvation.
For the author, the hero's submission to the Word, followed by
his quest for knowledge represents the meeting of myth and history, and the beginning of conflict in the human adventure, as
belief in God's eternal purpose diverges toward a belief in man's
historical purpose of ultimate self-sufficiency. The hero's adven-

ture is symbolic to this extent, but the experience he goes through is personal insofar as he feels simultaneously convinced and uncertain about the validity of both the Word and knowledge. At first, this uniqueness in what he represents may be hard to recognize.

We sense nonetheless something special about his mind and sensibility. This personal distinctiveness is shown in the manner of his involvement in an immediate moral and material situation. His distress as a man of faith outside the order of faith reflects a sense of death-in-life, experience of which no one else has had except the Madman. It is a feeling special to him, and as he tries to express it he enables the rest of us to know that our world lacks the capacity to believe in any purpose in human life other than man's own. So the book is not all mysticism and symbolism; it is primarily, perhaps, an expression of hope in a higher civilization — one that can make room for the sacred.

Ambiguous Adventure is in this respect a further expression of the concern Kane wrote about discursively in his essay, 'Comme si nous nous étions donné rendezvous'.[4] How could the writer of fiction be content with only a symbolic achievement of the 'véritable communauté spirituelle' he feels all of us should strive for? Samba achieves in his own being the unity this new civilization implies between Africans and westerners, Moslems and non-Moslems; between men who believe in man, science and history, and those who believe in God, the Word and myth. Kane evidently hopes that one day westerners as well as Africans will come to believe in the possibility of this seemingly impossible 'communauté de destin'. He doubtless sees Samba as a man who acts on this belief. Apparently Mme Goré does not, even though she has taken note of Kane's essay.

She leaves this aside, however, and pursues the evidence of mysticism in *Ambiguous Adventure* to the extent of suggesting that the book shows a complete divorce from the concerns of this world. More than one statement conveys this idea, for our hero, she says, the object of existence is not at all 'un humanisme qui épanouirait la créature, mais un théocentrisme axé sur le concept d'Unité Divine' (p. 181).[5] While the divine unity is, to be sure, central to his aspiration, the 'theocentrism' that Mme Goré feels dominates his mental life is actually complemented by an equally intense solicitude about man and human destiny.

She needlessly excludes this side of the matter in order to point up her discovery: 'Sa démarche initiale n'est pas recherche d'un équilibre et d'un épanouissement humain, elle procède infiniment plus du Soufisme . . . ' (p. 183).[6] Contradicting the first part of this assertion is the fact that Samba and his father, in more than one place, speak of a concern for what they both understand as 'l'équilibre de l'homme et de sa disponibilité' (p. 88).[7] Moreover, if the roots of Samba's pilgrimage lie in Sufism, they probably lie also, as the Most Royal Lady reminds us, in the paradox of everyday life that men who are not right win. The Diallobé want to know why this is so, and there is no indication in the book that Samba starts out to find the answer in asceticism or mysticism.

In a further expression of her disposition to see in Samba's attitude only pure spirituality dissociated from man's concerns, she mentions without qualification 'ce mépris de la vie qui pénètre toute l'*Aventure ambiguë*' (p. 186).[8] This leaves the regrettable impression of the book to some readers, who miss its interior motif. Samba does not recoil from life but from the death of the spirit. In going to the West his wish is to learn how to improve life, in accordance with the wishes of all the Diallobé, except Thierno, who wished to 'kill the life' in him but without succeeding. His role and purpose have to do with showing others how all life might be preserved, as his father indicates when speaking to the Frenchman Lacroix about the future he foresees for his son in 'la cité future' (p. 101).

These are some of the observations Mme Goré makes about the book in general; and, proceeding from a faulty general view, her treatment of Samba's solitude and death becomes less than reliable. One mistake, easy to make in the circumstances, is that she magnifies the author's meditation on the 'values of death'. Such stress would probably not have seemed warranted had due notice been taken of Kane's method of composition. He constructs the work as a dialectic. Meditation on the 'values of death' generates reflection on the values of life. The sacredness implied in the one appears in the other: life and death together are referable in Kane's perspective to the divine intention. Because he embraces the values of life he can believe in the eventual triumph of the spirit over the forces of aggression that would destroy life.

To the extent that he sees how life can be destroyed, he acknowledges the western sense of death as dissolution. In fact, he feels that survival is constantly threatened so long as man's purpose in life engenders antagonism. The conflict in Samba appears manifest when, assimilating western ideology at the European school, he begins to consider the ideal of life as human self-sufficiency, as he does at the end of part one of the story. His attempt to justify human effort without God makes him feel increasingly alienated from himself, from the Master and from his people. Thus ensues during his stay in the West the sense of death-in-life that will drive him to the verge of despair.

Mme Goré sees in Samba's death only an exemplification of the mystic's way. 'Samba Diallo choisit "la voie du blâme" ', she says, 'lorsqu'il réussit à se faire mettre à mort pour impiété par le Fou, ministre du Destin' (p. 186). She adds further on: 'Sa mort n'est pas suicide mais mort proprement mystique . . . ' (p. 188). Granted that his death is not suicide, it is self-willed, an act of surrender carried out as both a choice and a necessity. Perhaps what keeps it from being suicide is the necessity in its wilfulness, but this touches on its significance, a question considered further on.

As to Mme Goré's contention, at any rate, the author's imagination goes beyond what is known about the way of mystics. It invents a highly arresting scene in which the reader witnesses the consummation of life and death. Samba's 'sense of death' joins with the theme of his solitude and the theme of survival, announced early on in the story, to make the link between denouement and conclusion an unbroken event: the test and confirmation of eternal life in God. His dying is depicted in the interior monologue that ends the story, and we are made to accept its authenticity strictly as a revelation coming from his own fading consciousness of being in history. However, Mme Goré makes short shrift of a remarkable inventiveness when qualifying the hero's self-willed death as a mystical act. In doing so, she passes over the important question of whether the act emanating in his death becomes effective. Does the author, and does Samba, desire an effect that is purely personal? Or does their desire embrace the secret wishes of men generally who wish to believe but have yet to discover the way to a higher existence? At best Mme Goré's statement suggests that Samba feels a need to repent, and that the Madman feels a duty to impose such repentance. But this would seem to indicate that Samba's demeanour is not intended to affect his witnesses; yet, Kane has certainly made the reader as well as the Madman a witness to the character's wilfulness, thereby involving his audience in the act that the hero has been brought to commit. It is pertinent to the significance of the story as a whole to find out what 'blame' the reader himself must assume for this death; Mme Goré's statement hinges around this issue.

In the first place, Samba's act can hardly be construed to exclude the author's and the character's own concern with a collective 'blame' that must be shared by all men who have participated in eliminating the sacred from the world. Secondly, if in the adjective 'mystique' Mme Goré intends the idea of an intuitive belief more persuasive than reason, it may be noticed that Samba is not an absolute believer at the point where he is struck down by the Madman. He is simply like other men who wish to believe but without succeeding fully. Therefore, the intended effect, raised as a question above, has to do with the extent to which the reader is persuaded to believe in the regenerative power accruing to himself and to others as the will to die is carried out by a man who implicates the rest of us in his own half-hearted faith. The way the author makes this involvement seem real cannot be taken up in this paper, but some indications of the boldness of his imagination are offered hereafter regarding another matter that Mme Goré discusses concerning Samba's death.

Lastly and more to her point on Samba's death, she discerns something like stasis in his fading consciousness of historical being; but this mistakes the sense of Kane's conclusion. The depiction is that of a movement through eternity, an ascension outside historical time. So that Mme Goré is only partially right in her summing up, concerning Samba's passage from life to after-life: 'L'aventure mystique devient signe, l'évolution intérieure s'arrête net . . . ' (p. 187). There is little indication in this statement that the ending is especially revealing of the meaning of the total work. The interior monologue is, moreover, a distinct and integral creation in itself because it is carefully conceived and executed to suggest not a halt but endless development as an expansion of consciousness.

Contrary to Mme Goré's idea of stasis, there are five discernible stages through which Samba moves progressively toward being. If the mystical journey ends, as she says, the interior monologue reveals that life in the spirit begins anew, and this is the aspect of the book's conclusion that stands out — the author's guarantee through his imagination of the principle of illimitable becoming in man's enduring spirit. If such a vision has any significance at all, then clearly the author cannot have turned away from life; he shows us instead that even the impossible could be achieved if only the spirit could come back into the life we live every day.

This is all the more evident in that up to a certain point in the interior monologue, Samba is still a personal self; he is Samba Diallo the man. As his incomplete metamorphosis is transcended by the experience of being, the personal self becomes impersonal. His quest has been symbolic all along, whereas only at the end, in union with God, is Samba himself a symbol: he is man fulfilling his destiny.

The author's vision does not represent the reality reported by mystics but the reality of his personal intuition. He succeeds in making his hero's consciousness a synthesis of the Word and knowledge. (The two merging voices in the interior monologue are Samba's and the Master's, thus unification of the human and the divine.) We know of no other such instance of complete being, but we reflect on this one as a possibility for all men. As Samba and the Master articulate a common mind projecting '[cette] véritable communauté spirituelle', the reader understands this as Kane's conception of modern man's 'communauté de destin'. A new understanding of human destiny, in other words, is, for the reader, the effect of this imagination — an effect that finally becomes discernible thanks to the poetry of the depicted experience.

The author persuades the reader to believe the experience by making poetry of it. His appeal is to the heart first: by feeling the wholeness that Samba feels, we may apprehend his destiny as antagonisms dissolve. On the dissolution of a 'hybrid' existence — between being and nothingness — arises consciousness of a unified existence. The author makes us see the possibility of the human in union with the divine. Apparent in this is a broader implication: Samba's example points the way to a higher civilization. But this image of the hero in the flow of time is still not a symbol. Only through the character's own consciousness can we have any idea of what is happening to him. He testifies to attaining being, but generally people are little prepared to believe this since no one reading the book knows what it means to die. We can, on the other hand, believe in the possibility of Samba's personal regeneration.

Mme Goré seems to hardly recognize the personal self within the symbolic man, though in the quest she admits the final reconciliation of opposites (the Word and knowledge, etc). To this extent Kane's vision goes unnoticed for what it is. Actually, it assumes form by means of an illusion of time stopping; that is why, no doubt, Mme Goré speaks of a complete halt. But this is only an interval, an instant, in which the hero's total experience is unified as though to disclose its underlying significance. It is the hero's consciousness, detached from necessarily limiting experience in the uncertain and conditional world that now apprehends its own nature. His consciousness becomes a poetic confirmation of its own limitless possibilities. Kane is suggesting that personal existence in the present can extend endlessly outward toward an unknown horizon in eternity. In the first instance, therefore, the significance of the event is not merely symbolic.

To be a symbol, the image would have to refer to something we can conceive or already know; only in the personal testimony of this particular hero does ultimate being appear as a real possibility. His personal experience cannot be symbolic at all until his personal myth becomes generalized. This is the point evidently, that Kane is making. It is the motive of his imagination in the interior monologue, as can be recognized from the events preceding it, one of which is especially illuminating, namely Samba's exchange of ideas with the Pierre-Louis family. This scene shows Samba justifying his belief in an original identity common to westerners and others (pp. 180–2). Referring to 'cette contrariété de leurs destins', he finds the origin of antagonism not in nature but in history. Consequently, for him, historical time admits of the possible dissolution of differences. Non-westerners, because closer to nature, are the ones he sees leading the way back to nature — to a renewal of man's original participation in the divine intention. The task is written in their destiny, he thinks, as a necessity to be realized in history. Samba's faith embraces the personal myth of humanity unified by a renewal of the sacred, whereas he has found out in the West that men generally are dissociated in a world reflecting human powers only.

It is God's absence, he feels, that enables man to hold the centre of the stage in the cosmos; but human power, as he and his Parisian friends agree, is directed only towards 'l'objet' — the material reward of conquest over nature. The sense of man's omnipotence resulting from that triumph, Samba believes, is only an illusion because human power ignores the divine purpose. He stands thus all the more alone in the West. Does anyone else conceive how the sacred would magnify human possibilities both within and beyond history? Our hero encounters no one who understands his idea of a world at once human and divine, where the sense of death is the sense of a chance in life to make history a record of human accomplishment. This would be unlimited rather than limited to 'l'objet', as in contemporary civilization, because as knowledge and the Word become one, man's achievement goes beyond history and beyond imagination; it becomes, in eternity, achievement of the impossible. This is Samba's personal myth, the interior monologue being its elaboration.

Contrary, then, to Mme Goré's assertion, his inner development goes on — the image of the sea suggesting realization of being in the flux of time. To be sure, his self-unity definitely comes to pass and extends beyond the moment, in so far as it has exemplary value. But the example is that of an entirely new man, whose realness is hard to conceive in our world and thus hard to believe. His example communicates above all a deep faith in what man *can* be.

On this point Mme Goré uses much too strong a verb when she says, 'il incarne . . . la foi' (p. 181). The fact is that in the West Samba no longer feels the omnipresence of God and is in the process of questioning his faith in the light of western reason. It is precisely because he takes survival to be problematic, because he believes in man in spite of history, in spite of man's banishment of God, that his faith gains in validity in the reader's estimation. His example becomes ultimately more persuasive than if he were, as Mme Goré contends, a man of absolute faith. As a man of uncertainty he inspires belief in what he stands for, even though his personal knowledge of the human spirit regenerated and enduring remains his personal myth. Mme Goré unintentionally deprives him of this credit and limits his significance by making him a mystic and considering his adventure a pilgrimage. In fact, we can only wonder what sense she intends in her use of the word 'pèlerinage'; Samba's voyage to the West is not a voyage to a holy place but rather the opposite, and while there, he is far from abdicating reason, as Mme Goré implies that he does. Her position, emphasizing the completeness of his faith, compels a full response to put this aspect of Kane's hero in another perspective, which is to say, Samba might be seen simply as a man of faith distressed by the difficulty of faith in a profane world.

Mme Goré's idea is invalidated especially by the scene that ends part one of the book. It is here that Samba begins to question his faith in a long conversation with his father. His mind is becoming receptive to the foreigner's point of view, which he now knows obliges him, in fairness to himself, to examine his own heritage. The incident anticipates the denouement and establishes carefully the contours of the conclusion, where the interior monologue will elaborate a myth derived from faith refined by reason.

Part two, accordingly, develops the hero's gradual falling away from the faith. He reaches a moment of great significance when, in a letter from the chief of the Diallobé, he hears about the Master, who is near death. This moment of solitude is of a kind to rekindle in him the unquestioning faith of the Master, but Samba turns away from the place where he had once willingly submitted to the Word and where his people regretted his absence and his consequent relinquishment of his election as the teacher's heir. Now entirely alone, partly by circumstance but also by choice, he is obliged to work out his destiny with little or none of the assurance he had felt under the tutelage of the Master.

This scene links the conversation with his father to the conversation with the Madman in the denouement. In the former it is a question of honouring God and his intention; in the latter, a question of venerating the Master and his teaching. At issue in each instance is Samba's faith. In the first instance, his steadfast faith is signified by his acquiescence when his father calls him to pray as their conversation ends; and, in the second instance, by his refusal when the Madman urges him to pray. He refuses to avail himself of his last chance to regain the faith he knew as a child at the 'Glowing Hearth', though the Madman, taking up in effect the thread of the earlier discussion between father and son, now knows that only prayer will save the apparent apostate from the death-in-life he has suffered in the West. Thus, struck down by the Madman's weapon, Samba is dying, and now comes to full development the interior monologue which was already taking form at the end of part one as the hero complied with his father's bidding to pray.

The idea advanced by Mme Goré, that Samba is the embodiment of faith and dies in the manner of a mystic because he is insistent on attaining union with God, is hardly tenable in the light of the book's structural elements indicated above. In fact, if we notice what happens when Samba turns his back on the Master and his people, it is apparent that Mme Goré has overstated the mystical aspect of the crisis Samba is about to face. As the letter falls from his hands he seems no longer to remember nor to care what the issues are among his people: 'Que me font leurs problèmes? J'ai le droit de . . . me retirer au-dedans de moi-même. Après tout, je ne suis que moi-même. Je n'ai que moi' (p. 152). His thoughts are focused on his feeling of being separate and alone as he begins to face with a critical mind the mystery of life and death. He is continuing to question his faith.

The questioning will become a testing, already apparent in the supplication he is about to address to God. In the anguish of decision he borrows the 'unalterable accents' of the Sufis, says Mme

Goré, or the earlier cry of Chibli (pp. 185–6). The words deserve notice, first Samba's (in which the accents of the Sufis are underlined), then Chibli's, as cited by Mme Goré:

'Mon Dieu, Tu ne Te souviens donc pas? Je suis bien cette âme que Tu faisais pleurer en l'emplissant. . . . Je ne t'ai pas demandé de faire éclore cette lueur qui, un jour, perçut qu'elle ardait. Tu m'as voulu. Tu ne saurais m'oublier comme cela. Je n'accepterais pas, seul de nous deux, de pâtir de Ton éloignement. . . . ' (p. 152)

Celui qui est habitué à Ton intimité, ne peut supporter l'éloignement. Celui qui a été touché au coeur par Ton amour, ne peut supporter même la proximité. Si l'oeil ne te voit pas, le coeur t'a déjà vu (p. 186)

While Samba does express a sense of having been elected, he is still in the world where he must be in order for his people to learn how they can safeguard their heritage. He feels some responsibility toward others and is carrying out his function as the chosen one with a view to effecting the salvation of others as well as his own. The significant thing here is not that he uses the words of the Sufis (there is a fund of religious lore), but that the text is preparing in a structural way for the denouement. It is instructive to consider the 'unalterable accents' as a notation on the theme of solitude and death. Professor Gerald Moore chooses to quote them in *African Literature* and it is relevant to notice the way he comments: 'At once the final isolation of Samba Diallo is understood in all its desolation. In this light, his suicide itself becomes explicable, almost acceptable. . . . '[9]

If Mme Goré's position compels assent, it is obviously not without qualification. She has not overcome the reservation expressed by Roger Mercier who suggested that the denouement of *Ambiguous Adventure* risked sacrificing 'la vraisemblance',[10] nor the broader criticism levelled by Albert Gérard in his review of the book shortly after its appearance. He called Samba's death: ' . . . une mort absurde . . . fondée sur un malentendu, un malentendu . . . évitable, artificiel, arbitrairement machiné par un romancier encore malhabile, qui croit nécessaire de terminer son oeuvre sur une retentissante dissonnance.'[11] Then comes Professor Moore who seems less than convinced by Mme Goré's attempt to make Samba's death understandable in the light of the Sufi sayings despite her descant, late in her talk, that the death of Kane's hero is not suicide. Evidently, something is still wanting; we are back to the initial issue. How are we to understand Samba's self-willed death in relation to his life as a believer and unbeliever in a world where he is isolated because, it is said in the text, 'God is dead'? The question remains because the link established by Mme Goré that places Kane's hero in the tradition of Sufi mysticism, however illuminating in itself, needs to be broadened to take account of Samba's involvement in the profane world. I shall go on to expand this broader view.

Samba's isolation is the immediate consequence of his adventure beyond the order of the Word. He can no longer feel life as participation in the divine intention. God's purpose as he learned it at the 'Glowing Hearth' is not the purpose of men in the secular world. Here there is a contradiction of the order of things first given him by his teacher, who exacted his submission to the Word. Now, in place of the Word, authority for the permanent validity of his people's way of life, he finds that science, the keystone of human knowledge, is the promise of existence for men without God.

In the circumstances, he feels constrained to examine his own beliefs critically — the beliefs his people were seeking to safeguard in the first place when they sent him to find out 'how one can conquer without being in the right'. As a result of his experience of exile and desolation confronted with the awesome potential of science, they might eventually understand that knowledge itself generates the power to conquer both nature and people. Samba, himself, would similarly have to admit that if colonization was one manifestation of western power, his own seduction by western thought was another (p. 186). He sees, finally, in western ideology a risk to human survival; for in the absence of God he realizes that the life of men can hardly be regarded as sacred. In this connection he remarks with a certain poignancy:

> 'C'est le même geste de l'Occident, qui maîtrise la chose et nous colonise tout à la fois. Si nous n'éveillons pas l'Occident à la différence qui nous sépare de la chose, nous ne vaudrons pas plus qu'elle, et ne la maîtrieserons jamais. Et notre échec serait la fin du dernier humain de cette terre'. (p. 183)

Because, the West makes little distinction between people and things, the issue for Samba is humanity and its survival; and he feels that survival depends on non-westerners who must lead men back to the ideal of existence for God inculcated in him at the 'Glowing Hearth'.

In the foregoing summary of the general movement of the drama as it anticipates the denouement, it is perhaps sufficient to point out that in the development of events viewed as an intention executed by the author, what we find happening is this: while Samba's adventure remains ambiguous — consciousness of himself as a 'hybrid' isolated from participation in his own world as well as the foreigner's — his quest assumes the character of a dialectical examination of man's remaining chances in the world. He is about to take stock of his own remaining chances by invoking the thesis that God is necessary for survival, and then opposing it (as he inclines to do at the end of part one of the story) by considering the antithesis that survival depends on man alone. The 'hybrid' that he is becomes the empty forum wherein both positions are asserted by himself alone for his own hearing in his solitude. Uttering the former position is a voice firm and clear; uttering the latter is a distressed voice. Finally, in the calm of the divine presence both voices are heard again in the interior monologue, announcing the hero's release from solitude and his deliverance from ambiguity, while the two as one express the ultimate ambiguity of being in the divine solitude.

This *ambiguous* synthesis is anticipated by the problem of choice which Samba faces on the death of the Master and the subsequent passing of the original order of things. Now, all things are uncertain, even in the land of the Diallobé (as is evident in Samba's final encounter with the Madman). The choice to be made must presuppose that the unbeliever in himself can rejoin the believer, and that knowledge acquired in history can find accommodation with the enduring Word in eternity. Like his own self-unity, therefore, a renewal of the sacred is conceivable as a possibility. But the object in choosing, which is to say a humanity cognizant of the divine purpose, is shut out by the fact of the two opposing terms between which he must choose, namely existence for man or existence for God. It follows that God's presence among men can be only an object of imagination. Kane's imagination will attempt to make it real, at least for his hero, who must find a way to transcend the given opposition in the two choices. The only way, now that the Master is dead and there is no longer any certainty, is through death because this is the only guarantee in the contingent world.

Death, however, no longer justifies faith: the demise of the Master has not regenerated in Samba the life of the spirit; it has not brought him back to the faith. Death may or may not bear out the promise of the Word. Samba understands it in the only way he can, given his present state of mind; he understands that natural life ends. The same state of mind impels him to find out whether the regenerated spirit endures. The act by which he will do so becomes at the same time a renewal of his faith. It requires him to face death without the assurance he had felt under the teaching of the Master.

There, at the 'Glowing Hearth', he had felt assurance and security, even when at the Master's direction, he came face to face with death during the moments he was chanting litanies to warn people about the terrible Azraël, angel of death. He knew on his teacher's authority that Azraël could be at times benign. It is the now-deceased Master who understood best among the Diallobé 'les valeurs de mort'. Speaking to the Most Royal Lady on this subject, he had once insisted: 'Non, Madame. Ce sont des valeurs ultimes qui se tiendront encore au chevet du dernier humain' (p. 42). At home, then, Samba knew that giving up natural life need not mean dissolution of the spirit, that on the contrary surrender to God insures the preservation of life. The demise of the Master marks the end of that assurance and the beginning of his contemplating alone the values of death as well as the relation of God to man, a subject on which, in a letter from his father, he is reminded of the teaching of his religion (pp. 192–4). Now forlorn, he feels forsaken by the Master:

'Maître, appela-t-il en pensée, que me reste-t-il? Les ténèbres me gagnent. . . . ' Le visage du maître ne bougeait pas. Samba Diallo, de nouveau, l'invoqua. 'Toi . . . qui, seul, détiens la Parole . . . j'implore en grâce ta clameur dans l'ombre, l'éclat de ta voix, afin de me ressusciter à la tendresse secrète. . . . ' Mais le visage avait disparu (pp. 190–1)

Samba must try as best he can to reach God alone. From here the drama goes on in the solitude of an individual heart preparing to transcend the necessity of choosing between existence for man and existence for God.

This begins a test of his waning faith. Once again he articulates a supplication to God — in the same words as when learning earlier of the Master's last act in making Demba his heir: 'Tu ne saurais m'oublier comme cela. Je n'accepterai pas, seul de nous deux, de pâtir de Ton éloignement. Je n'accepterai pas. Non. . . . ' (p. 205). Expressing a will to surrender, he calls upon God to witness and relieve his solitude in the profane world. He brings God to testify to His presence among men so his faith can be renewed; otherwise he will have pierced the mystery of the Word by assimilating it to myth, thanks to a critical mind that still wishes to believe. If Samba does personify faith, as Mme Goré says, it is a faith he must test nonetheless; for, having relinquished his place as heir of the Master, he now has no alternative but to choose death for the sake of regenerating life — his own and all men's — in a world he feels can only survive by a meeting between knowledge and the Word. This is the synthesis his solitude has brought him to envisage in consequence of his adventure in the West.

Samba's solitude, then, arises from his difficulty of feeling at one with God. He has come to see his last remaining chance of realizing this unity not in the preservation of natural life but on the other side of it. In this connection there is a question as to why he has a need to *feel* God, given this teaching of his religion: 'Dieu n'est commensurable à rien. . . . Dieu n'est point notre parent' (pp. 192–3). Notwithstanding her special knowledge of Islam, Mme Goré leaves the question unanswered.

She tells us little more than we can know without reference to Islam, that: 'L'exile réel du héros en Europe vient de ce qu'il ne "sent" plus la présence divine. . . . ' (pp. 184–5). Finally, she simply poses the issue and leaves it virtually untouched, saying only: 'Or, curieusement, ce héros qui privilégie tellement le sentiment est celui-là même qui inscrit l'Absolu dans une transcendance adamantine' (p. 185). The oddness she sees in this development might have directed attention back to the cause of Samba's solitude, to the moment when he first felt alone. Mme Goré does not look for such a moment, though it could be an indication as to why in Europe he has a need he did not have at home within the order of the Word.

She might have found reason to choose a different direction from that taken near the heart of her exposition where she says: 'Tout le livre d'Hamidou est . . . dominé par une solitude radicale: celle de l'homme qui croit aux "valeurs de mort" ' (p. 179). This distinctiveness is pointed out also as follows: 'ce sens noir de la mort . . . est pour Hamidou Kane solitude primitive de tout homme antérieurement à une quelconque différenciation raciale', and the idea is extended with emphasis: 'la solitude de Samba Diallo, solitude fondamentale, n'est pas celle de l'opprimé, elle est celle de tout homme . . . ' (p. 180).

This very concise language attributes to Kane's vision the same inherent solitude it says is present in man. Samba's feeling of isolation from God is, accordingly, atavistic in nature; and we are apparently to understand that in this he is like other men. It is as a black man, Mme Goré seems to think, that Samba's loneness impels him toward death. The solitude she calls 'fundamental' is, in this view, a privileged sentiment, as is the 'feeling for death'. Samba's race, in other words, has preserved the sense of some fundamental truth about life and death. But how does this accord with the idea that he represents every man?

As if to give an answer, Mme Goré invokes a pre-historical, if not mythical, condition common to all men, which is now presumed to be in Samba a particularity of his race. This seems initially to be exactly what Samba means when he refers to 'cette nature originelle où éclate notre identité avec eux', going on to suggest that this original nature is preserved in his racial identity: 'Ce sentiment de notre absence . . . établit notre nécessité et indique notre tâche la plus urgente, qui est le déblaiement de la nature' (p. 182). Closeness to nature and hence harmony with God, would seem of itself to preclude solitude, but perhaps only a mystic could answer this presupposition. At any rate, there is little to convince us that Samba's solitude can properly be called 'primitive' or 'fundamental' when we remember that he began life in harmony with the Word. He begins to feel estrangement only when, on leaving the Koranic school, he comes in contact with western ideology, and the original harmony he felt is displaced.

Mme Goré offers what we might take as an alternative idea to 'primitive' and 'fundamental' solitude, and comes closer to the text, when she says: 'Mais la solitude de Samba Diallo lui est surtout intérieure' (p. 181). She quickly adds, however, this related remark that seems determined to make him a mystic from birth: 'Il doit à sa nature et à son éducation d'être pétri de l'oubli de soi. . . . ' (p. 181) This is a strange thing to say when he certainly does explain himself, his inner being, to his Parisian friends. What she considers his self-forgetting and isolation even in childhood is, more realistically, an austere demeanour and seriousness reflecting the discipline imposed on the pupil by the Master.

In a consistent manner, the 'feeling for death' in the pupil at the 'Glowing Hearth' is positive submission to the divine law. He accepts God's conditions for the preservation of life as shown by his two childhood encounters with death — when he learns the ways of Azraël, and later when he concludes about Old Rella that she could not have disappeared forever. Only later, in his despair of finding God, does his 'feeling for death' become a sense of the possible impermanence of the spirit. This occurs, like his feeling of solitude, under western tutelage where death means dissolution of life because permanently estranged from God, man is alone. Seen in the light of Kane's regret and critique of a world that makes no room for the sacred, the relation between Samba's 'feeling for death' and his feeling of solitude suggests, in the final analysis, that it has induced in him a will to die having this dual intention: to beseech God to assert His presence in the world, and, in a strangely detached way, to make a protest against the self — through the Madman as intermediary, his alter ego — as the image of all men who have lost God and are alone.[12] In the denouement he evinces a wilful approach to the mystery of God's absence from human life, a fact of his experience that makes natural life an experience of non-being. Yet, in the conclusion he makes us contemplate the mystery of mysteries: in union with God he is still alone. How can this be?

An understanding was in the offing, it seems, at the point in Mme Goré's discussion where she notes that 'la solitude de Samba Diallo est entée sur la solitude divine' (p. 181). This is a compelling observation and probably a key insight. One can only wish that Mme Goré had developed it, for it raises at the very least this two-fold question: is Samba's loneliness in life finally transmuted into bliss by his union with God; or does that union amount to a complete blank, a joining of the finite self with the infinite in an austere, solitary marriage without end? If Kane is depicting his hero in the latter light, his overall vision would seem to arise from a faith he feels to be strangely deceptive, or perhaps from an intuition that masks a certain scepticism. Mme Goré does not go into this, but her insight, so admirably phrased, might well have produced a new awareness of Kane's sensibility and the ultimate quality of his hero's experience of eternity. Finally, she seems to contradict her idea about the 'divine solitude' when she says of Samba's death as a mystical act that 'elle rompt enfin le cycle de ces solitudes' (p. 188).

However, what we actually find in the interior monologue, is solitude still in death. Though now the image of man with God, Samba is alone just as he was alone in life as the image of a split self: African and westerner, believer and unbeliever, the 'Master' and the Madman. But he has realized being, which turns out to be a two-ness like the two-ness he felt in life as nothingness. The book is saying something unrecognized so far, it seems, about being and nothingness as the analogue of two in one.

The foregoing analysis prompts the conclusion that Mme Goré's explanation of Samba Diallo's solitude and death is unconvincing in the final analysis; and strangely, this is plainly due to her great admiration for the black poet. She rightly considers Kane a poet whose artistic expression bears the stamp of his religion. Islam, she thinks, brings out the African character; thus, while the drama in *Ambiguous Adventure* is an interior drama, it is nonetheless exemplary, transposing to the intellectual level the legend of the black man's 'Holy Grail'. One can hardly quarrel with her up to this point. Her explanation begins to raise some difficulty when reminding us that Kane has referred to 'the exile of the soul'; in his view, she reports, westerners have broken away from the sources of life. When she tries to tell us how the black man has retained a closeness to those sources, the difficulty becomes full-blown. It may be that one can say in clear language what the white man has lost, and succeed more or less in describing the resultant state of being. It is altogether another problem to make clear what the black man has retained; and, regarding his state of being, an encapsulated description is not likely to prove satisfactory to many people. The consequence is far-reaching, for obviously an attempt to encode that state of being at all costs can be dangerous.

We see this in Mme Goré's appreciation. By a predilection for the black poet's 'soul', she is drawn into the position of having to tell us that Kane's representation of the African character amounts to a journey of discovery (a quest for the 'grail'); and she is forced to go further and contend that the journey of discovery is a movement backwards to what Georges Gusdorf, in another, though highly pertinent, discussion calls 'la conscience mythique'.[13] She seems to forget, having once mentioned it, that Kane's book features a people participating in 'la conscience intellectuelle' (another of Gusdorf's terms) while prolonging simultaneously 'la conscience mythique'.

They have indeed been thrust into the present by the western invaders, and the significance of this fact is evident, again, from Georges Gusdorf's observation as follows: 'l'homme d'à présent reconnaît implicitement la différence entre le monde quotidien, désacralisé, et la surréalité religieuse.'[14] What is not given sufficient notice, then, in Mme Goré's position is the Diallobés' presentday standpoint; in the age of 'la conscience intellectuelle', they are making the distinction between 'le monde désacralisé' and 'la surréalité religieuse'. The consciousness turned toward spiritual reality in Kane's depiction cannot, therefore, be that of a movement backwards to 'la conscience mythique'. The Diallobé are concerned with making known the real object of the myth in the present day, which is a renewal of the sacred in a secular world.

This spiritual objective in Kane's work is noted by Mme Goré as 'cette science secrète dont il sent qu'elle est toute la richnesse de son peuple . . . ' which one can accept. Remarking, however, that Kane himself has mentioned the failings of black cultures (and by interpolation one might imply a kind of primitive stasis or atavistic inertia), she goes on to say that these failings find a compensation in 'cette "intuition de la mort" ' that haunts the best pages of *Ambiguous Adventure* (p. 179). There is something troubling in this, for it seems to be an appreciation of the 'sense of death' as the poetry of a people whose feeling for the sacred gives their way of life an inorganic character.

If intellectuals like Kane feel that the historical process of such a culture is tantamount to marking time, the implicit standpoint is western but with the advantage of a broader ontological perspective, which westerners in the circumstances, such as the Frenchman Lacroix, are hardly likely to bring to their judgement. It is easy for them to assume, incorrectly, that 'le néant' is the essence of the feeling for the sacred. Persons open to this, on the other hand, like Mme Goré, seem to be extolling it for the wrong reason when suggesting that it keeps a people like the Diallobé close to a bygone mythical age. If in the end 'cette science secrète' is judged to be as valuable as that other science which in the West insures the evolution of human institutions, it is because the sacred in life becomes finally meaningful only after first being recognized as a poetic expression of a commitment to death.

It is not death, however, but spiritual life that the Diallobé feel in their world; an intuitive grasp of the divine intention reinforced by the Word has given the structure of their culture permanent validity, which is ontological, not historical. As the divine intention embraces death, the Diallobé's 'intuition de la mort' makes their lives whole.

In Europe, Samba's 'sense of death' contains regret that secular life is not whole. He is trying to make it whole, though not in the way he is presumed to be exemplifying the black man's 'intuition de la mort'. This is taken by Mme Goré, we have noticed, and by some other observers of black cultures, to signify a literal predisposition or fascination for something like the purity of nothingness or nonexistence. 'Self-naughting' is the term she says Sartre has used, and she sees a stark expression of 'self-naughting' behaviour in Kane's hero. Though she recognizes that the myth has been transposed to the intellectual level, she chooses to understand the content of the myth in a way that keeps it mythical. It follows, in her view, that Samba represents a people who have turned back from life; even from the intellectual standpoint, the sacred can point only to nothingness. The black man's spiritual reality must be myth! Thus, for Mme Goré, the black poet becomes like the voice of mystery telling God's secret — to all who unlike himself have lost the power to withdraw to man's original closeness to 'that secret wisdom'. Kane, she thinks, manifests this power to a remarkable degree and reaches a rare starkness of presentation. But in the writings of other Africans (and Afro-Americans too, she says, pointing to James Baldwin's expression of the 'sense of death') she sees a similar way of being that she considers the privilege of a race. This is an expression of appreciation, of course, though in a way it is unfortunate.

Many writers have contributed to the invention and use of such symbols as 'the night' and 'the darkness' in attempting to encode a distinctive racial trait, but this is not an easy matter to fathom. The quality of soul among persons of African heritage that Mme Goré calls asceticism and re-defines as 'l'intuition de la mort' turns out in the end to denote, because of partial understanding, an apparent sublime backwardness. This is easily thought to be very real in the behaviour of a race; the other side of the trait in question stands for naught, that is the affirmation of the human spirit in daily life. Not taking note of this, Mme Goré begins to sound like the Frenchman Lacroix in the story, her urbane and laudatory language notwithstanding, for she establishes this explicit contrast: 'Aux blancs la lumière, le progrès, l'histoire, la techniques; aux noirs la nuit, non point féconde et mère des hommes, mais solitaire et image de la mort' (p. 179). While this dangerous observation is meant to applaud, Lacroix expresses a similar view with no intention to applaud. He chides the Diallobé for not realizing that their absolute is merely nothingness and that 'cette fascination du néant' is only an exalted compensation for having nothing (p. 99). With different intentions, the critic and the character see almost the same thing.

In sum, the very concise treatment of Samba Diallo's solitude and death that Mme Goré offers, admittedly in limited space, is on the whole misleading, though perceptive here and there when she recalls the actual text. Despite a key insight of considerable significance, as has been mentioned, it contains a useful formulation of certain technical features of the book within a general exposition that nonetheless provokes considerable reservation.

NOTES

1. In *Actes du colloque sur la littérature africaine d'expression française*, Université de Dakar, Publications de la Faculté des Lettres et Sciences Humaines, Langue et Littérature, 14, 1965, pp. 177–88. (An English translation appears in *African Literature and the Universities*, Gerald Moore (ed.), Ibadan University Press, 1965, pp. 27–40.) All further page references to this paper, which are incorporated into the text, are to the Dakar edition.
2. Gerald Moore, 'Introduction', *African Literature*, op.cit., p. 4.
3. All further page references, which are incorporated into the text, refer to the original French edition of *Ambiguous Adventure*, Paris, Juillard, 1961. New York, Macmillan, 1969. London, Heinemann (AWS 119), 1972; Exeter, NH, Heinemann Inc.
4. *Esprit*, No. 299, Oct. 1961, pp. 375–87.
5. It may be useful to compare the original French with the Enᵹlish rendering of Mme Goré's words in this citation and, for further sampling, in the two succeeding citations. Here, the English translation reads: 'is not, as the humanists believe, the development of the creature, but the centring of the life on God, in obedience to the concept of the Divine Unity' (translator unnamed, in *African Literature and the Universities*, ed. Gerald Moore, p. 30).
6. Translation: 'The pilgrimage he describes does not begin as a search for the balanced development of man; its roots lie rather in Sufism . . . ' (in *African Literature*, ed. Gerald Moore, p. 32).
7. These words appear in the original text as follows: 'Est-il de civilisation hors l'équilibre de l'homme et sa disponibilité?' In the American edition the English translation reads: 'Is civilization outside the balance of man and his disposability?' (Katherine Woods, translator, *Ambiguous Adventure*, New York: Macmillan, 1969, p. 63).
8. Translation: 'the contempt for life by which the whole book is penetrated' (in *African Literature*, ed. Gerald Moore, p. 34).
9. Gerald Moore, op. cit., p. 4.
10. 'La Littérature Africaine d'Expression Française . . . ' in *Actes du colloque*, op.cit., p. 31.
11. 'Lettres africaines: *L'Aventure ambiguë*', La Revue Nouvelle, XXIV, 1961, 441–50, see p. 449.
12. The role of the Madman deserves full study. Suffice it to say here that when he sees in Samba a life force identical with that of the Master almost extinguished, he will violently reject this apparent proof that the Master no longer lives. Unable to cope with the image of his world dissolving in Samba, he will seek to reverse this demise of his own being by making Samba a victim of sacrifice to the reinstitution of the sacred in the world. Finally, he lives on, alone, without the 'Master'

who, for him, is Samba, and who dies to be reborn as the Master, the legitimate heir of Thierno. We thus hear in the interior monologue two voices in one.

13. Georges Gusdorf says: La conscience mythique oriente l'action humaine en fonction d'un horizon défini une fois pour toutes . . . ' *Mythe et métaphysique*, Paris, Flammarion, 1953, p. 22.

14. ibid., pp. 22–4.

Still a Victim?
Mariama Bâ's
Une si Longue Lettre

Femi Ojo-Ade

'Women are man's proletariat.' (Karl Marx)

'Woman is inferior to man and is his subject.' (*The Koran*)

'The head of every man is Christ; the head of every woman is man.' (*The Bible*)

Introduction

Since the first contact with the white world, black literature has remained a literature of the underprivileged, a voice of the victim, a mirror of man's inhumanity to man, a record of the revolt of the recalcitrant against the cultural rape perpetrated by the racist colonizer.[1] Unfortunately, the community has emerged worse off than the individual. From the long drawn-out struggle came self-determination, self-satisfaction, self-aggrandizement: the self before the other; the élite before the masses; man before woman. Black literature underscores the continued colonization of the race; for authentic decolonization can be achieved only when the equation changes from self-independence to society-independence, from male-superior/female-inferior to male-female.

Like the near impossible dream of genuine black emancipation in a world where confusion, conflagration and ever-changing complexities and complexes draw people away from a real effort to

Une si Longue Lettre is available in an English translation under the title *So Long a Letter*, Ibadan, New Horn and London, Heinemann 1981 (AWS 247), Charles Merrill, Columbus, Ohio.

solve basic problems, female liberation may remain just that, a dream frustrated by harsh, existential realities. The Bible gives us Adam and Eve. The Koran asserts male superiority. The twentieth century, the era of dynamism and progress, the age of decolonization and purification (some would quickly add decadence and pollution), presents a forum for feminism, even if the fad is viewed with a sneer by the chauvinistic community.

Feminism, an occidental phenomenon like many others, has spread ever so slowly but steadily to the forbidden land of Africa. Forbidden, because the continent where man supposedly first surfaced prides herself on her tradition and resilience against foreign cultural intrusion. Such 'aberrations' as feminism are abhorred by many who are, however, the very purveyors of the bastardization of that culture whose contents remain confusing to their civilized minds. Criticism does not stop feminism from rearing its head; for society is a dynamic entity condemned to change from within and without. The war between male and female is now a contemporary constant, and new literary voices from among the once silent minority[2] cry out to be heard, even if there is reason to doubt on whose behalf the revolt is being declared.

Grace Ogot, Efua Sutherland, Ama Ata Aidoo, Flora Nwapa, women writers all, constitute the 'old guard',[3] steeped in the traditions of the land, complaining of their sufferings as subjects of the male master, but seeking solace in a society that has proclaimed woman the mother. That group's conciliatory position has been superseded by a current of revolt. Compromise is replaced by criticism and condemnation. Respect turns into repudiation. Devotion is buried by divorce. Buchi Emecheta, Nafissatou Diallo, Mariama Bâ,[4] those are the voices currently crying out for the liberation of woman, the second-class citizen.[5] Not an easy struggle, that; for the vocal female victim, born of the delicate wedlock of tradition and colonialism, and therefore imbued with the modernizing notions of intellectualism and equality, cannot shed the cloak of womanhood, that glorified niche carved out of the birth-pangs that constitute every mother's everlasting joy. Contradiction is indeed inevitable. Hard choices have to be made, and commitment could be destructive. *Une si Longue Lettre* is a study of those contradictions.

Mariama Bâ, the author,[6] is Senegalese, an educated Senegalese, a member of several associations interested in enhancing the female position in a predominantly Moslem, male-oriented society. Her western education notwithstanding, she would like to be considered as an 'average Senegalese woman', 'a woman of the house'.[7] *Lettre* is her first novel and it is filled with autobiographical elements, expressing as it does the novelist's desires and dilemma's, tracing her life in a society caught between the established order of the past and the exigencies of the present. A traditionalist at heart, Bâ aspires to be a revolutionary. A maternal retiring figure through and through, she aspires to be a pioneer in female emancipation. Her family upbringing and the Koranic training have imbued her with the absolute law of 'divine wish': man is woman's overlord. Added to that is Bâ's fatalism. Destiny is a fixed reality, impossible to avoid.

> Destiny seizes whoever he wants, when he wants. If his desire tallies with yours, he brings you an overabundance of bliss. But most often, he unbalances and brings conflict. You can only submit yourself to his laws.[8]

However, such fatalistic tendencies are contradictory to the tenets of the white man's school where Bâ learned how to manipulate the French language. Submissiveness in the face of suffering is discouraged and the victim is told to demand total reform of the social order. Her 'letter' is written in the form of a notebook kept by the heroine named Ramatoulaye. Married for thirty years to Modou by whom she has twelve children, Ramatoulaye has been separated for five years from her husband who repudiated her and left her for a much younger woman. Her 'letter', ostensibly addressed to a bosom friend, a divorcee working as an interpreter in the Senegalese embassy in New York and due to return home very soon, is written immediately after Modou's death. It is a reflection of life in a psychological ghetto of mental torture and social disorder, where woman is a slave and a beast of prey. Divorce is a rarity but separation and infidelity are common. The life of the couple, far from being a haven of contentment and consideration, is a hell of conniving criminals and common cretins. According to Bâ, two camps are precisely delineated: the victimizer, the slave-master, the ruler of this hell on earth, is Man; the victimized, the slave driven at times to the point of mental exhaustion, is Woman.

The Male Victimizer

Man, the unfaithful husband; Man, the womanizer; Man, the victimizer — Bâ's novel describes him in all his negative forms, without an exception to console his pride. First, there is Ramatoulaye's spineless husband, Modou Fall, a successful lawyer, a trade-union leader turned company executive. Happily married for twenty-five years, he suddenly takes an interest in Binetou, a teenage school-girl and friend of his daughter, Daba. Before his first wife can sift through the maze of lies and manipulations, Modou has aban-doned the matrimonial home to live with his new wife and her mother. Ramatoulaye is left forever with the question unanswered: 'Madness? Spinelessness? Irresistible love? What internal upheaval deranged Modou Fall to make him marry Binetou?' (p. 22). Definitely the fault is not Ramatoulaye's; as she makes the reader understand, she has made a thorough self-analysis and has come up with nothing to explain her husband's behaviour. Modou himself has the following explanation: God has destined him to have a second wife. To which the victimized heroine quickly responds with a sneer similar to that of a perfect angel ogled by a lecherous wolf but adamant to keep her innocence intact.

Yet, there are indications that Modou may not be a totally lost case of male monstrosity. Ramatoulaye mentions the fact that Binetou, 'a bit timid, frail, ill-at-ease, visibly, in (the bourgeois) milieu' (p. 54), is a beautiful apple ripe for plucking by someone with eyes good enough to see. 'Her beauty shone, pure. The har-monious curves of her body could not pass unnoticed' (p. 54). There she was, all aglow, a constant visitor to the Fall household, God's beauty there for appreciating by the clear-sighted, handsome Modou. Besides, Binetou, beautiful and appreciative of beauty around her, takes in the concrete elements of comfort in the Fall home. Bourgeois bountifulness conflicts with peasant poverty and the young girl's mother drives home the point, incessantly. She 'wishes so much to get out of her mediocre condition' and begs her daughter to give her 'a happy ending, in a real house' (p. 55). So, the narrator depicts the mother as a materialistic, daughter-hawking monster while her daughter is the innocent victim.

Man is the symbol of evil. There is Modou's friend, Mawdo Bâ, an excellent doctor but an execrable husband. Like Modou, he is hap-pily married to Aïssatou, intelligent daughter of a goldsmith. The wife does the husband proud by raising her status in society: she becomes a teacher, leaving behind her the banal existence of the uncivilized for the bourgeois life of the civilized. Mawdo falls prey to his mother's jealousy and vengeful sentiments over her only son's relationship with Aïssatou, the simple peasant, and her poor, lower-class family. The narrator writes:

Your mother-in-law, who saw you glowing near her son, who saw her son frequent more and more your father's forge, who saw your mother become more robust and better dressed, your mother-in-law thought more and more of her vengeance. (p. 41)

The vengeance came in the form of a girl, the niece of Aunt Nabou, Mawdo's mother. She goes to her brother and brings back the young girl to live with Mawdo. Duty towards mother calls for devotion. Devotion to duty is concretely expressed in desire of the flesh. Little Nabou grows in girth quickly enough. A child is the natural outcome, and Aïssatou decides to put an end to her life with Mawdo. Her parting remarks to the irresponsible husband:

You wish to dissociate love pure and simple from physical love. I hurl back at you the accusation that carnal knowledge cannot be without the acceptance of the heart, no matter how minimal it is. . . . Man is one: grandeur and animality confused. No gesture on his part is pure ideal. No gesture on his part is pure bestiality. (p. 50)

If Mawdo is guilty of failing to control the sexual beast in him, one wonders whether he is any more guilty than the mother who makes him marry his beautiful cousin; or more guilty than Ramatoulaye who helps Aunt Nabou to raise and educate the wife-to-be in full knowledge of the facts, while Aïssatou is kept in total ignorance.

There is no redemption for man, the monster. There is the Senegalese doctor, Samba Diack, married to the Ivoirian Jacqueline. A stunning beauty, she disobeys her parents, marries the foreigner in Abidjan and leaves with him for Dakar. Landed in a world strange to her, she becomes disoriented and disillusioned. She is harried for being a Protestant in a Moslem society, and is treated as a bushwoman by the hostile Senegalese. Diack makes life worse by his constant escapades with the alluring Dakarois girls that he had missed so much during his Ivoirian sojourn. Jacqueline falls into nervous depression and is on the brink of insanity. Fortunately, she is saved by a competent, humane psychiatrist who helps rid her of the dark shadow dogging her footsteps. And Diack? Not much is really said about him in the novel. The bare facts of his disdainful nature are put before us. Jugement has been made by the narrator: Man is guilty, as usual. However, all the episodes described by the narrator prove beyond doubt that the victimizer, no matter how vile he is, no matter how mean he is, is an ever-present figure in woman's life.

Aïssatou: Divorce, a Solution in Solitude

Man's basic guilt, the root cause for his vilification, the main element of his vicious behaviour, is polygamy. Polygamy, the estate revered by traditionalists as a function of Africanity. Polygamy, once supported and even suggested by African woman as a socio-economic expediency. That, vows Aïssatou, is a thing of the past. Polygamy is now the bane of society. Polygamy is a vice to be dealt with not by procrastination but by divorce. So, Aïssatou Bâ leaves the beast called Mawdo.

Aïssatou is, like her friend Ramatoulaye, an intellectual, that rare breed especially among the female species. Excellent students in the white man's school, their intelligence is extolled by their peers, and they themselves set out to be pioneers in the emancipation of women. Ramatoulaye will forever remember the white woman who 'first wanted for [them] a destiny "out of the ordinary" '. She continues:

> We were real sisters destined for the same emancipatory mission. To free us from the prison of traditions, superstitions and local mores; to make us appreciate multiple civilizations without denying ours; to raise our vision of the world, to cultivate our personality, reinforce our qualities, checkmate our faults; bring to fruition in us the values of universal morals; there is the task that the admirable headmistress took upon herself. (pp. 27–8)

The civilizing mission of colonialism could not have succeeded better. Aïssatou and Ramatoulaye are, so to speak, among the select few, and the selectors are, naturally, the whites. Their light shines forth in all its splendour. The path is well traced out before them: to bring to reality the 'profound options of the new Africa, to promote the black woman', to liberate her from the frustrating taboos of traditional Africa. The lesson is taught with precision, and assimilated — the word is not used by chance — extraordinarily well: marriage is built on love. Parents have no right to choose a husband for a girl. Dowry is a materialistic institution. All that matters to the wife is her husband who belongs to her wholly and to whom she belongs wholly, irrespective of any family ties that he normally has. Polygamy underscores African savagery and man's dehumanization of woman.

Aïssatou has four children by Mawdo, but that is a secondary issue when the time of rupture arrives. Consideration for the children would be another example of the tenets of a society of tree-climbers. 'Innocent victim of an unjust cause and hardy pioneer of a new life' (p. 53), she rejects sharing her husband's vile existence. She prefers dignity to disgrace, chooses solitude instead of solidarity. Solidarity. The warmth of a touch, a smile, a gesture. The sound of human voices. The chatter of children playing under the tropical sun. The shouts of a shameless husband defending his sham cause. The anger of a tearful wife consoled by the presence of the human face near her late at night and in times of trouble. But such solidarity, without rhyme or reason, without logic, is unacceptable to the civilized, calculating mind. Aïssatou leaves Dakar for New York with her four children. The narrator leaves a lot of questions half-answered or unanswered, such as the following: is Aïssatou happy in her solitude? How does she survive through the cold, wintry New York nights? What is her present attitude to men? Ramatoulaye's story tends to imply that Aïssatou's departure is not an action taken in search of happiness; or if that is the motive, that the objective is never attained. The saving grace in Aïssatou's embattled existence is her career and, as any overworked administrator, or interpreter or intellectual, would admit, a career is aeons removed from human care; books, in the final analysis, beget boredom. In Ramatoulaye's opinion, Aïssatou is saved by her books. 'Having become [her] refuge, they supported [her]' (p. 51).

> The power of books, marvellous invention of man's astute intelligence. Various signs, associated into sounds; different sounds moulding the word. Arrangement of words from which idea, thought, history, science, life, spring out. Unique instrument of relationship and culture, unequalled means of giving and receiving. Books knit together generations in the same continuous labour towards progress. (p. 51)

This ode to knowledge, powerful in its poetic fervour, overwhelming in its declaration of the birth of life through books, is far from convincing as far as happiness is concerned, however. Indeed, Aïssatou's rupture from her husband allows her to develop her skills and utilize her intelligence, although no clear statement is made by the narrator as to how those possibilities exist more outside the family home than within. The suggested reason is the lady's opportunity to travel abroad, although again we are not told that there was ever any problem in the nature of the husband's refusing to allow his wife room to breathe and travel. Anyway, Aïssatou travels to France — and the myth of the metropolis, centre of civilization, bursts forth in all its splendour — and then she goes to

America. Ramatoulaye tells us what her friend's letters tell her: the sojourn in foreign lands and the immersion in her career help Aïssatou turn away resolutely from 'the searchers of ephemeral joy and of facile liaisons'. Still the questions already posed remain unanswered. To all intents and purposes, culture constitutes a mere consolation. The career has afforded the lady upward mobility. She makes a lot of money, enough to be able to buy a brand-new car for Ramatoulaye who feels greatly hurt by the sight of her husband's second wife dashing all over Dakar in her ever-changing Alfa Romeo sports cars. Now, a tendency to out-bourgeois the bourgeoisie is common among the lower classes. If Ramatoulaye is convinced that such is the case with her rival Binetou's mother, the same should be true for her friend Aïssatou.

The same Ramatoulaye who sees her friend's liberation through books, narrates to us a sad case of the search for knowledge, namely that of a French teacher in Dakar: 'Studies must have been the only distraction of her youth. Cross-grained, she must have blocked out all fits of passion. Her solitude no doubt made her seek change' (p. 66). The change found is a teaching assistantship in Senegal. Older and wiser, the French woman, still a spinster, seeks solace in the colony. Her dreams of evasion end up unrealized. Her hopes in exotic lands are destroyed. Disillusionment sets in. She ends up on a hospital bed, beaten, nailed down by a throat infection, awaiting repatriation to the homeland that she fled. Before the chosen day arrives, death chooses her as his victim, thus completing her destiny of distress. Books, as we have stated, often beget boredom. Life is with human beings, in spite of the setbacks, the sadness, and the suffering. No doubt the same essential element is lacking in Aïssatou's life.

Besides, what originality exists in the vocation of an interpreter? Like the translator, and the secretary, the interpreter is a mere messenger of a message, a carrier of a cargo. A vehicle. A voice. A slave. A shadow. And the vehicle sometimes lacks communication; and the voice at times turns hoarse and misinterprets the message. The slave is used and discarded by the master; the shadow can never become the being. So, while achieving a goal worthy of the black bourgeoisie — they are all slaves of their borrowed civilization — Aïssatou remains what she has been: a sad slave, a loveless loser. She and her children will have a story to tell upon their return from America and, if others' experience is anything to go by, that story will be one of alienation, racism and solitude.[9]

Ramatoulaye, or the Victim Turned Victimizer . . . and still Victim of Love and Life

If Aïssatou symbolizes female intransigence, Ramatoulaye represents compromise, or so it would appear. She is abandoned after twenty-five years of marriage. Her eldest daughter, the intrepid, revolutionary type named Daba, is totally in favour of divorce from her inhuman father. But Ramatoulaye hesitates, then decides against divorce. She stays in the family home with her children, while Modou moves to the new house with Binetou. A case of the victim accepting her situation? Not so, insists the heroine, because the 'letter' that constitutes the novel being studied, a 'point of support in [her] anguish', is a form of vengeance. The text is written after Modou's death; it therefore also represents, as the narrator affirms, 'confidential information that drowns distress'. Not for Modou the sweet memories of his widow, nor the valediction based on the departed soul's virtues. Modou had his way in life; in death, he becomes a victim of his wife's sharp idiomatic weapon.

However, that is only part of the story. Modou is not only one man, but all men. The narrator makes plenty of generalizations. All men are traitors. All are polygamous by nature. All are sexual animals. All are victimizers that must be victimized. Hence Ramatoulaye sets out to hurt all men. The way she chooses is to refuse all suitors. First, Tamsir, her husband's brother who, by tradition, has a right to her. She spits her venom at the ugly man:

> You forget that I have a heart, a mind, that I am not an object to be passed from hand to hand. You are ignorant of what marriage means to me: an act of faith and of love, a total gift of the self to the being that you've chosen and that has chosen you. (p. 85)

Thus the aspiring conqueror is destroyed by a deft move of the feminist tongue. The point is emphasized several times in the text: she chose to marry her husband; she chooses not to leave the family home; she chooses not to marry her brother-in-law, just as she chooses not to marry Daouda Dieng, the man of virtue and riches who was her first love.

But, as usual, certain questions remain unanswered: is it simply a matter of choice? Is Ramatoulaye's rejection of Tamsir not due to her desire for vengeance against a man who supported her husband's polygamy? Has her choice not to marry Dieng got something to do with his polygamous life and his age? Is her recalcitrant attitude symptomatic of her wish to be a trail-blazer? Her relationship with Dieng poses other questions, such as: is she really in love with the man? Is her decision not to marry him a result of her jealousy of his first wife? The affair shows that Ramatoulaye and Daouda are, indeed, in love. After her official mourning period, he visits her and proposes anew. She awaits his visit with anxiety. She is burning with love for the man's compliments. She is dying to be ogled, to be fawned upon. She exalts: 'To be a woman! To live like a woman! Ah, Aïssatou! That night, I was moved, pardon my feeling. The savour of life is love. The salt of life is again love' (p. 94). And when Daouda asks for her hand in marriage that second time, she experiences a moment of ecstasy, of 'drunkenness'. The gentleness of his words inebriates her, and she says that she is not ashamed to confess it. One wonders then why the following statement, made at the moment of decision: 'My heart does not love Daouda Dieng. My mind appreciates the man. But the heart and the mind are often discordant' (p. 96). Her letter to Daouda, in spite of its ambiguity and decorum — traits of bourgeois hypocrisy — is categorical on one score, that she abhors polygamy. Playing second fiddle is not her idea of marriage, yet she wishes to continue seeing the man. The latter rejects her offer of friendship.

The Dieng case is of the utmost importance in understanding the narrator's character. I have stated that all men are vilified by her, without exception. Daouda Dieng, to a certain extent, constitutes an exception, because he has all the virtues that the other men mentioned in the novel lack. Once that general assertion is made, however, we are once more confronted with the ambiguity that is present throughout the novel: what, in essence, is Dieng's virtue? The question is pertinent, and remains unanswered, because the man is guilty of the one sin that makes for the condemnation of all the others, namely, he is a polygamist. Ramatoulaye's softness towards him, her ability to see beyond polygamy for once, are proof of the love that binds them together. This critic's opinion is that the heroine decides not to marry Dieng because she stands a good chance of being accused of playing the destructive role filled by the likes of Binetou and little Nabou. That would be another element of the contradiction which is her life. Who knows, she might have found happiness and harmony with Daouda Dieng, even as one of his wives; but social constraints which she actually imposes upon herself, block her path. A case of the reactionary hidden in' a revolutionary's clothing.

The unequivocal rupture with Dieng brings us back to the beginning: Ramatoulaye the would-be victimizer remains a loving, willing victim to the end. 'Excessively sentimental' (p. 21), she finds it very difficult to assume the role of a pioneer of feminism. Unlike Aïssatou, she cannot forget the first fire lit in her by the irrepressible, irresistible Modou:

> Modou Fall, the very instant you bent before me to invite me to dance, I was convinced that you were the one I was waiting for. (p. 24)

In spite of the later days of abandonment and harshness, she is definitively marked by the earliest qualities of the man:

> Above all, you knew how to be tender. . . . The discovery of your sharp intelligence, your engaging sensitivity, your usefulness, your ambition, that admitted no mediocrity. (p. 24)

In spite of the wishes of the adult children, she decides to stay. And the consequence? Times of suffering. Tears of solitude. Despair aggravated by the man's death. 'I lived alone in a monotony only cut short by the purifying baths and change of mourning clothes, every Monday and Friday' (p. 18). In spite of everything, Ramatoulaye loves Modou, just as she has always loved Daouda Dieng. The picture that remains in the reader's mind is not that of the man packing and leaving the house; not that of the male brute sexually attacking the innocent Binetous and Nabous of Africa; not that of the wife vomiting her ire on the monstrous man and leaving Africa for healthier climes abroad. The engrossing picture is that of Ramatoulaye, suddenly called to her dead husband's hospital bed, overwhelmed by what she calls the 'atrocious tragedy', desperate in her desire to revive him, straining to take his lifeless hand but restrained by sympathizers, sincere and hypocritical ones alike. That love surpasses all class constraints and traditional taboos. Ramatoulaye's mother is reticent about her liaison with the 'too handsome, too perfect' Modou. The daughter insists, disobeys, goes with her man.

> Marriage without dowry, without pomp, under the disapproving looks of my father, before the painful indignation of my frustrated mother, under the sarcastic remarks of my surprised sisters, in our town silenced by astonishment. (p. 29)

And we might rush to state that all is a matter of love between the heroine and her man. But the ambiguity prevalent in the text exists here, too. Love in the colonial context — that society evolving toward the accepted zenith of materialistic civilization — is not detached from the material. Love of the man goes with love of his money. Love means care, and comfort — love of lovers, and the good life. Ramatoulaye's avowed engrossment in the metaphysical, soulful aspects of her marriage notwithstanding, her desires, her nature, her life, bear the indelible mark of the *évolué* woman. She can hardly stand her in-laws who, by their very existence, seem to constitute a threat to her oasis of plenty with Modou. And the reader remembers vividly the white colonial officer's wife up in the reservation; you must book an appointment before daring to go up there to disturb the peace of the master's ménage. The reader recalls encounters with his brother's foreign wife; blood does not absolve one from the sacrilegious act of visiting without warning or invitation. The black bourgeoisie and their white ways: Ramatoulaye, black as the night, sun-tans with pleasure on the beach of Ngor. 'The sea air incited us to good humour . . . discouragement and sadness went away replaced suddenly by feelings of plenitude and radiance' (p. 36). The beach is the refuge of the rich. Escape in suburbia is the privilege of the sophisticated. The whole picture brings to mind the contrast between the privileged and the impoverished; the healthy air of the sea as against the hellish air of the city; the mansions of the middle-class as against the miserable structures in which the masses are imprisoned. Ramatoulaye claims that some in-laws unjustly envy her material power and the power of her mind, and she sees nothing wrong in her own situation as compared with that of the pauper. The fact is, she has a choice; the pauper does. It is, indeed, that wish to exercise her freedom of choice that makes her marry Modou instead of Dieng. It is that love of freedom that makes her espouse western education, or is it? The freedom of feminism does not triumph totally, even when the feminist claims to hate man with all her heart:

> Some men called us crazy. Others called us little devils. But many wanted to possess us. How many dreams had we fed desperately, that could have been concretized in lasting happiness and that we have disappointed in order to embrace others that have pitiably blown up like soap-bubbles, leaving us empty-handed? (p. 26)

So love is not removed from lust, even in the psyche of our ardent feminists. Freedom is not far from imprisonment. Feminism cannot rid woman, African woman, of femininity. Ramatoulaye loves to be possessed; just as she finally, definitively, is possessed by Modou, Man.

If hate lies at the root of the autobiographical *Une si Longue Lettre*, love is ever-present too. Autobiography is itself a lesson in bitterness and scepticism in the face of the disappointments and failures of life. Bitterness is decidedly evident in the style of Bâ's novel. The omniscient, omnipresent narrator-heroine chooses her moments of perspicacity and paucity of knowledge rather dexterously, and always to the detriment of Man and mother-in-law. That technique raises questions of authenticity. How, for example, does Ramatoulaye know what goes on in the minds of others, besides those whom she talks to directly or those whom she learns about from others? Bitterness engenders bias. Extremism is the hallmark of this feminism even if, as partisans of any victimized group would quickly add, such a posture is often a necessity in the face of the all-too-powerful victimizer. Bitterness of the bourgeoisie: Ramatoulaye cannot comprehend 'the entrance of Modou, a personality, into that family of *ndol* [paupers]' (p. 59). Binetou, Modou's second wife, deserves all the pity in the world however; innocent and sincere, 'she did not know Modou's overwhelming will-power, his tenacity before the obstacle, his pride to vanquish, his resistance inspiring new assaults at every failure' (p. 60). The narrator asks the exculpatory question: 'What can a child do before a furious mother that howls her hunger and thirst for life?' (p. 60) However, we know that Binetou is more or less as old as Ramatoulaye was when, at the moment of marriage, she disobeyed her mother, chose Modou and rejected the mother's choice. And if Binetou is 'a sacrificial lamb, as are many others, before the altar of material', (p. 60) it is no less of a truth that Ramatoulaye, and Aïssatou, are avid worshippers before that very altar.

Indeed, the innocent victim named Ramatoulaye is mean. And Ramatoulaye the critic is a cheat. She establishes a hierarchy even among the female species. Aïssatou is superior to little Nabou; Nabou is superior to Binetou; Ramatoulaye, naturally, is superior to all. The yardstick for comparison is the level of civilization. Civilization, as in western culture. Civilization, as in acculturation. Civilization, as in capitalism. For the reader must be clear about one fact: Ramatoulaye's middle-class origins are to her a source of pride and her commitment as a pioneer is, first and foremost, to that class.

Conclusion: Elements of a Colonized Literature

Now, my way of bringing together class stratification and commitment to female freedom might be viewed as a contradiction which, indeed, it could be but is not. Ramatoulaye's feminism as an expression of freedom constitutues only a partial aspect of the total reality of African life. Femininity is the virtue of the traditionalist; feminism, the veneer of the progressive striving to become a man. The latter feels insecure, unfulfilled, incomplete. Colonialism has taught her the lessons of civilization. Equality. Emancipation. Independence. In short, the African woman has a right to enjoy the privileges of the man who is now the new master. Like the man, the feminist lives on borrowed training and thoughts. But the questions remain: what is freedom in de-colonized Africa? Is African literature as a whole truly de-colonized from a borrowed life, a borrowed language? We may recall that the French language continues to give the privileged position to the masculine; to a borrowed life, a borrowed literature. It is true that the best-known African writers are still those able to manipulate 'without a trace of accent or cultural cleavage', the master's tongue. Bâ's feminism, especially as expressed by Aïssatou the interpreter, smacks of Beauvoirism:[10] the traditional marriage is a deterrent to woman's promise. No marriage. No attachment. No master. The home becomes a transitory institution. Love is a passing sentiment secondary to other elements of existence. The emphasis is on the female self.

Simone de Beauvoir's existentialist stance is based upon concrete experiences within a particular Eurocentric context, which creates some problems for the European imitator, but grave difficulties for the African follower. Firstly, the European may find that her's is not an easy-to-generalize, true freedom. Secondly, the African finds that Beauvoirist liberation does not end up in real freedom for the woman; it engulfs the erstwhile victim in another abyss, solitude. The critic Albert Memmi is categorical about what the real objective of all oppressed beings ought to be: 'an oppressed person does not save himself all alone'.[11] The irony, the aggressiveness behind the fatalism, the oppressive stand taken by the feminist, the African feminist, cannot save her from her communal background, unless she decides to go into permanent exile, which in itself would constitute a facile, sham solution. Solidarity, human, man-woman (couple), man-child-woman (family) solidarity, that is the essence of life. The couple remains perhaps the best solution to solitude. Lack of children is an abstraction, a mutilation of life. It is significant that the Ramatoulayes of Africa have not decided to live without children. Beauvoirism preaches a fake freedom, a liberty that is no less a lie than the cataleptic civilization passed on to the colonized by the colonizer.

Female emancipation is fraught with ambiguities. Ramatoulaye is caught between tradition and progress. Though her declared choice is the latter, her lived experiences prove her attachment to the former. The picture of her daughters in slacks is, for her, an eyesore. Life without marriage is death. When all the tears are shed, when the tension subsides, she affirms: 'I remain convinced of the inevitable and necessary complementarity of man and woman' (p. 128). The harmony of the couple coalesces with the happiness of the country. The family is a microcosm of the nation. Success. Solidarity. It is symbolic that the narrator leaves to a man, Daouda Dieng, her feminist politician-friend, the last word on the female condition:

> Woman must no longer be the decorating accessory. The object that you displace, the companion that you flatter, or calm down with promises. Woman is the original, fundamental root of a nation where every contribution is established, from which every development emanates. Woman must be induced to be more interested in her country's destiny. (p. 90)

Ramatoulaye accepts the declaration like a silent goddess in the traditional setting,[12] which goes to show that the woman still needs the male on many an occasion, even where proof of her freedom is concerned. Daouda Dieng, the politician, the feminist, is as much a colonized person as Ramatoulaye, a fact probably hard to take but a fact all the same. Earlier in the novel the narrator states that one of the aims of the 'new' African woman, that is the educated, is to 'appreciate multiple civilizations without denying ours' (p. 27). Now, the problem that neither she nor Dieng has solved is, how to do just that. The age-old problem of the colonized: how to escape the colonial cage stifling black culture; how to remain black in a world becoming whiter every day. The black woman's problem, in the final analysis, is part of the bigger burden of being black in the world.

Marx has stated that woman is man's proletariat. A true statement, indeed, but only as far as western, or European, civilization is concerned. Therein lies the dilemma of Africa. She is caught between her own culture and the imported culture. Marx means economic enslavement, no doubt. But there is more to it: social and psychological alienation; cultural bastardization; a destiny of death. The black woman is confused; the black man too. She needs love and demands it from her man. Unfortunately, the burden of blackness and the confusion of his borrowed culture often prove too overwhelming to allow him time for love. He is too busy comparing himself to the white man and, ironically, the same self-destructive process is being desperately pursued by the woman. So, Ramatoulaye Fall, confused, civilized, committed, is still seeking solace somewhere. She will no doubt write 'such a long letter' again, to herself, to her sisters, to us her men. And she may find solace some day, and we may read her letter, or tear it up and throw it into the dustbin.

NOTES

1. In this context, black literature is that literature written in the language of the colonizer.
2. Minority, used here not in terms of number but sociologically, symbolizing the deprived, the oppressed, the enslaved. Of course, it is true that women outnumber men in many countries.
3. Ogot of Kenya; Sutherland and Aidoo of Ghana; Nwapa of Nigeria. The label of 'old guard' is used out of very general considerations. For example, Aidoo is as contemporary/revolutionary as any of the emerging writers.
4. Emecheta is Nigerian; Diallo and Bâ, Senegalese.
5. Title of one of Emecheta's novels.
6. Mariama Bâ, *Une si Longue Lettre*, Dakar, Les Nouvelles Editions Africaines, 1979. All translations from the novel are mine.
7. The descriptions are the publisher's, taken from the back cover of the novel.
8. *Une si Longue Lettre*, p. 8. Henceforth, any quotations from the novel will be marked simply by inserting the page number after the quoted passage.
9. Examples of literary expression of Africans' experience in America are numerous. See J. P. Clark, *America, their America*; Ayi Kwei Armah, *Why are we so Blest?*; Youssouf Guèye, *Sahéliennes*; Bernard Dadié, *Patron de New York*.

10. Simone de Beauvoir, one of the pioneers of female emancipation in France, renowned writer (*Le Deuxième Sexe, La Force de l'age*) was Jean-Paul Sartre's companion.

11. Albert Memmi, 'Plaidoyer d'un tyran' in *L'Homme dominé*, Paris, Gallimard, 1968, p. 171.

12. See Buchi Emecheta, *The Bride Price*, London, Fontana Books, 1978, p. 50. New York, Braziller, 1976. In Emecheta's opinion, the age of the silent goddess is long gone.

Sembène Ousmane as Griot: The Money-Order with White Genesis

Jonathan A. Peters

A Senegalese fable tells the story of three encounters by Fene-Falsehood and Deug-Truth who were companions on a journey. At the first village they are thrown out by a man whose wife is discourteous to both the strangers and her husband because Deug, when asked, suggests that she is the worst wife he has seen. An honest answer to the chief's enquiry in the second village similarly lands them in trouble: Deug tells him that the children are in charge in the village because they are the ones who share out the meat, reserving the choicest portions for themselves. But in the third, the king is forced to part with half of his wealth because Fene, now their spokesman, dupes him into believing that he can bring back to life not only his dead favourite, but his father and grandfather as well. The present king does not want to have to deal with the problems of three kings in a single kingdom, especially since his father had been a tyrannous king whom his son helped to put away. When they set out on their journey Fene had observed that God loved Deug-Truth more than him. But when he obtains half of the king's wealth as a result of his untruths he concludes that God may be on the side of truth but falsehood was the best way to succeed with men.[1]

Sembène Ousmane, the internationally famous film-maker from the village of Ziguinchor, Senegal, has suffered much the same fate as Deug-Truth in terms of the reception of his fiction and his films. After more than two decades of artistic output[2] he has so far received comparatively little critical attention deserving of his seven books of fiction and at least an equal number of films[3]; for, if numbers do not provide a compelling reason for serious study, the issues he raises as well as the artistic quality of his fiction — to say nothing of his films which earn him first place among African film-makers — are sufficient to deserve more extensive analyses of the kind that some writers with certainly no greater contribution to African letters have received. One reason, perhaps, for his neglect among English-speaking writers and readers stems from the fact that some of his early works have never been translated into English[4] while, among those translated, only his most widely praised novel, *Les Bouts de bois de Dieu* was almost immediately available in translation under the title *God's Bits of Wood*.[5]

Another more significant reason may be that what he sees and expounds on repeatedly is the uncomfortable and even repelling 'truth' that black people are still undergoing a form of slavery in this, the latter portion of the twentieth century. This theme is not to the fore in *Les Bouts de bois de Dieu* which celebrates a rare victory for the forces that oppose white oppression. It, however, pervades Sembène's first novel, *Le Docker noir* in which the hero-novelist (the black docker) tries to liberate himself and his pregnant fiancée from the misery of French slums and shipyards but ends up in chains, like the slaves in his own novel entitled 'Négrier Sirius', because he unintentionally kills a woman French novelist who published his work under her own name; likewise Sembène's collection of short stories one of which ('Terre promise') was transformed into a full-length feature film (*La Noire de . . .*), another film set during the Second World War (*Emitaï*) and his most recent — and controversial — film (*Ceddo*) which uses a slave-trade setting to comment on contemporary manifestations of black slavery. The intensely moral tone of many of these works is in keeping not only with the role of a truth-seeker, but also (more importantly) with the function of that truth-telling bard of old — the griot — who, in Sembène's own words, 'was not only the dynamic element in his tribe, clan or village but also the living witness of every occurrence . . . placing before all at village gatherings the facts about each in full detail'.[6] The story of truth and falsehood provides an excellent reference point for examining Sembène griot role as exemplified in his two novelettes, *Le Mandat* and *Véhi-Ciosane ou Blanche-Genèse*, both of which have been made into films.[7]

The major theme in both *The Money-Order* and *White Genesis* turns on the conflict between truth and falsehood in human affairs. The two stories in fact are studies on the value of morality. *White*

Genesis is more tragic in its development but its end holds out the hope that truth, in bondage over a long period, will again be resurrected. *The Money-Order*, depicting somewhat humorously the misfortunes that surround its hero, ends on a note of pessimism. It is a structural parallel of the story of truth and falsehood in that its hero, Dieng, decides to give up his truthfulness and honesty in favour of deception and lies. The preference for falsehood evident in the society portrayed in *White Genesis* is constantly undermined by the griot-hero to the point where Sembène is able to suggest a new beginning through the illegitimate child of Khar Diob. In *The Money-Order*, after a series of misfortunes in which Dieng loses more than the value of the money-order sent by his nephew from Paris, he also loses his gullibility declaring: 'I am going to put on the skin of the hyena. . . . Why? Because it is only cheating and lies that are true. Honesty is a crime nowadays.'[8]

White Genesis

White Genesis is a griot's story. Sembène himself remarks in the introduction that it is as old as the world itself. It is a story of incest set in the village of Santhiu-Niaye. Sembène introduces the story by describing the setting of the village close to the Atlantic Ocean in Senegal. The very monotony of this region which defies definition in terms of savannah or delta, steppe, grassland, etc., gives a parallel to the lack-lustre morality which permeates the village, threatening its life as much as the migration of its young men to the city in search of a better life.

· The longest section of *White Genesis* gives us an extended view of Ngone War Thiandum, the mother of Khar Madiagua Diob. Before the story opens Khar had become pregnant and at first the responsibility of her pregnancy had been laid on the *navetanekat*, a migrant labourer called Atoumane. In spite of his denials the Diob family had wanted him killed on the strength of the accusation that he has violated their family honour. Since he is poor and perhaps of a low caste marriage with Khar would be undesirable; so the gravity of his offence in getting a girl pregnant whom he could not marry and who would for ever be tainted by this episode in her life, is quite obvious. Khar's brother, the mad Tanor who served time during the Second World War, destroys the labourer's groundnut crop and a crowd of villagers (which include Khar's uncle Medoune Diob) pursues and hunts the *navetanekat* for several days and nights. The identity of Khar's real violator is only gradually revealed. In fact, Ngone War Thiandum is one of the last people in the village to know. The scene in which she finds out that her husband is the father of the child their daughter, Khar, is expecting is depicted by means of a flashback. Gnagna Guisse, the wife of the shoemaker-griot, Dethye Law, can then no longer deny the truth when Ngone War Thiandum confronts her with it.

The whole story of *White Genesis* is overshadowed by events which have taken place long before the commencement of the story. By presenting these past occurrences through the mind of Ngone who is herself only just finding out the truth, Sembène is able to concentrate the action of the story into the few days when things reach a climax. The climax itself is the scene in which Khar delivers the baby, but already in this first major encounter with Ngone and her family we have the major outlines of the conflict.

In the opening portion of this episode we see Ngone in bed with her husband, Guibril, whom she is now forced by circumstances to despise. There is a delicate balance, however, between this sense of contempt and the genuine warmth of affection that contact with her husband's body conjures up in her through pleasant memories of their past relationship. The closing scene of this episode is the accouchement of Khar and it fittingly ends the long section, promising a resolution of one kind or another to this drama of incest.

The theme of incest in *White Genesis* is connected with themes of honour and nobility as well as morality and justice; it is also related to the theme of truth on which the Senegalese fable I referred to earlier is based. Sembène manages to interweave all these themes together to form a moral world not only as things are or as they used to be but, perhaps more important, as they should be. In accordance with this vision, Sembène makes a statement used first as an epigraph to the story and then recalled in the following reflection by Ngone War Thiandum at the end of our first encounter with her:

> The words of the sage came, luminous, into her mind: 'Sometimes a child is born into the most ordinary low caste family who grows up and glorifies his name, the name of his father, of his mother, of his whole family, of his community, of his tribe. More often, in a so-called high caste family which glories in its past, a child comes into the world who, by his actions, sullies his entire heritage, and even robs the individual diambur-diambur [freeborn] of his dignity.' She repeated these words to herself, but still she hesitated to act. (p. 13)

The whole purport of the passage reflects Sembène's belief that honour and nobility are not a typical characteristic of people of high birth, operating in a closed circuit. Rather, honour and dishonour are qualities that mark out individuals whether they are of humble or noble origin. The reference to 'so-called high caste' emphasizes Sembène's point.

Although Ngone is anxious to preserve the good name of her family, this duty and desire are not confined to those of her rank only. Indeed the most outspoken and uncompromising seeker after truth is not a member of a high caste, but one who acknowledges his lowly status. It is Dethye Law the griot-shoemaker who incorporates in his character the old virtues which had made their society great and which are now being trampled upon. The inherent truth behind the words of the sage is dramatized through the story. What Sembène is saying, in essence, is that Guibril Guedj Diob who was born into a family with a noble past, disgraces the reputation of not only his own high lineage but also the ordinary free-born citizen like Dethye Law. At the same time, we can say that someone like Dethye Law, born into an ordinary home, a low-caste griot home, can ennoble his community by his steadfast witness to the truth. It is this simple truth that *White Genesis* is designed to demonstrate.

Sembène Ousmane goes to great pains to document the inbreeding that takes place within a society where truth is seen as the prerogative of a particular class, one in which morality is a stylized process of maintaining dignity even if this means disguising or denying the truth. The crime of Guibril and his daughter Khar, an exception to this rule, is open for all to see. But the machinations of his brother, Medoune Diob, first of all instigating the invocation of the death penalty for Guibril Guedj Diob and his daughter and when this fails inciting the mad Tanor to kill his father are the kind of concern that the griot has. This concern with the truth is displayed throughout the story by Dethye Law as well as by others like Massar. Thus following the deaths of Guibril Diob at the hand of his son and the suicide of Ngone War Thiandum, Dethye Law makes an attempt at leaving which is designed to test the will of the villagers to uphold the truth.

Dethye has always spoken against those who have left the village because their desertion threatens the very survival of Santhiu-Niaye. But when the machinations of Medoune Diob go on unchallenged and even condoned by the present Imam, Dethye begins to be afraid that people like him who speak the truth will be threatened: the unscrupulous will not hesitate to eliminate those who speak against them once the moral will of the people is broken. His announcement that he is going to leave is followed by these exchanges which emphasize above all the fact that freedom and truth are not confined to the rich or those of noble ancestry:

> Medoune Diob repeated the question:
> 'You haven't told us where you are going.'
> Part of Medoune Diob's face showed above the head-rest.
> 'I am going where, I hope, the truth will be the concern of honest minds and not a privilege of birth,' rejoined Dethye Law.
> 'True, one must be a griot to possess that freedom.'
> 'Freedom of thought has never been a gift, nor an inheritance. It has always been bought for a heavy price in blood. The ruler who opposes it will find himself undone, sooner or later.'
> 'And is that freedom denied here?'
> 'No. In truth, no. It is early yet. But the basis of our community has been undermined. If it is not said now, it will be one day. You are not our chief. You are your brother's murderer, and our community has lost its foundation.'
> 'Take care what you are saying, Dethye Law,' interrupted Medoune Diob, abruptly getting up. His eyes went from one elder to the next. Dethye Law continued:
> 'What have I said? People will not be able to say any more that truth is the weakness of Santhiu-Niaye.'
> 'My ancestors have always ruled Santhiu-Niaye, and yours have always served them.'
> 'That is indeed true. But that was in the past. I have inherited from my ancestors a concern for the truth which I shall preserve until the end.'
> 'Are you trying to say you are of noble blood?'
> 'Yes. The blood of truth is always noble, whatever its origin.'
> (pp. 65–6)

At the time that the hero, Dethye Law, engages in this dialogue the climax of the story has already been reached. Khar has delivered her baby. Her mother, true to her guelewar upbringing and motto — 'Rather die a thousand deaths in a thousand ways each more terrible than the other than endure an insult for a single day' (p. 23) — has already committed suicide. And Guibril Guedj Diob has been killed by his son Tanor, at the instigation of his uncle Medoune Diob. Tanor cannot succeed his father, not only because of his madness but also because of his patricide. Besides, the last we see of him is the scene where he is tied to a tree; the last we hear of him is Medoune's statement to the toubab-commandant that he has left for the city like many of the young men. Medoune Diob has now inherited everything. He has the chieftaincy, the pomp of receiving dignitaries like the white commandant on a tax-collecting mission — even Guibril Guedj's colourful parasol which Tanor, returning home from the war in Indochina, had brought his father. In the light of these developments — especially the role of Medoune Diob in the liquidation of the incestuous Guibril — Dethye's decision that he can no longer live in Santhiu-Niaye is understandable.

Dethye Law is right on another point. The inhabitants of Santhiu-Niaye are not ready, in spite of their village's increasing desolation, to sacrifice the truth completely — yet. At the mosque where the faithful respond to the griot's intoning of the call to prayer five times a day, almost all the adherents desert the present conniving Imam in favour of Palla, his old rival for the position. The shifting of religious adherents also reflects the political scene, for Medoune Diob becomes ostracized in much the same way as Guibril was isolated when his incest became established. The changed situation also gives added significance to Dethye's comment that *in the past* the caste system made members of his family servants to the Ndiobene's. Thus, a society will prosper only if it dedicates itself to truth not as 'a gift, nor an inheritance' but as an ideal since 'the blood of truth is always noble, whatever its origin'. If we adopt this view, many of the roles in the story are immediately reversed. Dethye's unflagging efforts to preserve the truth make him a man of noble blood while the blood of the Ndiobene's has become tainted by the attempts to destroy the truth no less than by the sin of incest. This is the core of Sembène's message in the story.

For the cleansing to be complete, however, the new leadership has to banish Khar and her child from the village. Before her death, Ngone War Thiandum had hoped that this grandchild/stepchild would be a boy. But it is a girl that Khar brings into the world amid the injurious gossip that goes on about her. Unlike the gossip-mongers and even Ngone herself, Sembène is careful throughout to avoid making either father or daughter the seducer in their incestous crime. Since the two of them say very little in *White Genesis*, we are forced to hold them equally guilty. Yet it is this act of banishment that holds out hope in an otherwise bleak ending. In a very short space of time Khar ceases to be a child and becomes a woman. She becomes even more precipitately an orphan caring for a new-born infant whose future, like hers, is unknown. Her attempt to abandon the child which would only handicap her bid to begin life afresh in a new environment, is merely a reflection on her dilemma. The instinctual maternal attachment of this child-mother-orphan to her daughter, Vehi-Ciosane Thiandum, restores the balance to the natural cycle. The child, then, becomes the symbol of hope, the nonracial 'white genesis' after a prolonged rule of dishonesty, corruption and evil.

The moralizing tone of the novelette is inevitable because of the virtual identity of subject and theme, and the signal role of Dethye Law as an exponent of these, a role of griot-moralist that echoes Sembène's own. All the same, a good portion of *White Genesis* concentrates on the lives of villagers outside the Ndiobene-Thiandum household. The favourite meeting spot for the men is under the shade of the beintan tree where the griot-shoemaker works. It is in its shade that intense contests take place between Badieye and Gornaru, two inveterate players of *yothe* (the local version of draughts complete with dry donkey droppings for counters) while the habitués discuss everything under the sun, from the moral dilemma that engulfs the village to bawdy dexterities such as the following:

> 'When you make love to a woman [Badieye says], either she loves you or is calculating the value of your harvest.'
>
> Amath, who was one of his supporters, seized Badieye's wrist and added:
>
> 'True! When you have an old woman in cold weather, you warm her with your body or with firewood.'
>
> 'Those two activities are not everlasting occupations. In both of them, you lose your skin,' capped Badieye, digging his stick sharply into the ground.
>
> There was a noisy outcry.
>
> 'You will never dare return to that hut,' said Gornaru, and, in his turn, he commented: 'Eating flesh, mounting flesh, and putting flesh inside flesh.' (p. 51)

Such episodes give body to the otherwise slim story of human calamity. It is essentially an internal conflict, for none of the strangers — the *navetanekat* or the white official and his retinue — change the dynamics of the village in any way. All the change comes from within. And the end of the story returns us to the sandy flats as Khar, unselfpityingly braces herself for the trip to a new life in Ndakaru with a child of infamous ancestry but who may well grow up to glorify an entire people.

The Money-Order

The locale in The Money-Order shifts from a desolate rural setting
to Dakar, capital of Senegal, for which Khar Madiagua Diob is
headed at the end of White Genesis. There is a difference also in
the central conflict between the two novelettes. The one in White
Genesis is, as we have seen, primarily an internal village conflict, the nexus of which is the high caste family of the
Ndiobene-Diob which is completely shattered at the end. By contrast, the inhabitants of the same quarters as Ibrahima Dieng, the
central character of The Money-Order, are virtually indistingu-
ishable in terms of birth and caste on account of their common
misery. They help and hurt each other by lending or sharing
small portions of the meagre foodstuffs and loans they manage to
scrounge out of the over-priced store of Mbarka; by exchanging
and spreading news and malicious gossip about the changing
society and about each other; and by their jealous outrage against
the petit bourgeois whose members include Mbarka and the new
western educated elite. The central conflict is, however, a personal one. An external agent in the form of a money-order from
Paris forces the jobless Dieng outside his familiar world into the
unfamiliar world of the Dakar bureaucracy, leaving him disillusioned in the end.

Perhaps the most emphatic distinction between White Genesis
and The Money-Order is one of tone. The intensely moralistic tone
of the former is probably suited to the intention of Sembène to deal
with a very serious issue affecting the health and welfare of a whole
society. The tone is in fact not confined to the sermonizing hero,
Dethye Law, but extends to others as well. Thus, Ngone War
Thiandum tells her family griot, Gnagna Guisse (wife of Dethye
Law): 'It is a sin to lie. It is unfriendly to lie to me' (p. 22). And
Gnagna Guisse defends to herself the prolonged cover-up of the
truth by recalling the wisdom of the appropriate sage: 'Any truth
that divides and brings discord among the members of the same
family is false. The falsehood that weaves, unites and cements people together is truth' (p. 49). In the middle of his frustrations over
the money-order, Ibrahima Dieng's wife, Mety, spreads the rumour
in the neighbourhood that their husband was robbed after he had
cashed the money-order. Dieng rebukes her in this way: 'You must
always speak the truth. However hard it is, you must always speak
the truth' (p. 121). But even as he says this, Dieng's faith in the truth
is beginning to wear thin. He will soon change his mind about the

truth when, ironically, he *is* robbed of the money not by pick-pockets but by a relative of Mety who pretends to be a friendly and honest helper. It is this element of irony which most distinguishes *The Money-Order* from *White Genesis*. In *White Genesis* Sembène is involved with his hero. In *The Money-Order*, he is somewhat detached.

The *Money-Order* is a study in irony. The propelling event for the story is the arrival from Paris of a money-order from Dieng's nephew Abdou who has disappeared without telling anyone and is just writing his first letter home. The money is intended to bring relief, however small, for Dieng and his sister: the larger portion of it will serve as the first deposit in a savings account for Abdou. The irony is that it leaves virtually all the relatives worse off at the end than at the beginning. As soon as she gets her own letter from her son, Abdou's mother (who is Dieng's eldest sister), comes all the way from her village to get her three-thousand francs, borrowing more than the one-thousand five-hundred she gets from her brother who has not yet been able to cash the money-order. Abdou himself loses roughly twenty-thousand francs (CFA) for Dieng only gets five-thousand francs when the money is finally cashed — plus a fifty kilo bag of rice which he begins to distribute in despair.

But the recipient, Dieng, is the worst sufferer of all. When the story opens Dieng is idle, the only one still without a job of the many employees who had gone on strike a year earlier. Let us see what the whole transaction ends up costing him. He loses Mety's gold earrings bought for eleven-thousand five-hundred francs and pawned over three days for a paltry two-thousand francs. His reply to Abdou assures him that he has apportioned the money as requested, meaning that he now owes Abdou twenty-thousand francs, since he only gets five-thousand of the original twenty-five-thousand-franc money-order. His losses are reduced by the five-thousand francs he gets from Mbaye whom he gave a power of attorney; the two-thousand francs he gets from pawning the jewel-lery; the eleven-hundred francs which a nephew with connections in the town hall gives him (reduced to six-hundred francs when a clerk prises three-hundred francs off him while Ambrose takes two-hundred francs); and the one-hundred francs an old man and his son thrust in his hand. To the net loss of about twenty-three-thousand francs we can also add the twenty-five francs he gives to a prostitute posing as a destitute and the expenses he has on a Sun-day. But in addition to his financial loss, Dieng also suffers from a broken nose at the hand of a practised apprentice of Ambrose, loses his credibility with many of those in his immediate circle and, above all, becomes cynical like the rest following his humiliation and his disillusionment with the truth.

What we have in *The Money-Order* is a crisis of faith. But it is not a crisis that is morbidly presented; rather we have a sequence in which Sembène places a good many characters, including Dieng himself, in ironic situations which point up the exploitative relationships that exist in the society at and between its successive levels. The role of protagonist fits Dieng because he remains one of those who have not yet become corrupted by the malaise and the indigence which permeate the quarter. Even his two wives are much wiser in the ways of the world than their husband whom they acknowledge as master in conformity with custom. In the face of the impatience that even his own wives show for his scruples and the vicious treatment he receives from the parasitic neighbours, the greatest plea for tolerance towards Dieng comes from Sembène himself in this comment about his hero:

> We must try and understand Ibrahima Dieng. Conditioned by years of blind, unconscious submissiveness, he fled from anything likely to cause him trouble, be it physical or moral. The blow of the fist he had received on his nose was an *atte Yallah*: the will of God. The money he had lost, too, it was ordained that it was not he who should spend it. If dishonesty seemed to have the upper hand, this was because the times were like that, not because Yallah wanted it so. These were times that refused to conform to the old tradition. In order to rid himself of his feeling of humiliation, Ibrahima Dieng invoked Yallah's omnipotence: for he was also a refuge, this Yallah. In the depths of his despair, and of the humiliation to which he had been subjected, the strength of his faith sustained him, releasing a subterranean stream of hope, but this stream also revealed vast areas of doubt. He did not, however, doubt the certainty that tomorrow would be better than today. Alas! Ibrahima Dieng did not know who would be the architect of this better tomorrow, this better tomorrow which he did not doubt. (p. 118)

The moral suasion of Dieng, when coupled with his simple approach to situations, stands in bold relief against a background of general cynicism, corruption and dishonesty. It is a major prop onto which much of the irony in the novelette is latched.

Although a good deal of the irony with which *White Genesis* is laced is verbal, this type of irony is often buttressed by irony of situation. We have already seen the ironic twist that the cashing of the money-order takes when Mbaye tells Dieng he has been robbed of his money. Mbaye uses the same story that Mety and Aram had invented to keep the neighbours from wheedling the money out of Dieng once it is cashed. In actual fact, Dieng has himself provided Mbaye with the story, after the dispute with Mbarka. Mbaye (a prototype for El Hadji Abdou Kader Beye, the hero of *Xala*, 1974) does not surprise us in his actions because we have been prepared for this outcome by Sembène's description of him as a member of the 'New Africa' generation, a breed of 'men who combined Cartesian logic with the influence of Islam and the atrophied energy of the Negro' (p. 127). Since no difficulty is beyond him, it is easy to appreciate the enterprising solution he brings to bear when he disabuses Dieng of the bulk of the money.

Dieng has throughout the story a good deal of difficulty in establishing his identity, because at every turn the bureaucratic functionaries 'want a piece of paper to prove who I am' (p. 92). This problem of identity is explored on other levels. It is related to his 'fine clothes' which Mbarka tells him are 'just wind'. When he is mauled by Ambrose's apprentice, he returns home via the back alleys so that his neighbours will not see him in his present undignified state. But these very clothes provoke some derisive remarks and help create his identity crisis. Thus the prostitute tells him that he looks like a marabout (p. 104); the letter-writer charges him with impersonating a marabout (p. 89) when he fails to pay fifty francs for having his letter read; Ambrose's apprentice calls him a 'fake marabout' (p. 115); and in his reply to his nephew, Abdou, he himself promises to consult a 'real marabout' (p. 131) on Abdou's account. But the incident that tops all is the one in which he recites verses from the Koran as he thanks his Dakar nephew for the great assistance he has given him. Sembène comments thus:

> The distant cousin let him have his way. Out of the corner of his eye, he saw a policeman approaching them, feeling his chest pocket. When he reached them, the policeman looked at the two pairs of hands, at the man's face, then at the marabout (for he thought Dieng was one), and he joined his hands to theirs. Dieng took hold of one of his thumbs. He raised his forehead and his lips moved. Two passers-by stopped and held out their hands. When he had finished murmuring, Dieng sprayed saliva all around. They all replied, 'Amine! Amine!' and rubbed their faces as they broke up. (p. 107)

Sembène's consistent depiction of Dieng and other characters in situations that are both ironical and laughable implies his conscious employment of satire. In a sense, it increases our sense of his detachment from the hero's predicament, in contrast to his apparent attachment to the moral stance of Dethye Law, the protagonist of *White Genesis*. The subtlety which characterizes the gently satiric tone of Sembène shows how painstaking and ingenious a craftsman he is. One will find *The Money-Order* full of structural irony only if one is ready to delve below the surface so as to discover the subterranean echoes and situational parallels that punctuate the narrative. Indeed, so replete is this work with satire and irony, that even the noble (if also humble) profession of griot is not left unscathed. Unlike Dieng's unintentional performance as a marabout, the unscrupulous Maissa, who is so determined to bilk Dieng of as much money as possible from whatever source without giving away any of his own, suddenly becomes a posturing griot 'extolling the noble lineage of a young man dressed in European clothes: the beauty of the women, the boundless generosity and bravery of the men, the nobility of their conduct, all of it redounding on the young man, pure blood . . . from the purest of blood' (pp. 90–1). Although the young man is indifferent to traditional praises, he is embarrassed enough to slip Maissa a hundred-franc note in the middle of his intoning that he sings not for money but 'to keep the tradition alive' (p. 91). And Dieng the 'marabout' who is at the police station trying to obtain an identity card admits that he knows 'nothing about life today', being 'overcome by Gorgui Maissa's lack of dignity in pretending to be a griot' (p. 91).

Dieng's naïvety is crucial in achieving Sembène's goal of social criticism in *The Money-Order*. Yet, in spite of the exaggerations necessary to satire and such absurdities as the small amount of money which so completely dominated Dieng's world — 25,000 francs CFA was the equivalent of approximately forty dollars in 1965[9] — what Cameroonian writer Mbella Sonne Dipoko describes as 'dynamic realism' permeates this 'minor masterpiece'.[10] This realism is even more poignant in the film. Indeed, Sembène has been widely praised and also widely upbraided, in the latter case for touches like the belching of Makhouredia Gueye (as Dieng) and an almost exclusive focus on the depressed areas of Dakar. Ironically, he has also been criticized for a lack of realism in his choice of costumes that are sometimes too colourful or dressy for the people portrayed in this and other films. The much wider audience that Sembène's films have received in both Senegal and elsewhere in Africa, justifies his badge of 'la meilleure école du soir' (the best night school)[11] for the cinema in his country, where illiterates (like the bewildered Ibrahima Dieng) account for virtually eighty-five per cent of the population. His didactic purpose is better realized in the film than in the short novel, because the longer film is largely in

Wolof with occasional dialogue in French among the educated Senegalese. An example of his subtle touches shows Mbaye callously carrying on a telephone discussion in French with a prospective buyer for a house while its unwitting and fiercely possessive owner, Dieng, is trustingly sitting down waiting for Mbaye's help.

The use of Wolof in *Le Mandat*, Sembène's first colour film, also serves a political function. Sembène has declared himself in favour of 'un cinéma militant'.[12] The bold use of a national language such as Wolof consequently represents a significant achievement in terms of breaking free from colonial domination, even though dependence on French came through in the process of making the film: the Wolof dialogue had to be written in French phrases that were literal translations of the as yet unwritten language of Wolof.

According to Paulin Vieyra, who has been Sembène's producer from *Le Mandat* on, adaptation of *The Money-Order* for the screen was considerably more successful than the conversion of *White Genesis* from fiction to the film *Niaye*.[13] He suggests the novelty for Sembène of adaptations from fiction to film, the lack of sufficient funds, and the obviousness of the message delivered by Dethye Law the narrator, as factors for the serious demerits of the film. *Niaye*, made in 1964, required more fundamental restructuring than the highly successful *Mandat*, the production of which more than three years later constituted a pioneering venture, replacing colonial criteria for depicting African landscapes and societies with African ones but attempting no technical innovation. *Niaye* has not been made available to the public; therefore its merits and demerits can be attested to only by the comparative few who were fortunate enough to view it at Tours and at Locarno. *Le Mandat*, however, has generated a lot of reactions and commentaries, verbal and written, both within Senegal and abroad, creating renewed interest in the narrative version but with little accompanying judgments for the record.

Taken together, *The Money-Order* and *White Genesis*, the stories on which these two films are based, provide interesting, complementary and artistic case studies on justice, morality and honesty. Sembène is interested in a society where there will be social equality, not one in which women, as wives, will be lorded over by husbands or have to share their spouses with one or more co-wives; nor one in which people will be divided into high and low classes or professions by virtue of their birth. Still far short of this ideal, society is now encumbered by a resigned fatalism which accepts every misfortune as the will of Yallah. It is moreover, a morally and religiously bankrupt society where, according to an elder in *White Genesis*:

> The scriptures are a dead letter. For never in this village, nor in the whole of Senegal, where mosques nevertheless proliferate, not once have the penalties laid down by the holy scriptures been carried out. Go and see the authorities! We respect them and we cherish them; that seems to be all. That leaves us with the adda, the heritage of our fathers. (p. 45)

In *The Money-Order* it is not just that the scriptures are set aside, but that the very day-to-day communications constantly operate in a climate of mutual distrust. Mety, one of Dieng's two wives, observes at one point, 'Tell them the truth? They wouldn't believe it. It's simple: the truth isn't any use any more!' (p. 121). Dieng himself falls prey to the malaise when he implicity affirms Mety's fabrication of the robbery: 'I have difficulty myself in believing it. Yet . . . well, honesty is a crime nowadays in this country.' The sponging Maissa tells his neighbour that 'people must help one another' and that 'man's remedy is man' (p. 113), but he deserts Dieng at a time of need. The group solidarity shown by neighbours when they bring gifts to Dieng after the faked robbery is a fragile truce. The postman's assurances to Dieng that in concert they will change society is a wan hope, recalling us to Mety's observation at the outset that hope can kill. For the moment, all the dissimulation and lies help to preserve a society turned against itself, a society in which a small group of 'children' — young bureaucrats and insolent functionaries — is, in distributing the meat of prosperity reserving the choicest bits for itself and distributing the remnants unevenly among the masses. Sembène, as artist-griot, lays bare a society which subscribes to the moral of the fable that men (in spite of Gorgui Maissa) love falsehood rather than truth.

NOTES

1. See Barbara D. Stanford with Gene Stanford, *Myths and Modern Man*, New York, Pocket Books, 1972. Paraphrased from *Rites*, ed. John Cafferata, New York, McGraw-Hill, 1975, p. 360.
2. Sembène Ousmane's first novel, the semi-autobiographical *Le Docker noir* (*The Black Docker*) was published in 1956. His latest film, *Ceddo*, was released in 1977.

3. Five novels have so far been published. They are *Le Docker noir*, 1956; *O pays, mon beau peuple!* (*O Country, My Beautiful People!*), 1957; *Les Bouts de bois de Dieu* (*God's Bits of Wood*), 1960, translated 1962; *L'Harmattan* (*The Harmattan*), 1964; and *Xala*, 1974, translated 1976; a volume of short stories, *Voltaïque*, 1962, was translated into English in 1974 as *Tribal Scars and other stories*; and two short novels, *Véhi Ciosane* and *Le Mandat* appeared in a single volume in 1965, translated 1972 (*The Money-Order with White Genesis*). *Le Dernier de l'Empire* will be published in 1981. The seven films released commercially are *Borom Sarret* (Cart Driver, 1962); *La Noire de . . .* (*Black Girl*, 1966); *Mandabi/Mandat* (in separate Wolof and French versions); *Taw* (*Tauw*, 1970; *Emitaï* (*Thunder Gods*, 1972; *Xala* (1974) and *Ceddo* (*Resisters*, 1977). Where applicable, films will be referred to by their French or Wolof titles to avoid possible confusion with the prose fiction.

4. The first two novels have so far not been translated. The second has been out of print for many years, others for shorter periods. *The Money-Order with White Genesis* came out seven years after the original French version, London, Heinemann (AWS 92), 1972; Exeter, NH, Heinemann Inc.

5. This was the 1962 New York edition. The English edition was published in London, Heinemann (AWS 63), 1969.

6. Quoted from the 'Avertissement de l'Auteur' of *L'Harmattan*, Paris, *Présence Africaine*, 1964, p. 8. The translation is mine.

7. *Niaye* (1964) was the first adaptation of a work of fiction by Sembène Ousmane, in this case, of *Véhi Ciosane*.

8. *The Money-Order with White Genesis*, London, Heinemann (AWS 92), 1972; Exeter, NH, Heinemann Inc., p. 136. All further quotations are from this translation and are referred to in the text by page number alone.

9. Cf., however, Sembène's remark, in an interview with *Jeune Afrique*, 26 Février–3 Mars 1968, that the actual amount was unknown to almost everyone outside Dieng's household.

10. See his 'Cultural Diplomacy in African Writing' in Per Wastberg (ed.), *The Writer in Modern Africa*, New York, Africana Publishing Corporation, 1969, p. 70.

11. Quoted from *Jeune Afrique*, 1 Juillet 1977, p. 91.

12. *Bingo*, 195, Avril 1969, quoted in Paulin S. Vieyra, *Ousmane Sembène: Cinéaste*, Paris, *Présence Africaine*, 1972, p. 180.

13. Paulin Vieyra, *op. cit.*, pp. 48–50. The material on *Niaye* in this discussion comes from Vieyra's study.

Taban lo Liyong's Narrative Art

Elizabeth Knight

Taban lo Liyong is a unique figure in East African literature both in his thought and work. A highly individualistic poet, critic, short-story and folk-literature writer, he draws his material from both traditional and modern life. The many facets of his character and work leave his critics and reviewers hiding behind such epithets as 'stimulating', 'prolific' and 'controversial'. However, his short stories fail to provoke much reaction and are all too often passed over as trivia in comparison with the longer, philosophical poems.

The short stories in Taban's two volumes, *Fixions*[1] and *The Uniformed Man*,[2] fall into three classes. There are the modern stories such as 'A Traveller's Tale' and traditional tales like 'Ododo pa Apwoyo Gin ki Lyech'. Many of the stories, though, overlap into a third category in which a traditional story is brought up to date or a modern tale is told in the manner of a *lucak wer*, the traditional oral artist. In reading the tales it is necessary to be constantly alive to certain aspects of Taban's thinking. There is, for example, his directive in the preface to *The Uniformed Man*:

> Rather than approach a story or a novel with the usual outlook, looking for introduction, exposition, rising action, etc., up to the climax, you just concentrate on each word, phrase, or sentence, and learn what it has to say or admire the way it is put together or get your titillation from it. Don't postpone your enjoyment to the end. (pp. xii–xiii)

Nor must the reader overlook the moral overtones to many of the stories. Taban's own parable-like interpretation of the *Iliad* in *The Last Word*[3] is an indication of his view of literary works being 'clothes-lines for displaying values'.

'Ododo pa Apwoyo Gin ki Lyech' in *Fixions* is a good illustration of the traditional story-teller's art. It is an animal fable with the stock Acoli characters of Master Hare and Master Elephant and the timeless setting of 'once upon a time'. The introduction of Hare forewarns the audience of a trickster tale in the Acoli manner but the jungle in which these events occur is most un-Acoli. It is more a convention of the western, 'exotic' tale and indeed its sole function seems to be an excuse for puns such as 'in the whole wide jungle' (*Fixions*, p. 54) with its shades of 'Black Sambo', 'what in the Jungle are you doing here?' (*Fixions*, p. 74) and 'beastly jungle' (*Fixions*, p. 71). It adds a certain facetious and self-conscious element to the tale and the author often parodies the conventions of his genre.

The simplicity of the language and sentence structure is one of the most obvious features of this genre although it is not so accentuated in this story as in 'The Old Man of Usumbura and His Misery', also included in *Fixions*. Here the second paragraph follows the same formula as the first, beginning:

> There was another old man of Kigali who was very poor. This old man of Kigali. He was thoroughly sunk in misery. This miserable man of Kigali. His eyes were always red with weeping. The eyes of the man of Kigali. He was rich once. This previously rich man of Kigali. . . . (*Fixions*, p. 2)

This technique is one line of advancement of the story followed by one line of recapitulation. It is a stylized exaggeration of the general oral technique that requires frequent recapitulations in order to maintain a clear story line amid the many variations and elaborations. The underlining of the story line is achieved in 'Stare Decisis Deo' by the use of song. Taban's stylized technique in 'The Old Man of Usumbura and His Misery' has a marked rhythmic, choric, effect and the repetitions add to the tale itself, as well as to the telling, becoming increasingly ironic. But the diction remains as simple as in 'Ododo pa Apwoyo Gin ki Lyech'.

Incorporated into this plain language are Luo features. The author said of the English language in *The Last Word*:

> If it is, say, English we have adopted, we will not have to stick to Queen's English; that is English for people in England. We have to tame the shrew and naturalize her so that she echoes local sentiments and figures of speech. (p. 80)

He grafts onto his English stock, traditional Acoli expressions together with modern allusions and Tabanisms. He describes for instance, Min Hare's throat in terms of classroom physics: 'The throat that tastes no food grows small-small-small-small and finally contracts like a tin full of vacuum' (*Fixions*, p. 56). The 'scientific' allusion also becomes a paradox, an illustration of the author's delight in word play. This is also found in the expression 'sunup till sundown' (*The Uniformed Man*, p. 58) which is more likely to be a result of Taban's logic than a deliberate Americanism, and in the depiction of the Snail as 'abominable slow man' (*Fixions*, p. 64). The introduction of modern allusions serves to bring the tales up-to-date and to make them more obviously relevant.[4] Tortoise becomes 'MD, DWD' (*Fixions*, p. 67), not simply witch-doctor, and a sinister element is introduced with his guard of 'special police' (*Fixions*, p. 70). In the Tortoise's tale in 'A Prescription for Idleness', Cuckle Cock is modernized into a twentieth-century city gent with bowler and umbrella and the beautiful heroine Miss Gazelle sounds like a Hollywood movie star of the 1950s with her name changed to Venus de Bois. An equally amusing modernization occurs in 'Asu the Great' where the shark is a Harvard graduate.[5]

Biblical allusions also occur throughout Taban lo Liyong's work. In *Fixions*, Jumbe is depicted in 'Ododo pa Apwoyo Gin ki Lyech' with his tail bolt upright like a wart-hog and a generic connection is thus made between this and the following reference to his Gadarene-swine-like actions, 'as if he was possessed by a legion of evil spirits' (*Fixions*, p. 74). In 'The Old Man of Usumbura and His Misery' the moral nature of the fable is further enhanced by Biblical language and echoes such as 'his wealth increased manifoldly' (*Fixions*, p. 2), 'worldly goods' (p. 2), 'erstwhile' (p. 2) and 'bereft' (p. 3). To charges that these modernizations and allusions from non-Acoli sources are adulterating his medium he counters in *The Last Word*:

> If the Acoli and Black People have been 'borrowers' and 'lenders', what is the rationale for imposing limits to borrowings and lendings now? Unconscious cultural absorptions take place every day without the reasoner's knowledge or sanction. (p. 149)

His language and thought, then, are a blend of the traditional and the modern, the western and the African.

Yet in a predominantly traditional tale such as 'Ododo pa Apwoyo Gin ki Lyech' the art of the oral teller of tales is well to the fore. The use made of repetition and recapitulation has already been touched on. Another feature, best exemplified in this tale, is the use of conversation. To maintain his audience's attention the oral raconteur had to vary his use of the voice as much as possible and conversation was one way of introducing different dialects, mannerisms and speech defects. In *The Last Word*, lo Liyong writes:

> To make the chief protagonist really exceptional, the story-teller makes use of a sub-dialect consisting of nasality, consonantal variants, and lisping. The mimicking of such a speech is fun, especially in the hands of a gifted raconteur. (p. 74)

This is the type of speech he uses for Hare.[6]

He introduces Hare's speech gradually to get the reader 'acclimatized' to it, beginning simply: 'Mama, you know how much I keya fo you' (*Fixions*, p. 56). Then he elaborates on this speech peculiarity: 'Jear Mama, waich foy anja week. I wench chu za gayjen yischajei and founj za pea noch yweji' (*Fixions*, p. 60). But the context always explains what Hare means for the benefit of the reader who cannot understand this cross between Donald Duck and Bug's Bunny. The speech defect ridicules Hare as well as individualizing him. A slight variation of speech occurs in 'Stare Decisis Deo' with Monkey addressing Python: 'Mistah, we don't call that "sittin". . . . Now, get seated like other folks' (*Fixions*, p. 24). The sub-dialect corresponds to the role of 'uncultured' and 'unintelligent' black to which Python has assigned Monkey. Other differences in speech depend upon the reader's imagination but an indication is given in this tale — 'Monkey said like that' — that Taban is constantly aware of vocal as opposed to visual variety.

The teller of tales frequently intervenes in the story but in a more direct and personal way than the omniscient narrator of western fiction. In 'A Prescription for Idleness' the author asks the reader questions, addressing him individually:

> Where did Brother Tortoise get such an appetite? Madam, he had no appetite at all. . . . Sir, this also applied to the other zoo animals. We focused on Brother Tortoise because our sympathies are more with him. (*Uniformed Man*, p. 1)

He also reveals his own feelings and awareness of himself as a writer. Such is the case, too, in 'Tombe 'Gworong's Own Story':

> To understand this story there are three things you must know. One is that I am a Tombe 'Gworong — that is, of the tribe that eats people. (*Fixions*, p. 26)

The address is direct to the reader and, although the 'I' is Tombe 'Gworong and not Taban, attention is still drawn to the conventions of story-telling. In 'Ododo pa Apwoyo Gin ki Lyech' it is lo Liyong, the writer, who addresses the audience: 'You see, he had tricked his mother into roasting all the peas; roasted peas cannot grow' (*Fixions*, p. 62). He delights in assuming dictatorial powers over his story and readers[7] which allow him to state the obvious, although in this case it must be remembered that the animal fables are designed for children, according to Taban.[8]

Incidents such as Jumbe in his rage (*Fixions*, p. 64) or Hare running through the fields (*Fixions*, p. 62) allow the artist to display his story-telling talents but he is still working within a medium that has certain conventions. The animal fable, for instance, is composed of stock characters, situations and solutions. In the Acoli tradition Hare is the trickster and as the author admits: 'Nowhere does a trickster escape scot-free' (*The Last Word*, p. 77). Hare always has a mother and his father is either unknown or insignificant.[9] Hare has the habit of claiming everyone for a friend, as this one does. Usually the stories require a search for a witch-doctor who knows how to trap the trickster, the wax maiden being a common means. Above all, the tale must have a moral for, as Taban comments: 'Nemesis was very efficient in putting people in the straight and narrow course' (*The Last Word*, p. 77). In 'A Prescription for Idleness' hasty Hare gets his just deserts, albeit a rough justice, for his vanity and senseless following of fashion.[10] So, too, the treatment Python receives in 'Stare Decisis Deo' is only poetic justice after his degrading treatment of Monkey. In contrast 'Tombe 'Gworong's Own Story' is a parody of the moral fable, perhaps understandably so as it is told from his viewpoint and not by an objective observer. His actual story takes up only the final paragraph and is all moral with little, if any, application to the preceding narration. In the test given to Jumbe by Tortoise in 'Ododo pa Apwoyo Gin ki Lyech' there is another sort of parody — that of the impossible task.

Major stock characters such as Hare and Monkey have certain obviously human characteristics under a veneer of animalism. Animal-like realism does occur, as in the bat incident when Jumbe, following the law of the jungle 'was about to squash him' (*Fixions*, p. 66) without batting an eyelid. But also in that tale the animals are engaged in human occupations like cultivation, and Hare acts just like a child when he tries to get round Min Hare. These human characteristics bring home the allegorical level of the tales. Particularly clever in this respect is the choice of Chameleon, with its mercurial nature, for a charlatan. The inter-relation of animal and human life in 'A Prescription for Idleness' further accentuates the symbolic value of the animals. The bank robber's escape has immediate relevance to the animals in the zoo and the description of Tortoise: '. . . a self-contained animal, with a floor, walls, and a roof to seal him in' (*Uniformed Man*, p. 2), reads like that of man's isolated and solitary existence within his little boxes. He is also the emblem of the thinker:

> Introverts of Brother Tortoise's calibre have an intensity of concentration and analysis which is little met with in extroverts like dogs. (*Uniformed Man*, p. 2)

His literary diversions further add to the human relevance of the tale as more than a piece of entertainment. Taban lo Liyong records in *The Last Word*:

> However long a tale may be, it is merely an elaborate way of illustrating an epigram, proverb or 'law' of life or nature. (p. 71)

This allegorical, educative nature of the fable[11] explains the strict morality found within them. In 'Ododo pa Apwoyo Gin ki Lyech' no one escapes blame, for Hare is wicked although cunning, Jumbe is foolish despite his good nature and Min Hare is excessively greedy. During the pea feast at Min Jumbe's: 'She ate, and ate, and ate, till she even ate one of her fingers' (*Fixions*, p. 61). The Good Neighbour Law of the Jungle throws into relief man's methods of punishing crime.

In 'The Old Man of Usumbura and His Misery' there is a strong element of fate. The sons of Usumbura become 'these worthy agents of fate' (*Fixions*, p. 4), the old man of Kigali is 'knowing' and 'prescient' (*Fixions*, p. 5) and in a position to judge and mete out rewards and punishments. There is something inexorable in the stark cry: 'Oh the fatal end. Death, you have reaped a rich harvest. Death that levels all' (*Fixions*, p. 7).

Akin to this fatalistic streak is the sombre realism and often horrific detail found in these otherwise lighthearted tales. Hasty Hare has three legs amputated[12] for the sake of fashion and then a horrific reality is introduced into the otherwise cartoon-like fable with the addition, 'these were retained as merchandise by the butcher'. (*Uniformed Man*, p. 4). The bat incident has already been noted; so, too, the dissection of Python. With remarkable phlegm the animals discuss the trimmings for their Master Hare's dinner and the attitude towards killing is deliberately casual in 'Tombe 'Gworong's Own Story'. All serve as reminders of the serious intent of the tales. The writer explains in *The Last Word* that in this genre, entertainment is only a means to an end, that end being education (p. 74) and not only the teaching of tribal philosophy.

Taban lo Liyong does not use the fable medium just for the sake of being traditional. He explains in his essay 'Traditional African Literature':

> It is not that we are to revive all things of our past. If a renaissance is just a device for reverting to past modes without justification, it is as good as retrogression. But there are things you can teach through a fable much better than through a poem or a novel. (*The Last Word*, p. 77)

On this basis the children of Usumbura illustrate mankind: 'these apathetic and reflective children' (p. 6) and 'these constant active few' (p. 6). The bundle they carry is the outward sign of an inward antagonism they feel towards each other. It is an illustration of the author's pessimistic view of a fragmented society. Yet he also expresses some optimism. In the Python and Monkey tale, for instance, both title and moral advocate the sanctity of the individual. Both views recur throughout his work.

In the preface to *The Uniformed Man*, Taban states his objective as an artist in the face of a disjointed society:

> Since, whether we know it or not, we are engaged in building (shaping, constructing) a new chain of being, the importance of thoughts, ideas, rather than of art should be our primary concern. (p. xiii)

So it is that the modern stories are more concerned with intellect than emotion, with ideas rather than form. The extreme example of this in *The Uniformed Man* is 'Project X' which is all plot and no form. It is, in fact, a do-it-yourself story with Taban trying to get the reader to be positive and creative. Similarly in 'A Traveller's Tale', an outline of setting and characters is given. Such effects can become annoying, particularly in view of the writer's ideas expressed in *The Last Word* about lazy readers (p. 8). Taban's outline stories encourage this laziness and stock response.

Often these stories are rambling with a quite arbitrary selection of incidents. Anecdotes such as the one about the boy and the fire which occurs in 'The Uniformed Man' and the stone-rolling episode in 'Herolette' seem quite irrelevant. Only in 'The Education of Taban lo Liyong' is there evidence of structuring, the framework of the story being established by Dr Panfacade's lecture. The thoughts that occur between the beginning and end of the class are either provoked by Dr Panfacade's words or are associated ideas in Taban's mind. Perhaps the more meandering tales reflect certain oral techniques but they lack the constant underlining of the storyline. The author continues to use Luo-isms such as the literal translation of *min-ot* in *Fixions* (p. 79) as 'mother house'. This may be a slight directed at the new political élite's ignorance of English or it may indicate the breakdown of traditional society, thus rendering traditional phrases and appellations meaningless. In 'It is Swallowing' the author introduces an expanded metaphor along traditional lines:

> Moreover, she would have had children. For don't husbands have brothers, or even cousins? What are their uses if they don't water a kinsman's garden to help sustain the family tree? A woman is the wife of the family — 'my people will be your people' — and that's that. (*Uniformed Man*, p. 51)

Referring to the womb as a seed-bed needing watering is a common conceit and Taban develops it logically to be the seed-bed for the genealogical tree.

The stories continue to mix prose and poetry — a common feature of the oral tradition.[13] This blurring of distinction is more apparent in the *Eating Chiefs*[14] pieces but it occurs here too, as in 'Asu the Great' (*Uniformed Man*, p. 42) which even includes choric and other elements more associated with drama. Taban often retains the teller of tale's manner of addressing the audience directly in these modern tales, and of adding his own comments as in 'Sages and Wages':

> As I was saying, that was during her first delivery. Our story, however, concerns the second delivery. . . . (Her trouble was not in her throat. I'll tell you where it was, if you really want to know.) (*Fixions*, p. 13)

This contact Taban lo Liyong maintains with his audience gives his writing that 'folksy' quality noted by Eldred Jones.[15]

Sometimes his intervention as writer is not just to create immediacy and contact with his audience but also to challenge them. This happens, for instance, in 'Sages and Wages' where the boring athlete's narration (*Fixions*, pp. 14–15) is deliberately so and broken words are introduced to see if the reader is still attentive. Again this is Taban delighting in his dictatorial powers. In 'Asu the Great' he intervenes to establish his sympathies and justify Asu's actions:

> Asu saw no good reason for hiding the evidence of the spoils at table. Dirty hands do not harm us as much as what comes from inside a man. That is an assurance from the best authority. (*Uniformed Man*, p. 43)

This kind of Biblical allusion is employed to great effect as a means of underlining his allegories or even his single points. In 'Sages and Wages', for example, a stranger intrudes into this land of athletic women with the words 'Why mourn ye?'; he declares the child merely asleep like Jairus's daughter and is himself described in Christlike terms: 'but of course he had to begin from the beginning — just like himself' (*Fixions*, p. 18). This Biblical sanction of the characters adds to the moral atmosphere of the Day-of-Judgement ending.

Nor is this moral and allegorical element lacking in the rest of these 'modern' tales, for Taban's viewpoint is that of the soaring eagle and the Platonist he so admires. By means of a question in *The Last Word* he asserts his ideas on the role of the writer, the intellectual in society, and African society in particular:

> ... should our intellectuals (mostly Aristotelians) not become critics (=evaluators) of everything, especially in our own countries where any Biafras or cultural revolutions will surely shed the blood of those we love? (*The Last Word*, p. 13)

He sets out to evaluate certain trends in society in his tales. 'Sages and Wages' is an indictment against an over-competitive society in which normal human feelings are totally disregarded. Much of the satire is reminiscent of Swift with the merits of pond-jumping paralleling those of rope-climbing. In stories like 'A Traveller's Tale' Taban illustrates the inhibitions and frustrations foisted on man by social conventions. Indeed the many instances of graphic, animalistic sex, as in 'Herolette', can be seen as his attempt to shock the reader into admitting his basic sexual drives. Society's conventions cause the woman's frustration and the negro bum's desires to be incommunicable.

It is these controls that are abandoned in 'It is Swallowing' and 'Tombe 'Gworong's Own Story', revealing the real callousness and brutality of man. In the former, lo Liyong writes:

Morals, mores, taboos and all forms of social control work when we can still be reasonable. But, as man must eat, when famine enters through the main gate, all forms of social control dissolve into nothingness; their original quality. (*Uniformed Man*, p. 54)

Rousseau's social contract is shown to be spurious and man's adherence to it superficial. Hence the corruption revealed in 'Fixions'. I feel Donald Carter dismisses the title story too easily.[16] He is aware of the author's delight in word play but ignores the peculiar suffix -fixion found in crucifixion. Such an analogy is in keeping with the theme, for the foreign power crucifies the developing country and the politician crucifies his erstwhile associates. The story tallies well with specific events in Kenya's history centring on the detention of Oginga Odinga, the former vice-president, on charges of concealing arms from China in his house. But the story could be generally applied to any Third World country caught in the economic stranglehold of one of the major powers.

These larger political themes are tackled in stories like 'The Uniformed Man' and 'Lexicographicide'. The latter portrays an authoritarian state, cut off from foreign influences and with one national language called Zed to signify the dead-end Taban feels such a nation has reached. The immediate application would seem to be Tanzania with its policy of rural development, self-sufficiency and its national language of Swahili. Taban is elsewhere[17] critical of these factors. The parallels are many though — the reduction of the vocabulary by 500 words each year is synonymous with less obvious forms of censorship as is the thought-detecting machine. Taban's stance is not so much political as individualistic. He attacks all forms of control on individual freedom. In another story, 'He and Him' it is the automated, categorized and regimented society he satirizes. In an uncharacteristically sympathetic appreciation of human emotions Taban says of his county bumpkin:

You understand, our man from the countryside is used to warmth in personal contact — nay, he even still has feelings for the beautiful, dirty, gruntling snub-nosed piglets, and he caresses hay. (*Fixions*, p. 34)

This contrasts favourably with the coldness of the town man who acts like a wooden soldier.

Disregard for normal feelings by a military regime is most brutally shown in 'The Uniformed Man'. Before the emblem of this regime is introduced though, Taban fires a few broadsides at the controls on individual freedom imposed by society in the form of gods or God (*Uniformed Man*, p. 58) and at the working and living conditions in Uganda's cotton ginneries (*Uniformed Man*, p. 61). The bitterness of his tone and the realistic, 'straight' depiction may indicate personal knowledge of these places that did so much to disrupt traditional Acoli life in particular. The uniformed man himself is little more than a caricature, an emblem of the military regime: 'He was a bundle all right — a bundle full of commands and obediences' (*Uniformed Man*, p. 67). The father's bike is commissioned by the soldier for a humanitarian mission. On mounting, the soldier kicks the sick child's head:

> After a while the head had been so well pounded, the white of the brain and blood had been so well pounded, the white of the brain and blood spread on the saddle like strawberry milkshake spilt.

> And now, with the obstacle cleared out of the way, our militant man settled his uniformed haunches on the saddle and rode triumphantly away to the dispensary. (*Uniformed Man*, p. 68)

Would it be stretching the reader's imagination too far to consider the child as a poor, sick country — Uganda — the commissioned bike as the hard-won gains of the working population? The soldier then becomes Idi Amin, ostensibly seeking to help the country but imposing his thick-soled jackboot on it instead and, having ruined it, going to the dispensary of foreign aid. Perhaps this is reading too much into the tale, but certainly the implications are there of the callousness and blind stupidity of military rule.

This callous, authoritarian state is the one that crushed Asu. Although this particular tale is very obscure, Asu does stand out as an example of uniqueness, of individualism and, perhaps, of intellectual freedom. All this in the midst of discrimination, the pressure of social conventions, cruelty and an atmosphere of fatalism, for at the very start of the story we are told of Asu's death. Such weird, sardonic humour is typical of Taban's response to the world as he sees it. Often his technique is to reduce to absurdity, as with the footnote to 'Herolette' on Zeno in which he 'proves' that all movement is impossible. Or there is the author's linking of Dr Leakey and Kenyatta in the image of the hooded men. They have their academic hooded gowns but the author is also referring to the hoods worn during the Emergency by the men who volunteered to

identify members of the Mau Mau — an incident in which the two
men took opposite sides, hence 'perfect symmetry' (*Uniformed
Man*, p. 25). Or there is the sordid 'rape' of 'A Traveller's Tale'
during which the African reads *The Faerie Queene* and the negro
bum leaves the woman with a kiss unplanted — echoes of 'Ode on a
Grecian Urn'.

Taban lo Liyong's humour is an assertion of his individualism
and integrity in the face of a fragmented society. He can overdo this
self-assertion and become simply pompous. Addressing the girls
in his English class he says:

> I used to sit dutifully like you until I found that most teachers were not
> keeping up with the pace of my thoughts but trailing miles behind.
> (*Uniformed Man*, p. 34)

Yet the context reveals his own thoughts to be tangential to Dr
Panfacade's and when he complains: 'Old De Quincey did it pur-
posely in order to hurt me, to embarrass me in this classroom full of
girls' (*Uniformed Man*, p. 35), it is obvious that it is himself he is
'sending up' — and he is just as ready to mock himself as others. In
this particular story he extends his criticism to the intellectual and
academic world. Perhaps the context of the story is a criticism of
American teaching and teachers in itself, for in the course of his
fifty-minute lecture Dr Panfacade manages to cover from *Oedipus
Rex* to Walpole and the Romantics, even including the major
philosophies of Coleridge and Shelley. His main criticism is, however, lack of creativity. He sees formal education, in a very
Wordsworthian passage, as one of the main imposers of social
controls that stifle positive action and creativity (*Uniformed
Man*, pp. 26–7). Taban views the world as often illogical with
only an arbitrary ordering of events (*The Last Word*, p. 21), and
society as a superficial constraint on man. In the face of such a
world, Taban laughs or asserts the individual's freedom of will.

His methods of portraying the world are both traditional and
modern, as are his specific themes, but the moral fable form, so
often used, indicates the universal applicability of what he has to
say. So Taban lo Liyong arrives at a synthesis, incorporating all his
experiences in his story-telling. He declares in the preface to *The
Uniformed Man*:

> In a world which is culturally in chaos; in which the old chain of being
> has been broken and the wheel of fate is still revolving without giving

us a chance to guess where the needle will point when it stops; in a world whose old cosmology has been splintered and the splinters are mixed with splinters from another cosmology or other broken cosmologies — in a world which has to make do with a jumble makeshift cosmology; in a world which is primarily fractured, what business have we to talk about unities, of Aristotle? Nature and culture are broken; art which mirrors them can only correctly register broken images. (pp. ix–x)

In *Fixions* and *The Uniformed Man* he attempts to register these images. The animal fables employ a fairly fixed formal structure and tradition, and in this medium Taban displays much skill as a raconteur. In the modern settings he focuses on contemporary themes and ideas rather than forms, the transition being equated with the disruption of one world view and its adulteration by another. However, he maintains a link with the older order in his strong critical and educative stance, and in many of his entertainment techniques of variety, personal appeal to the audience and humour. In this he fulfills his own hope expressed in 'Can we correct literary barrenness in East Africa?':

. . . that our grandchildren of folklorists, of fable-tellers still possess that story-telling passion. (*The Last Word*, p. 40)

NOTES

1. Taban lo Liyong, *Fixions*, London, Heinemann (AWS 69); Exeter, NH, Heinemann Inc., 1969.
2. Taban lo Liyong, *The Uniformed Man*, Nairobi, East African Publishing House, 1971.
3. Taban lo Liyong, *The Last Word*, Nairobi, East African Publishing House, 1969.
4. See *The Last Word*, p. 78.
5. See Okot p'Bitek, *Oral Literature and its Social Background among the Acoli and Lango*, B.Litt. thesis, Oxford, 1963, for an account of this fable indicating that it is not authentic.
6. Okot p'Bitek, op. cit., p. 398.
7. *The Last Word*, p. 8.
8. ibid., p. 69. Okot p'Bitek, op. cit., p. 393.
9. Okot p'Bitek, op. cit., p. 398.

10. For examples of these stock characteristics of Hare as copycat, see Okot p'Bitek, op. cit., p. 404.
11. Okot p'Bitek, op. cit., p. 419.
12. See Hare and Cock story in Okot p'Bitek, op. cit., pp. 404–6.
13. Ruth Finnegan, *Oral Literature in Africa*, London, OUP, 1970, p. 76; New York, OUP, 1976. Also Okot p'Bitek, op. cit., p. 434.
14. Taban lo Liyong, *Eating Chiefs*, London, Heinemann (AWS 74), 1970; Exeter, NH, Heinemann Inc.
15. Eldred Durosimi Jones (ed.), *African Literature Today*, 6, London, 1973, p. 177; New York, Africana Publishing Corporation, 1973.
16. Eldred Durosimi Jones (ed.), *African Literature Today*, 5, London, 1975, p. 142; New York, Africana Publishing Corporation, 1975.
17. Taban lo Liyong, *Frantz Fanon's Uneven Ribs*, London, Heinemann (AWS 90), 1971; Exeter, NH, Heinemann Inc. p. 119 and p. 146.

Revolutionary Aesthetics in Recent Nigerian Theatre

Olu Obafemi

Over the last decade, African studies — Humanities and the Social Sciences — have revealed an overt political commitment that has been described as 'radical' in their 'clear and growing tendency away from the conventional wisdom enshrined in the bulk of writings and teaching on Africa . . . in the West'.[1] Introducing the book which he co-edited with Gutkind on *African Social Studies*, Peter Waterman identifies the characteristics of radicalism in recent African writings:

> This is usually phrased in terms of opposition to imperialism (seen as a social system dominating Africa politically and exploiting it economically). And — more positively — in terms of concern for the African masses, and of a preference for socialist economic and political strategies.[2]

The development of a revolutionary approach to art and theatre (theatre being the most social of all art-forms) among young Nigerian writers forms part of this growing radical tendency. This development manifests itself in the young playwrights' commitment to the employment of the revolutionary potential of theatre to sharpen social awareness, adopt an alternative approach (socialist to be precise) to the obsolescence they find in the body politic of present-day Nigeria, and presenting recipes for social change. The remarkable point of departure between this young generation of dramatists in Nigeria (Femi Osofisan, Bode Sowande, Kole Omotoso, and James Iroha, to name a few) and their predecessors (Wole Soyinka and J. P. Clark) is the formers' conscious ideological commitment; their conviction that social change could come by the playwrights' ability to raise mass awareness to a positive

revolutionary alternative to social decadence. While their predecessors deal with universal verities and metaphysical profun-
dities such as the part psychic search for the meaning of life and
death in Soyinka's *The Road*, the young playwrights deal with
urgent contemporary social problems in Nigeria like the armed
robbery phenomenon in Osofisan's *Once Upon Four Robbers*, student violence in Sowande's *The Night Before*, and the obscenity of
undistributed property in Omotoso's *The Curse*.[3] These young
playwrights reject the tragic vision in their predecessors' work
which they attribute to their harping upon animist metaphysics. In
a series of interviews between this writer and some of these young
playwrights, there emerges a rejection of social vision which opts
for individual heroism. Osofisan finds it bourgeois and tragic:

> I think it is inevitable that he (Soyinka) arrives at these tragic conclu-
> sions because if you are always thinking of individuals creating history,
> history will always look like a series of tragedies. The revolution itself is
> a mass of people always doing things together.[4]

In a similar frame, Bode Sowande finds the cult of individuality
and messianism hypocritical and ineffective as a way of achieving
social revolution:

> Revolution has to be collective. If any man believes he can go it alone,
> he is fooling himself. The forces that he is fighting are enorm-
> ous. . . . Let us start from history, none of the revolutionaries worked
> alone. The kind of characters you have in Soyinka's plays who are
> individualists are so perhaps because of Soyinka's ideals. But I don't
> think it is realistic. You cannot make it as an individual.[5]

This socialist belief in collectivism as opposed to the 'protagonist's
ego' of bourgeois art[6] is evident in the Farmers' Movement in
Sowande's *Farewell to Babylon*; the recruitment of slaves, guards
and the rank and file for social revolution by the enlightened few
(Leje and Sontri) in Osofisan's *The Chattering and the Song*;[7] and
the confrontation of the proletariat (the working masses) with the
power élite — the intellectuals, businessmen and military rulers —
in Omotoso's *The Curse*.

This article examines two plays of Femi Osofisan, *The Chattering and the Song* and *Once Upon Four Robbers*, as examples of the
radical ideological stance through the theatrical medium of young
playwrights in Nigeria. The ideological character of their work is a
response (perhaps an unwitting one) to the invitation made by

Fiebach to African playwrights to allow their 'theatrical thinking' to be stimulated by Brecht's fundamental approach to theatre — 'the ideological character of a work of art'.[8] Osofisan told Enekwe in an interview that this ideological bent in the work of his generation of writers is the significant line of separation between them and their predecessors:

> A number of us the younger generation in fact share this perspective. . . . You may say we are Leftists without being essentially dogmatic about Marxism. But our essentially socialist leanings and convictions separate us from the older writers by a wide margin. . . . We wanted to create an alternative tradition . . . from a materialist perspective. We look at literature as a social force, an ideological weapon.[9]

From the standpoint of these two plays, my article attempts to assess this trend towards revolutionary aesthetics in the Nigerian theatre in English today which makes emphatic political statements through powerful theatrical aesthetics.[10] A basic dilemma that confronts these playwrights is how to create a theatre that will form part of the socio-historical crisis in Nigeria as well as 'transcend the banality of everyday experience'.[11] Osofisan is deeply aware of this dilemma facing a dramatist who is committed to projecting a socialist viewpoint of art as well as giving an aesthetically valid art. He expresses the enormity of the task in an interview with this writer:

> For those who want a certain profundity in their art, a lot of the things we do will be very disappointing, because you can't really get to the depths of experience. And I suppose that this is why one is still working and writing . . . that one should get what will be very socially relevant and at the same time have some depth.[12]

We must understand from the outset that this dilemma is not unique to these young playwrights. It is, to be sure, at the heart of Marxist criticism. It takes the shape of conflict between 'orthodox Marxism' after Lenin and Plekhanov who see literature as a 'cog and screw of one single democratic machine' inseparably linked with the working class movement,[13] and the 'vulgar Marxists' after Engels, Lukàcs and Althusser viewing the impress of history in the literary work, not in 'social documentation'.[14] While Edwin Piscator, in his appeal for a 'tendentious drama' and 'direct action' theatre, denounces aesthetic pursuit believing that it is not the main concern of the theatre to 'create art but to carry on political propaganda',[15] Brecht's dramatic theory (epic-theatre) is world famous because of its aesthetic process achieved through constant practice. In more recent times, Imamu Amiri Baraka, the black American revolutionary dramatist and Marxist ideologue, finds himself caught up in the dilemma of creating art that is aesthetically powerful and also politically effective. Taking his artistic credo from Mao Tse-Tung's book, *Yenam Forum on Art and Literature*, Baraka aims at a revolutionary aesthetics:

> You have to learn the art of writing the play; the question is how successfully can you bring to bear your ideology within this particular artifact you are creating.[16]

How Osofisan employs the theatrical medium to propose a socialist ethical perspective for society in *The Chattering and the Song* and *Once Upon Four Robbers* is the focus of this paper. The first part deals with his revolutionary vision; the second with his use of dramatic techniques to embody the vision.

The Plays

Both plays depict Osofisan's radical approach to historical and social realities and the urgent need for a social revolution that will give birth to a socialist state in Nigeria. *The Chattering and the Song* deals with a revolt led by a group of enlightened radical youths challenging the forces of rot, corruption and dictatorship, ending in the offer of a model for a new society that will replace autocracy in all its forms. This theme comes out positively in the central dramatic scene of the play which is also a play-within-a-play. Here, Osofisan recreates — even rewrites — the history of Oyo during the chaotic period of the rebellious Bashorun Gaha who overthrew the reigning Alafin and set up a reign of terror, killing all the princes of Oyo except Abiodun who was crippled in one leg. Abiodun grew up to challenge and overthrow this despot, re-establishing law and order. But as Professor Moore rightly observes, Osofisan is against all forms of autocracy, however benevolent: for him, 'heroism is a collective, not a kingly virtue'.[17] Osofisan throws his sympathy with Latoye, the rebel, to demonstrate the essence of a social revolution that will liberate society from the yoke of oppression. Latoye defies the Alafin by summoning his creative powers to raise the consciousness of the oppressed, represented in the play by the king's bodyguards (acted by the musicians). Instead of portraying the aspect of history where the old — the authoritative Alafin — uses his magical powers to subdue the young rebel, Osofisan depicts the successful challenge to traditional tyranny.

The young friends, Yanji, Mokan, Leje and Sontri constitute themselves into the Farmers' Movement which will carry out the inevitable social revolution and overthrow corrupt authority. These young intellectuals supply the necessary awareness of change as well as giving ideological direction to the revolution called the Farmers' Movement — the movement of workers and peasants against aggressive capitalism. The play reveals a Marxist vision which states that the proletariat, 'the comradeship of the downtrodden' will achieve revolutionary change in society. Individuals are just 'mere threads in the loom of state' (*The Chattering*, p. 54). This is vividly stated in the short epigram that precedes the Epilogue during the ideological indoctrination of Funlola by Leje;

> Didun nile oloyin . . .
> Say I am the thread
> And you the shuttle
> . . . in the loom of state. (*The Chattering*, p. 49)

In a Marxist framework, the playwright envisages collective action in the wake of mass political awareness. Leje, in a discussion which is at once a courting exercise as well as the political indoctrination of Funlola, the artist of the ivory tower (this game repeats the riddling game of courtship between Yanji and Sontri at the beginning of the play), explains the futility of the search by the police for revolutionary heroes whom they could silence:

Funlola: You are the one wanted by the police!
Leje: The police are ignorant. What is a single man in a revolution, it will run its course, with or without those who served to spark it off. History will remember us.
Funlola: So why do you want me?
Leje: The movement needs all capable people. The whole world, you see, is a farm, and all hands must toil both to cultivate it and to eat out of its fruit. (*The Chattering*, p. 54)

Like Herbert Marcuse[18] before him, Osofisan holds that revolution is a seminal, biological necessity. It is organic and capable of regenerating itself. Art as a part of social development must be committed to the social cause. The artist who commits his art to social change will be renewed, since he has sunk his roots in the communal soil where he will escape the withering that the ivory-tower artist suffers. This is the main message of the dialogue (or political education) between Leje and Funlola. A committed artist has no business fearing alienation:

Funlola:	Yes, what will happen?
Leje:	Renewal, I always answer. No one who commits himself will ever be asked to break with his ancestral roots.
Funlola:	. . . Your faith must run deep . . .
Leje:	Listen, that's how the tribe renews itself, that's how we all survive together.
Funlola:	By giving our life to the cause?
Leje:	By extending that life into myriad seedlings.
Funlola:	To get involved?
Leje:	Like putting out new roots. (*The Chattering*, p. 54)

What we have here is a potent use of biological metaphor for social revolution. The farm is the state to be transformed. The seeds to be sown are the masses to be enlightened on liberation. Osofisan's earlier appeal to writers to 'sow regenerative seeds in the community's flesh'[19] — to go beyond merely reflecting the despair and incoherence in an oppressive society by offering an ethical perspective and revealing possibilities beyond the present — is met in this play. Political awareness is followed by collective action, 'dancing together /in the loom of state' and weaving 'new patterns out of our world' (*The Chattering*, p. 55).

But if Osofisan appropriates the historical past for his social vision in *The Chattering and the Song*, he confronts contemporary reality in *Once Upon Four Robbers* which is a metaphorical treatment of the phenomenon of armed robbery. His dialectic treatment of history (this will come out clearly when we talk of his dramatic techniques) in the first play is continued in this new play, where he looks at the Nigerian condition from a purely Marxist viewpoint. He regards the armed robbers — Alhaja, Hassan, Angola and Major — as products of an unjust social system. The social vision of this play can best be understood in the context of Marxist theory as set out in Marx's preface to *The Critique of Political Economy* regarding the economic base and superstructures in society, social relations and consciousness. It states that men enter into 'definite' relations according to the 'social production of their life':

The sum total of these relations constitutes the economic structures of society, the real foundation on which rises a legal and political super-structure and to which correspond definite forms of social consciousness. The mode of production of material life conditions the social, political and intellectual life process in general.[20]

In the programme notes for the première of *Once Upon Four Robbers*, Osofisan describes the robbers as a tiny part of the Nigerian masses who have been brutalized by social stratification — the existence of two extremely distinct social classes — in Nigeria. He attributes the violence of armed robbery to this social structure:

Take a look at our salary structures, at our sprawling slums and ghettoes, our congested hospitals and crowded schools, our impossible markets . . . and then take another look at the fast proliferations of motor-cars, insurance agencies, supermarkets, chemist shops, boutiques, etc. The callous contradiction of our oil-doomed fantasies of rapid modernization.[21]

In a Fanonist mode,[22] Angola, one of the robbers in the play, finds violence inevitable in a capitalist society where 'too many people ride cars along the sore-ridden backs of the poor' (*Four Robbers*, p. 21). To restore primordial sanity, there must be a radical change in society; the weaverbirds in the earlier play must sing the song of social revolution if the Bar Beach Show (a swift description of the Nigerian firing squad) is not to continue unabated. Osofisan told me:

If in a certain situation one would rather choose crime than starvation . . . at least, somebody has to live, keep the family and all that. So, some people are condemned to be shot at the Bar Beach.[23]

The salient issue of armed robbery, a grave social malaise in post Civil War Nigeria, is the central theatrical metaphor in *Once Upon Four Robbers*. The enormity of this moral problem in contemporary Nigeria validates the claim of this playwright to social relevance in dealing with it. The armed robbers in this play are the remnants of a tightly organized band whose co-ordinator's corpse has just graced the beach when the play opens. The law hounds those involved without taking a look at the unjust social system that produces armed robbery. The point of optimism in the play is that the economic structure of the country will change, thereby changing social relationships and consciousness as well as social mentality. The poverty-stricken of today will have the law (that is, the superstructure which includes force and ideology) once they control the means of production (the base). Major anticipates this social revolution while tied to the stakes where he is going to be 'legally slaughtered'. He tells the Sergeant:

Major: Yes. The day is beautiful. Your stomach proves it. *(laughter)* But Man is so fragile, so easy to kill. Especially if he robs and lies, if he wantonly breaks the law. Serg, today that law is on the side of those who have, and in abundance, who are fed and bulging, who have several concubines. But tomorrow, that law will change. The poor will seize it and twist its neck. The starving will smash the gates of the supermarkets, the homeless will no longer yield to the fear of your bulldozers. *(Four Robbers, p. 60)*

That men's social relationship is determined by their economic (material) position, genetic bonds being only accidental, comes out in the discussion between Hassan the robber and Sergeant, his half-brother, who will order his killing. Their blood relationship no longer counts as they belong to different classes: Sergeant the hunting class, the wealthy and the powerful; Hassan the hunted class, poor and powerless:

Hassan: . . . you know what's going on everywhere, what's happening to people like us, so how can you remain unmoved?
Sergeant: Who said I'm unmoved? I enlisted, didn't I?
Hassan: From one bloody corner to another, the world getting narrower, shrinking around us, to give a few more bastards more room to fart.
Alhaja: Go on Hassan, tell him.
Major: He enlisted. His stomach grows. As they fatten a sacrificial ram.
Sergeant: Quiet! I signed my life. I joined the victors.
Alhaja: So keep running, beast of prey, among the hunting dogs. *(Four Robbers, p. 63)*

The episode that follows reveals the consequence of an unjust social system. It wrecks youthful dreams of high moral ideals and makes even market-women 'chop each other's heads to bits at the jingle of coins'. The social structure, in an establishment that exists only for the privileged few, turns the masses into victims. With increasing social demands (there is the family to feed, tax to pay and school bills to foot), the majority, who have no access to the means of production, are brutalized to the point of hacking at each other's limbs.

The play demonstrates the struggles in different ways of the poor masses, the unemployed, the market-women and the underpaid, to release themselves from the shackles of oppression and exploitation. The playwright's treatment of the historical conditions that produce the violence unleashed on society by armed robbery is dialectical: he confronts the hunters, represented by the Sergeant and his squad, with the strong arguments of the hunted, the armed robbers. In the process, we are invited through this confrontation to see how man's social being and the way he organizes his material life, conditions his thinking. The market-women, who are at each other's throats to make enough money to keep their families, clamour at the end of the play for the execution of the armed robbers. Yet they also belong to the same class — the exploited. The argument of the play clearly suggests that to change man's social behaviour and attitudes, precisely in order to curb armed robbery, the whole body politic must be changed.

Dramatic Techniques

In both plays, there is a genuine search for a theatre style that is linked to revolutionary politics. Osofisan employs in a dialectical and progressive fashion the medium of *total theatre* already pursued by Wole Soyinka in his work, especially in the theatrically ambitious *A Dance of the Forests*. This concept has been aptly described by Professor Adedeji as 'an ensemble where the conscious and the unconscious, the real and the unreal, poetry, song and dance, intermingle with elements of traditional theatre both sacred and secular'.[24] The playwright maintains an objective distance from the elements of myth, folk-tale, magic, music, dance and poetry so as to achieve a dialectical treatment of them, using them to convey his political viewpoint. This is similar to Brecht's unorthodox appropriation of classical material and of Shakespearean plays, described by Professor Yuill as 'cultural vandalism'.[25] This tendency to create an instructive contrast between history, magic and theatrical elements and his contemporary use of it in these plays has been accounted for by Osofisan in an interview:

> Obviously I may use myth or ritual, but only from a subversive perspective. I borrow ancient forms specifically to unmask them, to use theatrical magic to undermine the magic of superstition. All these gods and their inviolability . . . one is tired of them.[26]

An example from each play reveals his experimental and dialectical treatment of poetry, history and magic by demystifying and adapting them for progressive, artistic and ideological effects in a single dramatic experience. In the play-within-a-play, which is also the central dramatic scene in *The Chattering and the Song*, we see elements of history, magic and incantation taken together to dramatize an ideological position, namely the triumph of a social revolution over a reactionary and exploitative (although pre-capitalist) establishment. Latoye (who fittingly is acted by Leje, the leader of the Farmers' Movement, also called Osongangan) threatens Alafin Abiodun (who represents the forces of reaction) with dethronement. The success of this revolt is a recreation of history. Latoye employs his own creative energies to appeal to the inner feelings of the Alafin's guards, seeking *human* identification with them against the sympathetic identification of magic on which Alafin Abiodun relies. He awakens their consciousness to the depravity and squalor of their existence, asking them to liberate themselves from the hypnotic powers of Abiodun's magical reign. In a scene which because of its physicality (expressive body movements, mimetic quality, and rhythms of incantation and lyrical speech) and creativity achieves a dramatic effect aiding audience perception, Osofisan confronts magic with anti-magic. Latoye first exposes the truth of their existence to the guards with the aim of raising their consciousness to the positive alternative of freedom:

> Latoye: Look around you. Look into your past, look into your future. What do you see? Always the same unending tale of oppression, of poverty, of squalor and disease. Why? Ah. You and your people, you are the soil on which Alafin's tree is nourished, tended until it is overladen with fruit! And yet, when you stretch out your hands, there are no fruits for you. . . . I am begging you, please fly out of your narrow nests. Come follow me, raise a song of freedom now. (*The Chattering*, p. 42)

This appeal to the reason and feelings of the guards is accompanied by a combination of the magical effect of Ifa incantation, freed from traditional complexity and rendered in free-flowing prose without losing the potency of its magical effect, with the body rhythms and the mimed 'freezing' of the guards. The magical effect of Latoye's incantation negates the effect of Alafin Abiodun's magical powers. He triumphs over him by appealing to the people's consciousness using his own creative energies. The effectiveness of both magic and anti-magic to demonstrate a historical dialectic thus presenting an ideological viewpoint is realized in the guards' shout of freedom and rush to mob the Alafin.

The shocking reaction which this 'vandalism' — the unfamiliar treatment of familiar history and cultural elements — elicits in *The Chattering and the Song* is also pursued in *Once Upon Four Robbers* where a dialogue develops between the armed robbers tied to the stakes and their executioners. This gives a theatrical twist to the arm of contemporary history. There is a process of self-justification by all the segments of society — firing squad, the market-women and the robbers — in a heated argument which is also a condemnation of the system that produces such mental and social consciousness (aggressive materialism). Magical effect through incantations, taught by Aafa to the four robbers, brings liberation. The 'unexpected phenomenon', namely the chanting of Angola's formula of *Ofo* (an Ifa poetic verse for ransoming death), bewilders Sergeant and the death sentence is not enacted until the other robbers say their parts. Dancing replaces shooting. A stalemate is produced, enabling a democratic involvement of the audience in resolving the plot. The audience are required to give a referendum, having heard the reasoning of the robbers — the oppressed, and the oppressor represented by the Sergeant and his soldiers. In both plays, reasoning is evoked rather than empathy, because the playwright does not merely document reality, but 'subverts' it. The remote history of Oyo and the contemporary phenomenon of armed robbery are both treated objectively in an unconventional way so as to shock the audience into awareness.

The traditional story-telling technique features prominently in Osofisan's dramatic idiom. In *The Chattering and the Song*, it is the riddling game that is utilized for theatrical purposes. The play opens with Sontri and Yanji acting out various kinds of riddles built around an Ifa motif, specifically *Iwori Otura*,[27] dealing with unfolding of meanings. The insertion of this motif unexplained into the riddle-pattern could obscure the effect of entertainment and instruction which the playwright intends. The riddles (Alo-Apamo) which punctuate the action between the two 'intending' lovers are both literally and symbolically meaningful. The central metaphor in the series of role-playing scenes through the riddle-medium is the prey-predator phenomenon which the playwright shows dominating society. The frog preys upon the fish, the hawk on the hen, the stag upon the doe. In these mimed riddles, Osofisan highlights the evils of class inequality in society; Sontri in his role as hawk says to Yanji the hen, 'I'm swooping down with my beak of steel' (The Chattering, p. 2) — the suppression of the poor by the powerful using superior weapons. Other social maladies such as the callousness of the strong towards the poor and hypocrisy are portrayed: 'a bad conscience does wear a mane'.

But the great riddle which these smaller riddles prepare us for, is that Sontri is about to prey on Yanji. The dance of courtship replaces the riddling-game. Both the riddle and the dance of marriage which follows it represent the end of an engagement (between Mokan and Yanji) and the beginning of a new relationship between Sontri and Yanji whose wedding supplies a pretext for the atmosphere and is the main background event in the play. Mutual unravelling of riddles leads to marriage, but beyond that leads to courtship and political indoctrination between Leje and Funlola at the end of the play. By using the folk-tale technique of riddles, not in its conventional form but in mime, Osofisan succeeds in creating an expansive mood between the audience and the stage, having used a medium familiar to both. Rapport is achieved by taking images from the flora and fauna of the environment, and by stimulating participation through the riddles and gestures of the mime. He also makes a significant political statement about a society comprising two classes — the predators and the prey, the hunter and the hunted, with the downtrodden struggling in pain — 'the strangled scream of the people . . . the shout suppressed by power' (The Chattering, p. 4). It is a development of this which occurs at the end of the play when a riddling game becomes an exercise in political propaganda and Funlola is recruited into the liberation movement.

This use of the story-telling technique to generate a full-blooded audience involvement in the theatrical process is also used in Once Upon Four Robbers. The playwright employs the traditional story-telling technique with a narrator who is also a performer telling a contemporary tale in an acted form. The late Kola Ogunmola used this technique to realize the theme in his play The Palm-Wine Drinkard. J. P. Clark used the traditional folk-tale to open his play Ozidi. The remarkable difference between Osofisan's use of the story-telling technique and his predecessors' is that while Clark and Ogunmola used it for what was purely traditional folk-lore (folk-tale in Ogunmola's play and a mythical epic in Clark's), Osofisan uses the technique as a metaphor for a contemporary event. In the prologue, a story-teller is revealed in the moonlight in a performing mood. He comes with a sekere (castanets) to announce with a shout the formular beginning of a sung fable in the contemporary mode. The technique is traditional but the content is modern. The stage directions acknowledge the inheritance and the effectiveness of the form in modern theatrical usage:

> Commanding the spotlight is the Story-teller, with a set of castanets or a sekere. He shouts out the traditional introductory formula: Alo O! As usual everybody replies: Aaalo! He repeats this, gets the same response and playing his instrument, begins his song. The audience picks up the simple refrain — Alugbinrin Gbinrin! after each line.
> (Four Robbers, p. 1)

The purpose which underlies the formula, both in the traditional form and in its modern recreation — is its use as a mode of instruction. A folk-tale must point a simple moral. Osofisan enlarges this function by using the folk-tale to project an ideological viewpoint. The whole play is about the disruptive violence produced by an aggressive capitalist society. By using the technique whereby the actors come out of the audience and seem part of them, the playwright puts the message across that the criminals are there to dramatize an aspect of common human experience.

The dramatic techniques of role-playing and mime play a significant part in achieving socio-political criticism in the play. The use of multiple role-playing, which has been perfected in Soyinka's plays especially Madmen and Specialists[28] is central to the realization of theme in Osofisan's plays. In The Chattering and the Song, Osofisan formalizes the device of a 'play-within-a-play', with the characters who are known actors of particular roles coming out in full view of the audience to take on new parts. In Once Upon Four Robbers, the characters initially are part of the audience but come out after the play begins to act out the role of four robbers. By this device, the playwright achieves two effects.

Firstly, in a purely Brechtian manner of realizing particular social crises,[29] the whole cast confront the audience with the performance of an historical event. This is particularly so in the central dramatic scene of The Chattering and the Song. We are shown men in the process of liberating themselves and determining their own destinies. The audience are shown the action during the process of its being produced. In this scene, the characters show us as we move from the level of the 'real' play to the level of multiple role-playing, that they are actors within a play rather than individuals in the 'real life' of the main play. The actors of the main play who assume new roles in the central dramatic scene, pick up their costumes right on the stage in the full view of the audience to show that they are actors in a major play (*The Chattering*), acting new roles in a sub-play (the historical scene referred to above). We see Sontri, for instance, fitting himself into the role of Alafin Abiodun. The stage directions warn would-be directors not to miss the element of showing the actors as role-players in a play-within-a-play:

> During the 'play', we must feel the characters — especially Sontri — at first searching for words and attitudes, until they gradually, if consciously merge with the figures they are trying to impersonate. One possible way of showing this would be in the change of verbal rhythms and tonation. (*The Chattering*, p. 34)

What is achieved to some extent and what the playwright aims at, is best described by Brecht's 'alienation effect' where actors dissociate themselves emotionally from the stage characters. What is demonstrated is how characters and actions are historically produced, revealing 'how they could have been and still can be' (what Terry Eagleton described as actors showing 'the characters they act and showing themselves showing them'). In terms of ideology, the action demonstrates how society can be changed and has always been changed historically through self-liberating effort taken collectively, but led by the socially aware, like Latoye.

Secondly, and with regard to *Once Upon Four Robbers*, by making the actors come out from among the audience and pick up their costumes from the stage to get themselves into the roles they are to play, the playwright makes the conscious effort of implanting into the actors' minds the fact that they are not to immerse their personalities in the roles they play. It also impresses upon the audience that the actors (who are part of them) are on the stage to perform a story about armed robbers which is a familiar phenomenon to them. The stage directions spell this out:

> Already the actors and musicians have gathered on the stage, evidently all in a light mood, as they recognize one another and exchange warm greetings. Then discovering the costumes, they begin to pick and choose, and then to dress up, gradually establishing the various roles they will be playing. (*Four Robbers*, p. 3)

The effect is to avoid any emotional attachment to these actors either in sympathy or repulsion. Osofisan uses this experiment to present a view of society where, as Professor Williams says of

Brecht's efforts, 'the spectator confronts something and is made to study what he sees'.[30] Awakening audience awareness is intended, as opposed to portraying a verisimilitude of life that might distract the audience's attention and reasoning as does conventional drama in the Aristotelian mode. It is in the light of this that the democratization of the theatrical form and thematic resolution which occurs at the end of this play makes sense. The dialogue between the robbers and their executioners, as well as between the market-women, prepares the spectators for the referendum given by Aafa the story-teller in the final scene, without which the play cannot end — just as *The Chattering and the Song* did not end! The playwright's interest is to promote a reaction from the audience, albeit a shocked reaction.

Music plays a significant part in Osofisan's drama. In fact, the plays are realized to a great extent in music. Apart from the main role in *The Chattering and the Song* of the orchestra located on the stage as a separate theatrical element of the play, there are songs designed mainly to communicate the playwright's strong political bent. There are instances of speeches supplying a naturalistic pre-text for musical pieces with a propagandist intent. For instance, Yanji's mere mention of 'crawling things' at the sight of a lizard recalls one of Sontri's revolutionary songs, 'Dance of the Crawling Things' which provokes dancing, miming and singing. It entertains as well as makes a statement — the spinelessness and apathy of the nation as symbolized by the millipede with 'myriad feet':

> He has no bite, he has no fist
> He has no tongue to voice protest
> This haughty thing is a millipede.
>
> This millipede, a curious thing . . .
> It signifies our nation now . . .
>
> But in our shells, behind our grins,
> Behind our embroidered gowns
> Is coming the piercing knife of truth. (*The Chattering*, p. 14)

The whole body politic of the nation is pointedly satirized in this incidental music revealing the playwright's optimism about the imminence of social change, 'the piercing knife of truth'. Entertainment and instruction are achieved through song, dance and miming.

The same musical elements dominate *Once Upon Four Robbers* both in terms of dramaturgy and statement. For instance, songs and dances add to the potency of Aafa's incantatory magical formula used by the robbers for 'unarmed robbery', as well as producing the stalemate at the end of the play. But songs are also used for satirical effect; all the songs of Aafa, which provide the story-line of the play are satirical. They condemn armed robbery and human greed which bring misery to the robbed families. Listen to the praise name of the robbers in the sung fable:

Itan mi dori o dori	A modern tale I will tell you
Dori olosa merin o	A tale of four armed robbers
Danon danon apani lekun	Dangerous highwaymen
Awodi jeun epe	Freebooters, source of tears
Ron ni sorun apanandodo	Life kites, eaters of accursed food
(*Four Robbers*, p. 2)	(*Four Robbers*, p. 72)

The other songs analyse the evil of armed robbery and the reasons men get involved in the business — the race to get-rich-quick in an exploitative society. In both plays, we see therefore the theatrical form of music employed to achieve aesthetic as well as political purpose.

The two plays discussed in this article show Osofisan's employment of the revolutionary potential of theatre to embody the political and ideological character of his work. Like his contemporaries, he aims to propose a socialist ethical perspective for Nigeria by first reawakening the people's consciousness to a reality beyond the decadence of the present. There are dangers inherent in such a commitment. As these young playwrights are aware, one of the grave dangers is that artistic depth might be sacrificed for political content; that the writers might resort to sheer propaganda as in the Farmers' Anthem in *The Chattering and the Song*. A more serious fault is Osofisan's inability, occasionally, to carry through a theatrical device set in motion in certain episodes. An example is the way Mokan's emotion gets in the way of his successful completion of his role as Aresa, the Alafin's chief bodyguard. His vindictiveness makes him reveal himself, for the first time, as a secret policeman. This sudden revelation of identity and his arrest of Sontri and Yanji, puzzlingly blurs the device and changes the mood of the play. A macabre dimension is thus attained from the position of a wedding entertainment play. But such faults are very few, as Osofisan appreciably succeeds in employing theatrical mechanics to harmonize the related arts of music, dance, mime and verbal arts, achieving an impressive aesthetic quality which gives authenticity to his strong political bent. This must be the trend of a theatre like Nigeria's which is growing more and more revolutionary. In spite of its growing social relevance, our theatre must have eternal values. Even Plekhanov, often taken as the father of the concept of the 'social equivalent of art' believes that a politically committed art must also be aesthetically valid. He says:

> Sociology must not slam the door in the face of aesthetics but rather fling it open wide. The second art of any consequent materialistic critique must therefore, just as for idealistic kinds, involve a judgement as to the aesthetic value of the production in question. . . . The characteristics of the artistic production of a given period stand in the closest causal relationship to the social mentality expressed in it. The determination of the social equivalent of a given literary work would therefore remain incomplete, and consequently inexact, if the critic abdicated any judgement as to the aesthetic value.[31]

NOTES

1. Two scholarly movements give expression to this 'radical' approach to art and society. (a) 'The Nigerian Anthropology and Sociology Association' with prominent champions such as Osoba, Onogie, Usman; (b) 'The Ibadan-Ife Group' dominated by Osofisan, Omotoso, Jeyifo. Their last conference, subtitled 'Radical Perspectives on African Literature and Society' in Ibadan in December 1977, brought to a head the running ideological battle between them and their predecessors, notably Wole Soyinka.

2. See Peter Waterman's introductory article 'On Radicalism in African Studies' in Gutkind and Waterman (eds.), *African Social Studies*, London, Heinemann, 1977. New York, Monthly Review Press.

3. *Once Upon Four Robbers* by Femi Osofisan is at the time of writing in its final form as manuscript and was kindly lent to this writer by the playwright. *The Night Before* by Bode Sowande, forms part of his maiden volume of plays entitled *Farewell to Babylon and other plays*, London, Longman, 1979. *The Curse* by Kole Omotoso, Ibadan, New Horn Press, 1976.

4. Olu Obafemi, interview with Femi Osofisan in Ibadan, 11 November 1978, to be published in a forthcoming Ph.D. thesis on Nigerian Contemporary Theatre.

5. Olu Obafemi, interview with Bode Sowande in Ibadan, 8 November 1978.

6. The de-individualization of characters in favour of collective-heroism is an important element of the proletarian theatre of this younger generation of playwrights.

7. Femi Osofisan, *The Chattering and the Song*, first published by New Horn Press, Ibadan, 1976. References here to Ibadan University Press, 1977 edition.

8. J.F. Fiebach, 'On the Social Function of Modern African Theatre and Brecht', in R. Ngethe (ed.) *Darlite*, IV, 2, Dar es Salaam, March, 1970.

9. Essie O. Enekwe interviewing Femi Osofisan, Ibadan, 1978. (Unpublished)

10. No attempt is made here to define 'Revolutionary Aesthetics' beyond the fact that I find it a suitable term to describe a revolutionary approach to art.

11. Expression used by Osofisan in a reply to Ofeimun's article, 'Criticism As Homicide', in *Afriscope*, VII, 8, 1978, p. 26.

12. Olu Obafemi interviewing Osofisan, op. cit.

13. Lenin's phrases quoted in Terry Eagleton, *Marxism and Literary Criticism*, London, Methuen, 1976, p. 40, and Berkeley, University of California Press. The Proletkut Theatre in Germany, in fact, goes further to recommend that art should be used as a party weapon; while Piscator's Political Theatre urges the 'direct action' of theatre.

14. Georg Lukács' position as evident in his book, *Studies in European Realism*, translated by Edith Bones, London, The Merlin Press, 1972, following Engels after the Hegelian tradition of art.

15. Piscator in fact bans the word 'art' in his programme for the formation of his Proletarian Theatre in Berlin in March 1919. The statement is quoted by Ernst Schumader in 'Piscator's Political Theatre' in P. Dementz (ed.), *Brecht*, Englewood Cliffs, NJ, Prentice Hall, 1962.

16. Amiri Baraka in an interview with G.W. Gibsby in *Theatre Quarterly*, VIII, 31, 1978, p. 33.

17. Gerald Moore, 'Against the Titans in Nigerian Literature', *Afriscope*, VII, 7, 1976, p. 19.

18. Herbert Marcuse holds that revolution is a seminal, biological necessity in his book, *Essay on Liberation*, London, Pelican, 1972. Boston, Beacon Press.

19. Osofisan, 'Anubis Resurgent', in Wole Soyinka (ed.), *Ch'Indaba*, II, 2, 1976.

20. Marx and Engels, *Selected Works*, London, 1974, p. 47.

21. *Once Upon Four Robbers*, Programme notes, p. 1 (iii).

22. Frantz Fanon expresses the view that the very fact of colonialism and imperialism imply violence, *The Wretched of the Earth*, London, Penguin, 1967. New York, Grove Press, 1965.

23. Olu Obafemi interviewing Osofisan, op. cit.

24. Joel Adedeji, 'A Profile of Nigerian Theatre, 1960–1970', *Nigeria Magazine*, 107–109, December–August 1971, p. 3.

25. Professor Yuill in 'The Art of Vandalism: Bertolt Brecht and the English Drama', Inaugural Address, Bedford College, 1977, p. 7.

26. Essie O. Enekwe interviewing Femi Osofisan, Ibadan, 1978. (Unpublished)

27. Iwori Otura, a combination of two of the principal figures of Ifa Divination used here, shunting its 'pernicious reverence' as Brecht would say, for perceptual effect.

28. Osofisan in his article, 'Tiger on Stage', on Soyinka, in Ogunba and Irele (eds.), *Theatre in Africa*, Ibadan, 1978, reveals Soyinka's inspirational influence on most young (and old) Nigerian playwrights like Sowande, Omotoso, himself, Gbadamosi, etc.

29. Although Brecht, like Osofisan later, is concerned with the whole range of historical and contemporary crisis, he concentrates on the realization of a particular crisis in any single dramatic experience. Raymond Williams cites an example of an early scene in *Fear and Misery in the Third Reich* where a stormtrooper encourages a worker to act out a grumbler in a food queue. See R. Williams, *Drama from Ibsen to Brecht*, London, Pelican, 1968, p. 319. New York, OUP, 1969.

30. R. Williams, *Drama from Ibsen to Brecht*, op. cit.

31. G.V. Plekhanov, quoted in Henry Arvon, *Marxist Aesthetics*, London, 1973 (Introduction, p. x). Ithaca, New York, Cornell University Press.

Abbreviations
1. *The Chattering: The Chattering and the Song*
2. *Four Robbers: Once Upon Four Robbers*.

Ola Rotimi: How Significant?

Alex C. Johnson

The production of *Our Husband Has Gone Mad Again* and *The Gods Are Not to Blame* at the Yale School of Drama in 1966 and the Ife Festival of Arts in 1968 respectively, signalled the emergence of a new talent on the African stage. Ola Rotimi has since published two historical plays, *Kurunmi* and *Ovonramwen Nogbaisi*, and produced others such as *Cast the First Stone, Holding Talks* and more recently *If*.[1]

Rotimi, who was until recently senior research fellow at the Institute of African Studies at the University of Ife, and is now head of the creative arts section and arts director at the University of Port Harcourt, has made a study of traditional African drama and African ritual drama.[2] His deep knowledge of these forms underlies his more innovative plays. He also acknowledges an interest in the 'use of indigenous cultural elements as viable ingredients in the creation of a distinct form of drama' in Soyinka and Clark, and the influence of the 'use of language, particularly proverbs' in the work of the Nigerian folk opera groups.[3] He also lists features of the African theatre, of which he is one of the main pioneers, such as music, dance, the use of crowds, communal participation and 'themes and situations . . . which relate directly . . . to African preoccupations and anxieties'.[4]

Rotimi's reputation was established by *The Gods Are Not to Blame*, a successful adaptation of the Oedipus legend which is innovative both on the level of the medium and in the development of the African theatre. It is his commitment to his audience which decided the distinctive character of the medium in this play. His intention was to reach a very wide, many-layered audience, hence his attempt to create a new idiom, a kind of language close to the rhythms and speech patterns of his native language but not deviating too radically from standard English and adequate to carry the weight of his themes.[5] It is in these two areas — language and the African theatre — as much as in the themes themselves that his significance as a new talent depends. In the three plays discussed here, Rotimi uses these ingredients to make an important contribution to African literature.

In *Our Husband Has Gone Mad Again*, Rotimi has written a delightful, light-hearted satirical comedy which is more hilarious and farcical than satirical. The ingredients in this comedy are: an extravagant political figure rather than politics itself; the comic and absurd situations in a polygamous marriage with an attendant cultural conflict; and the crucial but disruptive influence of women in politics, well-known and accepted attitudes to politics, power, social prestige and society.

Major Rahman Taslim Lejoka-Brown leaves his assured and lucrative cocoa business for the rough-and-tumble of party politics: 'It is war! Politics is war' (p. 7), because there are rich gains:

> Are you there . . . ? Politics is the thing now in Nigeria, mate. You want to be famous? Politics. You want to chop life? No, no — you want to chop a big slice of the national cake? Na Politics. (p. 4)

Another factor is social prestige for himself, one of his wives and his friend, lawyer G. A. Okonkwo:

> 'Ladies and Gentlemen, I have pleasure in introducing to you this evening, the chairlady of this august occasion . . . ' (*people clap — pra-pra-pra-pra-pra . . .*) 'She is the one and only Dr Mrs Elizabeth Lejoka-Brown, MD, MSc, wife of . . . (*drops his voice*) . . . an Ijebu-Ijesha cocoa farmer!' Now listen to this: (*more robust voice*)
> ' . . . She is the one and only Dr the Honourable Mrs Elizabeth Lejoka-Brown, MD(Yale), MSc (Gynaecology), wife of the one and only Federal Government Minister of Agriculture and Housing, Mister the Honourable Major Rahman Taslim Akinjide Lejoka-Brown, ON, MHR, Esquire!' (p. 29)

Even though he has retired from the army, Lejoka-Brown still cherishes the romantic vigour of his military past and the audience is reminded of this by his army songs, physical exercises, anecdotes of heroic action, and some absurd posturing such as his surprise-and-attack political strategy. The playwright uses these as the bases for much effective comedy.

His father has married him to his deceased elder brother's oldest wife, Mama Rashida, while he was serving in the Congo and with-

out his consent only two days before he was to marry Liza, a
Catholic Kenyan nurse. Whilst Liza goes to the USA to study
medicine, he returns home, plunges into politics and marries Sikira, 'for emergency', since 'we need women's votes, man, if we must
win the next elections' and Sikira is the 'daughter of the President
of the Nigerian Union of Market Women' (p. 10). Liza knows
nothing of the other women though they both know about her; she
is expected back after the elections which Brown confidently
expects his party to win, and when:

> Everything would have worked out according to plan once the elections
> were over. See? I give Sikira lump sum capital to go and trade and look
> for another man or something like that; Mama Rashida remains right in
> this house of my fathers; and I move into Minister's quarters on Victoria
> Island. Liza joins me there, everybody is happy. But now look at it.
> (p. 10)

What has destroyed Brown's carefully worked-out plan is a cable
announcing Liza's immediate arrival; while he and Okonkwo dash
off to the airport to forestall a premature meeting of the three
women, Liza arrives ahead of schedule and the much feared meeting takes place.

From this point on, the comedy which is both verbal and situational, turns on the domestic and political fortunes of Lejoka-
Brown. The domestic comedy centres on Lejoka-Brown and the
three women in his life. Mama Rashida, the sensible matronly
traditionalist, accepts the situation with equanimity and her main
concern is to maintain decorum in her household, pursue her
chicken and egg trade, and direct her junior sister-in-marriage,
Sikira. The latter is a rebellious, unsettled, untraditional, indecor-
ous and aggressively impudent young girl who is immediately
suspicious of Liza and is determined to stand up to her, even if it
means being more insolent than usual. Her attitude is summed up
thus:

> That black-white woman who spent her whole life roaming the streets
> of America! . . . Ha! I know her kind. They think because they've been
> to England or to America — Toronto, they can kick everybody round
> and round like a . . . football. (pp. 15–16)

Liza is an educated, westernized and very sophisticated young
woman with a different system of cultural values which doesn't
allow for polygamy.

Splendid comedy ensues when these characters are thrown together but there is nothing innovative or specifically African about the situations which the playwright develops. Rotimi works within the usual conventions of mistaken identity, conflict between the sexes and different cultures, since Liza as a Catholic cannot accept a polygamous marriage and what she sees as Lejoka-Brown's deceitfulness.

This domestic aspect to the comedy is extended in the airport scene where Polycarp, the steward, informs the waiting Lejoka-Brown and Okonkwo of Liza's unscheduled arrival. This is perhaps the highest point in this comedy, as Lejoka-Brown realizes the full import of Polycarp's message and the implications for his carefully constructed deception:

> (*Slowly, speechlessly, Lejoka-Brown begins to sink down, absently, ending up in a vulgar squat — the way one does over a pit toilet. Okonkwo watches him curiously then beckons to Polycarp.*)

Okonkwo:	(*with impish delight*): Here boy.
	(*hands Polycarp a coin*)
	Looks like your master needs toilet paper!
	(*Polycarp stands confused*)
	Hurry, go buy some!
	(*Polycarp takes off*)
Lejoka-Brown:	(*peremptorily*): Hey! What's the matter? Hunh?
	(*Polycarp halts*)
	Madman, where are you going?
Polycarp:	I dey go buy toilet paper sah.
Lejoka-Brown:	I see . . . for who?
Polycarp:	(*respectfully*): For you sah.
Lejoka-Brown:	Ehen? I see. . . . Na so your papa dey take shit? Hunh? Answer. When your papa wan go latrine, he go take shokoto put for nyash; he carry damask agbada cover body, take cap knock for head finish, then he come butu dey shit for International Airport? (pp. 30–1)

The comic potential here is enormous and, with good acting, could be devastating; this is true of most of the humorous situations in the play.

Rotimi appears to change the direction of the comedy after the initial conflicts, for Liza's presence, instead of generating clashes in a polygamous situation, soon proves subversive in the household, yet she reaches an agreement with the women. She becomes Sikira's mentor, giving her provocative ideas about 'women's lib', precipitating more comic fights with Lejoka-Brown in the process. These account for much of the comedy in the play and seem an important aspect of Rotimi's concept of comic theatre. There is nothing surprising about this state of affairs in view of Liza's position; what is surprising and rather far-fetched about this amicable co-existence is that she teaches Rashida the laws of supply and demand, and the rather childish delight she takes in repeating them, though it might be expected that an experienced trader would not find them a novelty. Sikira is too rebellious to learn notions like the equality of men and women only from Liza.

The link between the domestic and political aspects of the comedy is Lejoka-Brown and Sikira, both of whom belong to these two worlds. A major source of fun here is the way Lejoka-Brown's military career infringes on politics. The most important of these situations is his extraordinary surprise-and-attack political strategy;[6] then there is the press conference where members of the press are forced to lie flat on their faces while Brown threatens them with a matchet and gun so that Liza can pass unobserved in her bikini, ending up with a toast and a hymn! This outrageous situation is incredible and far-fetched, generating laughter and astonishment. Another instance of this strange combination is when Brown drags Liza around the room teaching her the ten basic firing positions in preparation for a fight with the authorities who, he thinks, want to pull down his house. What is more surprising in this is his response to the news that he has been dropped by his party, in the middle of which he effects a reconciliation with Liza. The reconciliation occurs after Brown's craziest antics and stretches credulity to the utmost. A few minutes earlier, even the placid Rashida had left to pursue her chicken and egg trade in the village, thus clearing the stage for the happy ending which began with Sikira's exit after yet another fight with Brown.

That the playwright should contrive some of these situations points to an unsureness in his comic conception. There is no deep engagement with the problem facing Lejoka-Brown and Liza, and their reconciliation seems wholly gratuitous in order to provide a happy ending. Indeed, this lack of engagement is reflected in the artificiality and absence of feeling in Liza's language just before the reconciliation, when she expresses her regret that Brown has become 'a depraved, no-good scoundrel with the tastes of a pig, obsessed with the putrescent values of a maggot' (p. 70). A similarly artificial register is used during what should have been a serious and passionate row between Lejoka-Brown and Liza about her newly discovered polygamous status. Instead she takes his pulse and begins a diagnosis on the health risks caused by unnecessary agitation:

> . . . your pulse-rate now gives cause for alarm. Your adrenal glands, on top of your kidneys, are working themselves terribly hard. Your liver too is being badly affected; so are your nerves. What will happen next? Psychosomatic breakdown! . . . Take your choice: peptic ulcer; high blood pressure; asthma; obesity; dermatitis; neuralgia; headache; insomnia; migraine; cardio-vascular . . . (p. 40)

The ebullient and energetic Lejoka-Brown becomes an incredible character if he is seen as the usual comic figure. He appears to be a deliberately farcical creation, for to accept him even as a normal comic figure would be to take him too seriously. He is not a dimwit whom we laugh at, neither is he the kind of threat to society which Jero represents; he seems more of a threat to himself. We are invited to laugh at and occasionally with him as he cheerfully extricates himself from untenable positions, gracefully accepting his loss of face and sensibly retreating. It is therefore difficult to see a serious political commentary behind the play and the writer's implied intention seems to underline this.[7] Sikira goes through too many rapid transitions, from apprehension to confrontation and reconciliation with Liza to rebellion against Lejoka-Brown, until she finally becomes an election candidate replacing her husband. Rashida, in her turn, seems far too contented and committed to desert her husband because of better financial gains. Wouldn't she have known all along that conditions were better in the villages than in Lagos? Rotimi's treatment of his themes suggests a lack of focus and a failure to sustain a specific point of view. The execution of themes is uncertain and the inadequate motivation cumulative, thus minimizing the significance of the comedy.

However, these faults tend to disappear on stage and there is a sustained comic atmosphere. Rotimi shows great skill in building a comic structure with pertinently related parts. Language contributes to this as the convention embraces pidgin, various styles of English some of which represent local languages, and the liberal use of Yoruba and Arabic terms. The pidgin facilitates an immediacy of communication which any audience will appreciate, and some of the styles of English enhance characterization and add to the comedy. For example, Lejoka-Brown's colleague Mallam Gaskiya uses the inflated style of the older generation:

And, aside from the fact that the present leader of our party is so
old-fashioned and autocratic about the risky implementation of his
whimsical strategy, this whole mumbo-jumbo about military exercise
in a political set-up is a sham! (p. 52)

Madam Ajanaku, Sikira's mother, injects aphorisms and proverbs
into her pidgin which makes it a splendid index of characterization. There are linguistic infelicities and the text needs a good
deal of editing; nevertheless, *Our Husband Has Gone Mad Again*
is a successful stage comedy and a refreshing departure from the
more depressing treatment of political and social themes by
some other dramatists. Perhaps the realities of the West African
situation compelled Rotimi to abandon this kind of comedy in
favour of more serious concerns in the tragedy, *The Gods Are
Not to Blame*, the two historical plays, and the pessimistic but
polemical and rather sentimental play *If*.[8]

Kurunmi has as its subject the internecine Yoruba wars in the
kingdom of Oyo in the 19th century. It explores the conflict between the major power blocks of Ibadan and Ijaiye within the
empire, when the Alafin of Oyo declares his son, Adelu, his heir
instead of requiring him to commit suicide when he dies, as was
the custom. The play clearly shows that the conflict was due as
much to divergent views on tradition and the constitution as to
factionalism, personal jealousies and rivalry between the individual chiefs and war-lords of the empire. It focuses on the major
figures in conflict who dominate and determine the character of the
drama, especially Kurunmi, Ibikunle and Ogunmola of Ibadan;
also including a Christian missionary presence represented by the
activities of the Rev. and Mrs Mann. It traces the conflict of personalities and the course of the war culminating in Kurunmi's
death and the subjugation of Ijaiye.

Rotimi injects a contemporary political and social relevance into
this historical subject. He explores the themes of collective political and military leadership; social change and development in a
traditional society; responsible leadership; control and accountability in society. Oyo had reached a stage of development where
tradition had to be modified to maintain internal advancement and
facilitate adaptation in the face of encroaching modern values and
western power. But the arch-conservative opposed to change also
exercises almost absolute power and due to his abilities has gained
the ascendancy. Kurunmi rejects progress in the name of tradition
but his justification is untenable and mistaken:

When the gaboon viper dies,
its children take up its habits,
poison and all.
The plantain dies,
its saplings take its place,
broad leaves and all . . . (p. 15)

His analogies refer to natural phenomena which are renewing and life-sustaining through their cycle of death, birth and growth, and are not sterile and immutable like his own conception of tradition: 'We have tradition, and tradition is tradition. Time may pass but the laws of our fathers, tested and hallowed by the ways of men, live on. That is tradition' (p. 20). Tradition should be relevant and vital, serving the needs of society not constraining its development or denying its vitality. As Timi Ede reminds him, 'you forget that time passes and the ways of men must change with time' (p. 20).

Kurunmi rejects discussion and consultation, asserting his personal judgment and will on the state, impatiently dismissing the other leaders and showing scant regard for their legitimate concern over the military unpreparedness of Ijaiye for war. This causes a temporary rebellion as it breeds considerable resentment:

Amodu:	You have grown too powerful, my lord.
Fanyaka:	Landed property,
	Kurunmi.
	The farms,
	Kurunmi.
	The air we breathe,
	Kurunmi.
	The gods of our fathers,
	Kurunmi.
Warriors:	Kurunmi,
	Kurunmi,
	Kurunmi!
	Abah! (p. 39)

This conflict of opinion assumes dangerous proportions not only because of personal considerations, but more importantly because Kurunmi has the stature, resources and following to challenge the collective decision of the state and he is prepared to use these weapons. Hence he becomes a potent threat to society at large by virtue of his arrogance and ultimately reckless use of power and authority. Society too might be blamed for not curbing his excessive power when it had the opportunity to do so.

The other leaders in conflict against Kurunmi, who support the Alafin, may not appreciate the significance of their actions but they represent social change and the need for accountability which Kurunmi rejects. Rotimi distinguishes between them as individuals but shows by their deliberations that they accept the principle of consultation. Ogunmola is rash, precipitate and extreme and his attitude is coloured by personal rivalry with Kurunmi. Ibikunle, who is much more cautious and conciliatory, proposes negotiation and a peaceful solution, mainly because he appreciates the horrors of internecine war: 'a man cannot be so angry with his own head that he seizes the cap from that head and dons his buttocks with it' (p. 46). Ibikunle's cool and calculated rationality is sustained even under the pressure of war, but Ogunmola, though a good fighter, almost cracks in the face of the Egba intervention.

This intervention on the side of Ijaiye comes after Kurunmi has experienced serious military reverses and when he needed help most: 'one does not know the joy of a dog without a tail' (p. 74) but he could not dictate terms or oppose the decisions of the Egba war chiefs. But these decisions on common battlefield tactics prove to be more gratuitous and capricious than rational or considered and are catastrophic for Kurunmi. His appreciation of the course of events in proverbial language just before his suicide is an honest acceptance of his faults:

A cow gave birth to a fire.
She wanted to lick it
But
it burned her.
She wanted to leave it
but
she could not
because it was her own . . .
her own child,
her own . . .
child. (p. 94)

Kurunmi dominates the play as the most important character in the drama, being much more developed than the others. He is pre-eminent and strong-willed but ultimately over-reaches himself, though his stature is essentially tragic for he is honest although misguided; as well as his personal faults, an inevitable chain of events causes his destruction.

The introduction of white characters seems a flaw in Rotimi's total conception. Thematically, they are not well integrated into the dramatic texture and the focus is not clear. Perhaps Kurunmi's rejection of Christianity can be seen in relation to his rigid stand on tradition; in connection with this, the Rev. Mann reports that Ibadan has accepted 'the Word'.[9] The Rev. Mann is also used to bring out other aspects of Kurunmi's character, his sarcasm and common sense for example. Dramatically, the Manns' function is to comment on the flow of the conflict and report developments at crucial stages, thus ensuring an economical and clean dramatic presentation. But the Rev. Mann is a comic figure who emerges as a self-consciously pious, pompous and pontifical missionary, anxious to be seen in the tradition of Christian martyrs. This comic portrayal can be seen by the absurd situations he appears in and by his distinct verbal register which is inappropriate to its context. The Rev. Mann's language is formal and elevated with a ponderous and involved syntax; his vocabulary is pompous, archaic and overtly biblical. It is a religious register which he uses to preach at rather than to converse with people. Rotimi uses language effectively to distinguish him. With this kind of portrayal, it is difficult to see what serious role he plays in the elucidation of the themes.

Language plays as significant a role in *Kurunmi* as in *The Gods Are Not to Blame*, for besides using it to differentiate characters, Rotimi develops an idiom close to African speech. This is an English verbal register containing proverbs, figures of speech, special idioms, expressions, syntactic and lexical features. The differentiation may be seen in the two Ibadan leaders who use these to a lesser degree than Kurunmi; even among them, Ogunmola is noted for his animal and abusive lexical choices. However, it is Kurunmi who is distinguished by language more than any other character. For example, he consistently switches from prose to verse and back when playing specific roles or experiencing extreme feeling, for verse seems to represent a heightened idiom, as when he pours libation to Ogun or invokes spiritual support at his *agbo'le*. He also uses a great deal of proverbs and figurative language both during these formal roles and in normal speech situations. In his vocabulary there is a predominance of animal terms used either literally or figuratively to show his scorn and contempt for opponents.

The emphasis on African theatre in this play may be discerned by the unique character which those elements of traditional society give to the drama. Song, dance, mass and individual movements and ritual libation all add spectacle, facilitating the mechanics of the play and even defining character. War spectacle is minimized in favour of a cinematic technique, using the Rev. and Mrs Mann who report the flow of action and indicate its scale.

This aspect of African theatre is developed even more extensively in Rotimi's second historical play, *Ovonramwen Nogbaisi*, which continues the themes of political and military leadership in a period of crisis. These themes give historical plays a contemporary relevance and underline their significance in the modern African context. The British punitive expedition to Benin in 1897 which destroyed the empire is the subject used to work out these themes. The play shows the Oba Ovonramwen under pressure from internal dissension and external attack. In Act 1 he strenuously attempts to contain the serious assault on the unity and cohesion of the Benin empire caused by the striving of his chiefs for greater independence. His response is swift, decisive and summarily harsh at the expense, it seems, of a deeper, unexpected loyalty from his subjects. Ovonramwen appears not to exercise the necessary qualities of astuteness and leadership needed to generate the support needed in the face of British attacks.

This British encroachment is a formidable and potently destructive imperialist force with an undisguised colonialist and aggressively commercial motive. The Oba needs all his resources to contain this threat. The killing of British envoys is merely a pretext for invading and subjugating Benin. Oba Ovonramwen has no solution to this, neither does he have the material resources to counter the enormous firepower of the invaders. While the British deploy massive resources in the interests of colonialist expansion, traditional society stands no chance, especially in conditions of doubtful loyalty and uncertain leadership. The dramatist here relates character to situation because in such a situation character becomes crucial, especially when political leadership is called for.

The Oba does not show the necessary tact and firmness, and a superstitious streak unnerves and disorientates him after an unfavourable divination which actually predicts the sacking of Benin: 'Your Highness . . . the death I see here is not the death of one man. Bodies of men . . . fire . . . and blood — bodies floating' (p. 15). In spite of this prediction, even because of it, he becomes irresolute instead of cautious and inadvertently encourages a dilution of his own authority. He cannot exercise the kind of influence on his war-lords necessary for effective leadership. The delegation of responsibility for the defence of the empire to one of the chiefs prepares the ground for independent action, since they later interpret his inaction as either a sign of weakness or a sly test of their loyalty and initiative in the face of unprovoked British encroachments during the sacred Ague Festival. Oba Ovonramwen hesitates, allowing the initiative to pass from him to his war-lords and the British, after which his fall is rapid. The scale of this fall is represented by the symbolic and emotional homage he is forced to pay to the British resident, Roupell, after the occupation of Benin.

Like Kurunmi, Ovonramwen is the dominant character in this play, thus continuing Rotimi's tendency to concentrate on a hero. The Oba towers above all others in tragic stature and dignity, honour and ceremony. His fear of the British is justifiable and reasonable; their injustice forces him to resist even in a hopeless situation and against overwhelming odds, but he ultimately shows enough pragmatism to surrender. Thus the external pressure from the British is crucially important in an assessment of his leadership. When he says to Moor, 'Tell Queen Victoria that at last the big pot of corn has been toppled; now mother hen and her children may rejoice' (p. 78), he is expressing his understanding of the final triumph of superior forces. He becomes the victim of a changing and developing world in which superior modern armaments are decisive for survival in the event of a determined onslaught by opponents. The other indigenous characters stand for the collective will of the empire, giving Oba Ovonramwen the kind of support the leadership needs, but none of them has the significance he has.

European characters are important in Rotimi's dramatic texture but they are not presented objectively; his emotional involvement in and partisan attitude to the events of 1897 is apparent. The British are pictured as ruthless, unashamedly and crudely riding rough-shod over justice and human rights, deliberately provoking a confrontation with the Binis. Perhaps given the historical facts he could not have done otherwise, but the presentation is too biased. Although this portrayal may reflect his degree of commitment, it nevertheless detracts from the literary and artistic qualities of *Ovonramwen Nogbaisi*.

Language plays a significant part in this play. It is an important aspect of Rotimi's technique: he uses it to differentiate characters; to develop an appropriate setting; to create a convention which achieves consistency and which is an integral part of the dramatic texture. Here, as in *Kurunmi*, the characters may be classified and the categories correlated with various linguistic features. In both plays there are white characters and ethnic characters; given the geographical setting, the latter are Yorubas in *Kurunmi* and Edos in *Ovonramwen*.

The whites use a formal, standard English variety with occasional, appropriate modifications in particular situations as when Moor slips into momentary colloquialisms and uses simplified language, or when Phillips switches to a non-standard variety as he addresses his orderly: 'Good man, when you come back, I give you dash plenty-plenty' (p. 32). The ethnic characters whose English in the text represents their native language comprise the largest group and it is here that there is effective individual character differentiation. There is a distinct difference between Oba Ovonramwen's language and character in the early part of Act I and the rest of the play. Initially, he is a dignified, assured and royal figure who asserts his authority swiftly and decisively, using an elevated style which is marked by a distinctive syntax, use of proverbs and imagery:

> Because the moon is dim, the eyes of little stars cast a carefree glitter. Obaduagbon, Esasoyen, and the rest of you . . . your stars have this day consumed themselves in the heat of their own unwisdom. This night you all die. I have spoken. (p. 6)

Subsequently there is an alteration in his style due partly to the changed circumstances and also to the psychological disorientation caused by the divination. The distinctive syntax is gone, and although proverbs and imagery occur more frequently in his speech than in that of the other characters, the dignified reflexive imagery is no longer in evidence.

The third group of characters who appear in *Ovonramwen* speak either pidgin or show various degrees of competence in the use of non-standard English, and might be arranged in a cline of bilingualism. Rotimi's intention here is to show the maximum fidelity to the diachronic and socio-linguistic features of the setting while at the same time differentiating characters. The use of pidgin and other non-standard English varieties enriches the stage presentation; even though the convention is not always consistent, it is nevertheless good entertainment.

Ovonramwen is more firmly in the developing African theatre than *Kurunmi* or *The Gods Are Not To Blame*, for in it Rotimi deploys the full resources of traditional society, using the cultural and linguistic setting of traditional West Africa to give it rich dramatic texture. For example, Rotimi uses Edo, the local language, in songs, expressions and greetings making the play more accessible to a local audience but conceding translations for a wider audience. The English is modified and injected with special features to make it represent the local language; these include syntax, vocabulary, idioms and expressions, proverbs and figurative language. With figurative usage the ground, tenor and vehicle of the implied or explicit comparisons emphasize their West African origins, suggesting the resources of the local language, while proverbs are employed as obvious indicators of the cultural background. Syntax, idiom and vocabulary deviate deliberately, thereby suggesting by their unusual semantic values and structures the underlying indigenous language. Here are two examples:

> My brothers-at-arms, is this how we must dangle the rest of our lives? (p. 33)

> Our fear became heavy when the whitemen began to come to Benin (p. 59)

Song and mime are also important. In the prologue and epilogue, there is a symbolic mime consisting of prisoners in chains in various agonizing postures; this represents on the one hand the enslavement of those who rebelled against the Oba, and on the other, the traumatic historical events depicted in the play. Mime invariably goes with song, and this constitutes an important choric accompaniment to many of the crucial points in the action. It adds to the ritual spectacle and setting and, being so pervasive, communicates much of the ceremony and splendour surrounding the Oba.

Mass movement as an important feature of the spectacle can be witnessed, for example, in the trial scene where the interaction of the audience and cast creates a communal involvement in historical events as well as in the momentous societal disaster being enacted. Other dramatic moments, when war is imminent, for example, are presented economically using dance, symbolic movements and mime with music. A cinematic technique which involves the rapid alternate exposure of short scenes, encapsulating the contrast between the two sides on several levels, is used to show the preparation for the attack on and defence of Benin. The crucial encounter representing the final conflict and the defeat of Benin is mimed by Moor and Ologbosere. This is a more advanced technique than anything used in *Kurunmi* which suggests Rotimi's development as a playwright.

A further development is the integration of traditional aspects of the setting into the plot, thus contributing to the historical authenticity of the situation. The British intrusion occurs during the Ague Festival and is interpreted as an insult, a desecration and a challenge which the Benin empire has to respond to:

> It is the custom that for seven days while this ceremony of Ague goes on, there must be no drumming in the land, and no visits to Benin by strangers. (pp. 27–8)

Hence the war council meeting, the Oba's indecision, the unwelcome initiative of the war-lords and the subsequent chain of events ending in the destruction of Benin.

A language of the theatre has been forged out of ingredients from traditional African society and these advance the themes, contribute to characterization, and create a drama which is a triumph of stage spectacle. Some of these techniques, however, make excessive demands on both actors and producer and there is the need for expert choreography since much of the spectacle is rooted in a specific cultural environment, thus becoming a limitation.

The three plays discussed above are dramatically successful and confirm the important talent introduced by *The Gods Are Not to Blame*. This significance derives not only from the themes, his treatment of which confers a topicality and relevance that transcends the historical subjects, but also in Rotimi's experimentation with his medium and his development of traditional African theatre. His innovations in the linguistic convention are an important aspect of his significance. However, the convention is not always used consistently and the extensive inclusion of native language items becomes a limitation. For example, the group of characters who speak English in the style of a second language in *Ovonramwen* were, prior to the trial of the Oba and his chiefs, Benin warriors, and it is not clear how they have acquired this linguistic knowledge.

Modern African writers are concerned with the state of contemporary West African society. Rotimi's emphasis and concern differ from other contemporary dramatists only in degree; for just as a playwright like Soyinka has an acute imagination with a deep awareness of current social and political problems reflecting an instinctive sensitivity to the quality of life, Rotimi's awareness is merely a shift in emphasis showing an interest in the individual caught up in a chain of events whose fortunes are tied up with his society. In *The Gods Are Not to Blame* stability is achieved after the exile of Odewale, but in the historical plays society suffers almost the same fate as the pre-eminent individual. Since his themes represent only a difference in emphasis, his particular genius may lie in the successful modification of traditional dramatic form and content, and the attempt to create a consistent linguistic convention in correlation with this development of form. Rotimi is not content to work within established modes, and his ultimate place in African literature may, in the final analysis, depend on his competence within these chosen fields.

NOTES

1. Published plays:

   The Gods Are Not to Blame, London, OUP, 1971.
   Kurunmi, Ibadan, OUP, 1971. (All subsequent quotes in the text refer to this edition).
   Ovonramwen Nogbaisi, Ibadan/Benin City, OUP/Ethiope Publishing Corporation, 1974. (All subsequent quotes in the text refer to this edition.)
   Our Husband Has Gone Mad Again, London, OUP, 1977. (All subsequent quotes in the text refer to this edition.)

   Unpublished plays:

   Cast the First Stone
   Holding Talks
   If
2. 'Traditional Nigerian Drama', *Introduction to Nigerian Literature*, Bruce King (ed.), Lagos, Evans, 1971, pp. 36–49.
3. 'Ola Rotimi interviewed', *New Theatre Magazine*, XII, 2, 1972, pp. 5–7.
4. ibid.
5. This intention has its roots in Rotimi's awareness of the linguistic problems facing the African writer in English and in his desire to reach a wide local audience: ' . . . in handling the English language in my plays, I strive to temper its phraseology to the ear of both the dominant semi-literate as well as the literate classes, ensuring that my dialogue reaches out to both groups with ease in assimilation and clarity in identification' *Dem Say: Interviews with Eight Nigerian Writers*, Bernth Lindfors (ed.), African and Afro-American Studies and Research Centre, Austin, Texas, 1974, p. 60.

6. This is too long to quote in full yet the tremendous comic potential can only be discerned in an extended quotation.
7. Robert M. Wren quotes Rotimi as saying of this character: 'Lejoka-Brown is an ordinary Lagos man who does things our more sophisticated moral inhibitions won't allow us to do.' In 'Ola Rotimi: A Major New Talent', *African Report*, XVIII, 5, September–October 1973, p. 31.
8. *If* was performed at Ibadan in June 1979. The playwright appears to have got carried away by the social and economic tensions in Nigerian society. The ideological, didactic, humanistic aspects and the traditional element, especially the songs, are poorly assimilated into the drama. The play would appear to need much revision.
9. One reviewer refers to this 'nebulous' area of the play and quite correctly raises questions about the Manns' role; Oluropo Sekoni, *Ba Shiru*, VII, 1, 1976, pp. 80–1.

A Modern Afro-Islamic Vision through Art

Bahadur Tejani

Heirs to the Past by Driss Chraibi is one of the best expressions of the Afro-Islamic world view as seen through literature and art. It is not so much a work of fiction as an intense poetic metaphor which deals with many of the relevant issues in the modern African and Arab world. The title of the novel is clearly intended as a symbol and the story involves a quest for the heirs of Haj Ferdi, a deeply spiritual and powerful billionaire. The quest-motive is an old one in literature and needs originality of conception and technique to be of recurrent interest. With Chraibi, a rich blend of traditional Islamic values and ultra-modern European literary concepts, allow him to present the quest with profound historical and human insights.

The plot of the novel is representative of the search for a balanced identity and an aim in life which has continued to preoccupy many writers in Africa and Asia and in other parts of the world where European power and education has created social and individual schisms. For his setting Chraibi chooses the two contrasting cultures of metropolitan France and Morocco's Casablanca. His hero is an exceptional Moroccan Arab who has spent sixteen years in France away from his family, country and religion. He attempts complete integration by marrying a Christian. Called Driss, he is portrayed with humour which is characteristic of Chraibi throughout the novel: 'A real camel, one of those mules from Morocco that experts admire. Antibiotics? I don't even know what the word means. Truly. Listen — I've eaten stones. And believe me, when I say stones I mean stones.'[1] This robust solid man is possessed by such a deep neurosis of alienation that his doctor resolves to withdraw into himself rather than treat the patient. Driss's mind is in total revolt against the dehumanized technological sterility of modern society. The doctor realizes that he will have to question the basis of his own life and of western civilization and religion in general, to endure and cure his patient.

In a sense Driss knows too much, but his knowledge has added to his sensitivity and reaction towards the West. His expectations of the 'metropolitan parent' civilization are indeed classic. They are typical of the expectations of many young minds from the Third World and they continue to recur as much today as in the past. Chraibi is aware of the dependent-status syndrome and writes of it as such. In this quote, the hero is addressing an imaginary French audience in his mind:

> 'Tell me, madame, tell me, monsieur, young lad, little girl, tell me that I'm not mistaken, that you've only just got rid of the German occupying forces and that you'll soon again be the worthy people, warm-hearted and fraternal, whom your great company of writers, philosophers and humanists have told me about. Do, please. It's all I ask of you. Please. I'm not living on poems or selected verses, I'm entering on manhood. I'm not the only one in my case, there are several like me, a whole crowd of colonized and protected people. The twenty-five million of us over there were unable to come, but it's just as if we all had.' (pp. 16–17)

Europe and its representative, the scientifically trained doctor, have no idea of the torrent of emotions running through the subterranean gullies of Third World minds. Though the hero is living among the French, his neighbours are blissfully ignorant of the cultural dislocation created in his world by their past empires. Chraibi's highly dramatic technique raises the tension to a crisis. The hero is on the threshold of a total nervous breakdown when the phone rings to tell him that his father is dead. His arrival home in Morocco is heralded by two scenes, which are classic in the way that they typify the temptations many naïve men and women are prey to, in their assessment of their own past and the present. The two situations are related to comparative perspectives on European and non-European cultures and the self-image of individuals in the two cultures.

The first is the confrontation between the hero and the European intellectual on the plane. In his capacity as a master of 'words', the intellectual personifies a modern version of the nineteenth-century European colonialist concept with a Christian God at the centre of the universe. He represents a refined version of the massive onslaught through education, the media and scholarship with which Europe continues to lure the unwary to its own world view, its own concept of the universe and universality. Baptized informally as *homo sapiens miserabilis*, this liberal intellectual is appropriately abstract and carefree about life's real problems. He is preparing to deliver a lecture to the Arabs on cultural co-operation while their children scrounge in dustbins in the waste-land of cities shattered by colonial wars. The superbly fallacious flights of sensitivity with which he effortlessly rises above dis-cord and engagement are as tempting as they are dangerous: 'It is art in the end, that will draw us together again, after all this kil-ling, isn't that so? Art is greater than man and the condition of man. It survives him' (p. 20). Many African writers, especially the Negritude-visionaries, have rejected this European thesis as pro-art but anti-life. Its epigrammatic simplicity denotes strong beliefs and assumptions. The novelist has his own strong view-point, which is that when faced with acute suffering and poverty of the masses, this high-level philosophic abstraction is a mere disguise for avoiding life's problems. The writer's anger at such dissolute irrelevant dialogue is seen in the reply which his hero gives to the intellectual:

> 'If I've understood correctly, you've come to our African countries to give lectures and also to ferret out works of art. Look — I doubt that you'll find any here. Stones, yes, you'll find as many as you like of them, whole truck-loads. The government has just launched Operation Stone-removing. But before you go collecting stones, wouldn't you do better to collect the human remains?' (p. 21)

The rejection of universalism as propounded by the West is complemented by the betrayal within his own Arab world. This defines the second temptation where the Europeanized man turns upon the world of his father and curses what he sees there. Chraibi's highly poetic method of narration makes him draw the scene with great economy and intensity, allowing the situation to open a time-vista of many decades within a few pages. Also on the plane is an Arab taking his French wife home for the first time. She is: 'Orderly and methodical in . . . work as in . . . private life, con-scientious and realistic . . . symbolic of the West' (p. 14). Casually the Arab tells her lies of a grand heritage and culture, painting a vision of comfort and finesse. He talks in a loud voice, overheard by the passengers, all of whom will soon be aware of the monstrous lie and of the public betrayal by the son of his father. At the airport, an old man covered from head to foot in mud, riding a donkey and shouting loud enough for the whole world to bear witness, is straining to break the police barriers to meet his profligate son. The tragi-comedy is as natural as it is inevitable. The son refuses to acknowledge 'that dirty old man our servant'. In his wrath the father assaults the policeman, with natural consequences. The former's vehemence is as comic as it is terrible to behold. The sacred and the profane, time past and time present, get inexplicably and intricately entwined to create a dramatic picture which demonstrates Chraibi's superb control of language and of the art of fiction:

> 'In the name of God, the Compassionate, the Merciful, I sold my father's field, amen. And my brother's field, amen. And the one I robbed my neighbour of, my neighbour of, my neighbour of. The sheep, the billy-goats and the nanny-goat, the hens, the mattress, the army rifle, all sold. Amen. Thy will be done, O Lord, in this century of science, decolonization and independence. Money-order, sixty money-orders, plus the postage. So that he might be worthy of my unworthiness. And three of my sons have died at their work, wretched are we, and turned to dust shall we be, amen. And now he is ashamed of his father. The road is long, so very long, back to the village, and I am weary, so very weary, Lord, I no longer even wish to die, I no longer wish for anything.'
>
> 'And now, come along with me,' said the policeman, getting to his feet. He spoke gently, as though to a sick child; but he was looking surly. 'Come on, I'm taking you to the station. I told you to keep away from that barrier. Come on, grandad, come on.'
>
> Just then the donkey appeared, seemingly from nowhere. It finished chewing a blade of grass and then raised its old man's head to the sky and started to bray. (pp. 27–8)

In word and in deed, the world around the hero seems to offer no positive values. His inner life is full of agony; what he perceives of outward realities provides no solace either. Yet like another great existential hero, Raskolnikov in Dostoevsky's *Crime and Punishment*, Driss Haj's heart throbs with compassion for the wretched and the displaced of the oil-rich Arab countries. The following passage gives us a good insight into the doubts raging in his mind and his compassion for the masses. As a Muslim, he shouldn't follow Christian rites, but this mad, sad hero can no longer question rationally:

> I have gone into cathedrals built of stone and I've listened, I've watched and I've been moved. I had no right to take Communion, but I did. *Thou shalt not kill!* While across the sea the Koran declares in clear and intelligible Arabic: *To kill a single human being is to kill the whole of the human race.* So what do those religions of a glorious morrow mean? Christ is crucified again every day. As for Islam, has it ever existed? (p. 19)

The stage is thus set for dramatic rediscoveries. As Driss Haj revolves around the opposite pole of Islamic faith and belief, he enters the house of his dead father with much doubt and mixed feelings.

His father's character has a great deal to do with the scope of the discovery and the extent to which it draws the reader into the deeper aspects of Islamic spiritual thought. He is drawn with the keenest of artistic perceptions, much like a faceless statue which in form, movement and energy radiates a grand idea and overwhelming power. While alive, he was wise, disciplined, responsible and generous in the best traditions of Islamic piety. Although rich, he was a tremendously earthy character. He never touched alcohol and he could understand and appreciate life's contradictions, while being close to the deeper currents of spiritual energy needed by the world to help humankind become united and progressive. All in all, the father represents the best as well as the worst of the traditional world, being both generous and yet authoritarian. From the writer's point of view, in word, thought and deed he is symbolic of the message of Islam, uniting the family, community and humanity in death, as he strove to do while living. At his graveside, with the rain pouring down, the sky weeping symbolically, the hero makes his first discovery. Sixteen years and a cosmic belief away from this marvellous man, the impulse of Islam which his father practised is as alive in himself as when he was a child chanting the first verses of the Koran. The discovery of his roots begins here. The passage is worth quoting in full, both for the centrality of the idea and the poetic intensity of the language, which sustained by the atmosphere of collective consciousness marks an epic moment in a Moslem's life:

What he chanted was of no importance. It was not the words nor the meaning, nor even the symbolism, which moved our hearts, the men, women and children who were there. We forgot why we were there the moment he began to chant. It was the incantation, and the end of our woes and miserable little problems, the aching and yet serene longing for that other life which is ours and to which we are all destined to return, the victors and the defeated, the fully developed and those still at the larva stage, the faithful and the atheists, through God's great compassion. There was all of that in the voice of the man who stood chanting in the sun, and we were in his voice, I was in his voice despite the vast legacy of incredulity that I had received from the West. When he reached the end of a verse, he paused, and so it came about — an outburst of fervour. And while he chanted it was like a man in the wilderness chanting his faith. And the voice rose and swelled, changed in tone, became tragic, soared and then floated down on our heads like a seagull gliding gently and softly, little more than a whisper. And so — never, never again will I go in search of intellectuals, of written truths, synthetic truths, of collections of hybrid ideas which are nothing but ideas. Never again will I travel the world in search of a shadow of justice, fairness, progress of schemes calculated to change mankind. I was weary and I was returning to my clan. That man who was not even aware of his voice or his faith was alive and held the secret of life — a man who could not even have been a dustman in this world of founts of knowledge and of civilization. Peace and everlasting truth were in him and in his voice, while all was crumbling around him and on the continents. (pp. 43–4)

The common bond of a shared experience created by the invocation of the Koran, gives us an idea of what the hero is searching for in himself. For as long as he can remember, this unity between word and deed, between the individual and the community has been shattered. Thus to see himself and everyone else joined together in this collective experience is profoundly moving. Nor is the spiritual moment limited to Moslems only but transcends to a compassion for all humanity in the finest sense. At the end of the funeral we discover the hero's brother Madini, confiding in him the distilled essence of this compassion for mankind. If people can unite so well in death, if suffering is common to us all, he asks:

'I want . . . to know why all these people who were here a little while ago and who know what human suffering is — I just want to know why they become animals. . . . I want to understand, understand, to know why these people, not so long ago, caught an old Jew in the street, a poor old fellow who just happened to be passing, poured petrol over him and burned him alive. . . . It's not the advice given by my father that keeps going through my head, but the awful screams of that Jew. Tell me brother. You're educated, you've read a lot of books. Can you explain it?' (pp. 45–6)

As a representative of human wisdom, the father is not only a symbolic unity of spiritual principles but also a manifestation of real power. His power is wealth. He owns fleets of taxis, trucks, estates and urban property. Whatever the billionaire's character and his influence over people, human desire for his property must manifest itself. Hence a vast herd of relatives and dependents have come together to hear the will read. Like the rest of them, the hero is intensely curious regarding the fate of the world after the death of his father. Here Chraibi's accomplished technique enhances the symbolic scope of the whole story so that the hero's curiosity and his quest become a spiritual message for others. A dramatic shock awaits the audience. There is no will to be read. Instead the notary presses a switch and Haj Ferdi's voice rises from the dead to give each according to his need and his virtue. It is here that the writer's own Islamic vision is propounded; what follows is Chraibi's own version of Islam in the modern world. It is based upon the assumption that fundamentalist and authoritarian Islam with its traditional structure and unity is no longer possible, as symbolized in the death of the father who held it all together. Implicitly, therefore, the question is posed. Because of the impact of modernity, confluence of cultures, races and ideas, what can be put in its place?

To introduce his modern Islamic philosophy, the writer provides Haj Ferdi with six different offspring, all of them male. Each one has a unique social quality and like the father, is an extended symbol in himself. The most outstanding and forceful one is Nagib whose main qualities are thus presented by his father in the tape-recorded will:

> 'To go around lifting a truck with your hands, taking the heads of two people you don't like the look of and knocking them together as you roar with laughter, eating a leg of mutton for your breakfast, fornicating more than is natural — we pity the women you spend a night with — and having a fight when there's something you don't understand, and drowning your sorrows in drink — is that the whole of your existence?' (p. 77)

He is the strong man of the family and of the financial empire, yet incapable of a vision of the future or an aim in life. There is no inheritance for him then but the job of a foreman and money according to his work. The burden of holding together the kingdom of heaven on earth falls not on the eldest son Camel, the traditional choice, but the sad and sensitive Madini. Camel is dismissed with seventy-five million because the father knows too well that his bureaucratic, legal mind would destroy the hard-earned harmony of the family. Another of the sons, Jaad, is condemned to live in everlasting poverty because 'given a cornfield he would make a dustbowl of it'. His heart and manner of life are those of a beggar and it would be against the laws of nature to give him a helping hand. Abdel Krim, the youngest, has developed an abnormal sensitivity and feigns madness in the best sense, rather like Edgar in

King Lear. Described in the will as 'our consolation, our poetry and our laughter', he is told to carry on: 'go out on the roads and wherever you please! Our solicitor here has instructions to keep you supplied with sufficient funds to live and laugh to the end of your days' (p. 82).

The ending of the will is as dramatic as the beginning. There is no mention of the hero, the roving intellectual, the one with learning but without faith. The public blow isn't the end of his quest. A private reckoning with the father awaits him. Through a friend, the father has sent him a parcel full of bank notes with a message: 'For your expenses here. Search.' His return and his disappointment have been anticipated. Thus chastened, enlightened and sobered he begins to search all over again, continuing the quest. This time he comes face to face with the noble, self-denying qualities of his father. Haj Ferdi died of cancer but had voluntarily exiled himself from home for the last five years to spare the family and the community the distress and trauma of the gradual decomposition of body and morale.

There are several discoveries which involve both the hero and the audience in this quest for identity and towards wider horizons. The first one discussed above is of course the power of the Koran at the graveside. Although this is mainly subjective since we feel it through the emotions of the hero, the sense of united grief and the recitation of Islamic wisdom by all present make it a mutual human experience. The father's momentous sacrifice and his dedication to the welfare of those who come after him, is another such discovery. But the most positive and objective discovery of all is his assessment of his children. As mentioned before, each of them represents an extended world in himself. In assessing them the father is naturally passing judgment on the many aspects of life itself, particularly on the artistic, intellectual, material, financial, social and military aspects. Intrigued by his father's assessments, the hero 'interviews' his brothers. He discovers that deep down, each of them is really satisfied with the judgment. This includes his own reconciliation with his father and therefore with his private self. Thus we are treated to an objective viewpoint and conclude that modern Islamic vision as portrayed by the father's will should reconcile the many contrasting forces of life, while maintaining a basic spiritual unity.

Chraibi even deals with one of the most sensitive problems of Moslem life: the position of women in Islam. The portrait which the hero draws of his mother, a sensitive bird-like person, is disturbing and needs both attention and an answer. Although she accepts sacrifice, economic dependence and hard work as her lot, her spirit is profoundly restless within her. Chraibi is realistic enough not to provide any simple or ready-made answers to the position of women. Instead he makes the son run away from the seemingly unbearable burden of his mother:

'Do you understand, Driss? The whole world has grown older, much older, and the worst of it is that I've remained a child. Oh, I've no illusions, I can look at myself in the mirror. No matter how much I tried to rattle a tambourine and sing and dance, there would always be one thing I know to halt me and dry up the song on my lips — the world has left me behind, Driss, it's hurrying faster than I can even in my imagination. I've never said all this to anyone, not even the Seigneur. Oh, I try to reason with myself, and Madini has taken me out in the car and even in a motor-boat — "To give me some fresh air," he says, "to take my mind off the dead" — but all to no use. It's not the dead that I'm thinking of. The best place for me is here, in this house. In this house which, following the ancient custom that Islamic law reserved for women, has been my prison for thirty years.'
'Please, mother, that's enough!'
She did not seem to have heard.
'For thirty years. And now we're told that we're all free. But I ask you — doesn't an old prisoner like me end by liking her prison? A prison, whether it's big or small, is still a prison.' (p. 99)

Thus we are made aware of the intense, unreleased energy burning inside her. At the end of the novel, when the hero decides to return 'home to France' we are not sure if his quest is over. Perhaps such a quest can never have an ending. But the discoveries and rediscoveries he has made in the Moslem world, are likely to raise his personal and social life to a new level.

NOTE

1. Driss Chraibi, *Heirs to the Past*, London, Heinemann (AWS 79), 1972; Exeter, NH, Heinemann Inc., p. 4. (All further page references in the text are to this edition.)

Structure and Theme in Munonye's *Oil Man of Obange*

Charles E. Nnolim

The more John Munonye writes, it seems, the more critics seem determined to ignore him. Don Carter's very favourable review of his first novel, The Only Son, and the reviewer's speculation whether 'Achebe's place has not in this regard been challenged, and by a fellow Igbo, John Munonye',[1] seem equally to have fallen on critical deaf ears. Undoubtedly one of the most prolific novelists in Nigeria with six full-length novels to his credit, Munonye is in danger of remaining for far too long in critical limbo. For a writer of his training and ambition, to be totally ignored by the critics is disheartening.

After six full-length novels, it is not hard to discern what has kept Munonye in critical limbo. Matthew Arnold stated that Wordsworth might have been a greater poet than he was, had he read enough. It is time perhaps to wonder aloud whether Munonye and many other African writers like him read enough — not necessarily novels — but literary criticism about the art of the novel, especially criticism about the art of the great practitioners and writers of the novel the world over. The African reader — the ultimate consumer of the African literary product — has grown quite sophisticated of late and has come to want more than a story from the writer. One day, a clever and courageous reader may collect into one giant heap what have so far passed for novels in Africa, staple on top of this giant bundle Umeasiegbu's The Way We Lived as a suitable title, dump this bundle with its effete contents into the River Niger and, turning round, demand in an impatient and angry voice that African novelists should now *write* novels. This eventually might come to pass because many African writers have not seen the need to go beyond writing what Charles Larson (in *The Emergence of African Fiction*)[2] called 'the archetypal African novel' in which the stock situation has been the cultural conflict resulting from our collective colonial experience.

Munonye has not been his own critical best friend. After six novels, he might ask himself what, beyond the story itself, he has brought to his own art and what technical innovations he has contributed by way of narrative style, characterization, and point of view. One of the factors, I think, that has long kept Munonye in critical limbo is his apparent lack of seriousness. He seems unusually delighted with frivolous scenes where adolescent boys and girls frolic, either wrestling or fighting or throwing stones at one another. In Munonye's work, there is never a confrontation between a troubled mind and the consequences of his actions, no conflict between the human agent and his destiny, no character with a 'dark power' in his psyche that he has to purge, no conscious encounter of the personality with the stranger within, no casting round of a great soul athwart the mighty purposes of existence in a world full of insoluble tensions where the problem of 'how to be' becomes a burning question. No one seems to have been stimulated to point out any particular philosophy of life in any of Munonye's work, either through utterances by his characters or through the narrative. No great moral conflicts or issues beg for argument in any of his novels. Nor does Munonye's language carry with it the lodestars of what Longinus calls 'the sublime' which, with its nobility of diction, grandeur of expression, and impressiveness of thought creates in the reader a sense of being carried to new heights of passionate experience thus making a minor work, whatever its defects, appear truly impressive.

But *Oil Man of Obange* is in a class by itself among Munonye's work; it is the one novel that deserves a second reading. Here, most of the flaws that encumber his other books are surprisingly absent. It has the high seriousness that is lacking in his other novels. The story it tells is timeless. There is skilful composition, a miniature canvas but painted with intensity of feeling. In *The Only Son*, Munonye was playing the proverbial sedulous ape to Achebe's *Things Fall Apart*. *The Only Son* was a first novel with the usual flaws — formlessness, authorial intrusions into purely narrative passages, boring digressions that lead nowhere other than the privileged glimpses they give of the Igbo cultural milieu, and a lack of thematic depth. His second novel, *Obi*, was scarcely an improvement. His initial faults persisted, while new ones disturbingly intruded — no innuendo, no mystery, no foreshadowing, nothing left to puzzle the mind and tantalize the imagination — in other words, a poor concept of plot. The conclusion one is forced to draw after reading *Obi* is that even though Munonye succeeds quite often in evoking almost the same situational scenes as Achebe, he falls far short of the latter in his handling of plot, in creating characters with the complexity and dignified stature of Ezeulu, and in his narrative technique. *A Wreath for the Maidens* reads almost exactly like Ekwensi's *Survive the Peace*. Both are topical novels about the Nigerian civil war — shallow, reportorial, and doomed to die a natural death once the issues that keep them current fade into the limbo of memory. *A Dancer of Fortune* borders on farce unrelieved by its great narrative skill or the profundity of its thematic concerns; while the latest novel, *Bridge to a Wedding*, which continues the odyssey of Joe and Anna in *Obi*, contains no exciting new developments worth noting.

But *Oil Man of Obange*, Munonye's third novel, has the makings of a classic, if we understand a classic as a work of art that is among the best of its kind. A classic, one must also add, starts with what is traditional in its genre but goes further, since ultimately it advances the whole tradition, dealing with eternal truths presented in such a way that it pleases generation after generation. *Oil Man of Obange* is such a work. It first arrests the reader by the felicity of its narrative style which engages both the interest and the emotions of the reader. One of the scenes, where Jeri mounts his bicycle, fully loaded with six tins of oil precariously perched behind, is worth quoting here:

> But for the load, he would have tilted the bicycle to the right and then swung his right leg expertly over the saddle. Instead, Jeri held the bicycle erect and hopped upon the pedal, bearing himself stiffly. Then, he lifted his right leg up . . . slowly, steadily . . . over the crossbar, to the right side . . . He sat down.[3]

The emotional involvement of the reader in Jeri's plight is inescapable in this passage. One's heart seems to stop for a moment and stays arrested until Jeri is safely mounted. One might contrast the slow motion of the above passage with the rapidity of movement in another tense but emotionally engaging moment much later, when Jeri falls from his bicycle:

> 'What!' The brakes had snapped. The wheels were completely free. The bicycle bumped and rolled; the tins knocked. 'What!' (p. 126)

This second passage, with its short sentences reveals that Munonye is capable of a variety of styles to suit each situation. But the following passage reveals even more forcefully, a writer who seems sure of himself. One cannot but observe the sureness of touch and the relaxed, even avuncular, tone of the author as he discusses the collective opinion of people about Jeri:

> Why, they asked, did he not know that it was the season of rest? He should go home and rest: go home and look after himself for two weeks or so: go home and rest and forget everything to do with money for just a brief period. (p. 44)

But it is time to turn from Munonye's style to the major concern of this study — the theme and structure of the novel under discussion. However, it must be borne in mind that a full discussion of the author's narrative technique would reveal his thematic and structural concerns in bold relief. The theme of *Oil Man of Obange* is engaging. The view of tragedy which Munonye presents in the novel is in linear dimensions. In Jeri, we see a man, one of us, following an ill-advised course that leads only to darkness. The sad outcome derives ultimately from the usual root cause of tragedy in all human affairs — that of free choice. Jeri, in choosing a certain course of action, treads a path which, although it has its temporary palliatives and doubtful compensations, leads inevitably to disaster. When Jeri decides to abandon his father's ancestral lands and chart his course as an oil man rather than remain a farmer, his sister calls him a madman. When he decides that all his six children must receive a good education, all paid for from his very meagre income, his sister, Onugo, and other kinsmen give him up for lost. In Jeri, then, we are face to face with the view of tragedy which states that man cannot escape the consequences of his choices and of his actions. Tragedy results, as is usually the case with the genre, because man revolts against his own limitations, so that in *Oil Man of Obange* the more Jeri suffers reverses in the oil trade the more he rebelliously insists on continuing with it and keeping all his six children at school.

Munonye writes what reads like a classic naturalistic novel. In the so-called naturalistic novel, the real motivating forces are self-preservation, hunger, fear, sex, and ambition in a cruel and unsympathetic world. So we see that Munonye's Jeri is a man engaged in an endlessly brutal struggle for survival. He is portrayed as the victim of socio-economic forces, for in a world where successful oil men like Mr Brown deal in drums and can store almost limitless quantities while waiting for fair market prices in order to make a good profit, Jeri is restricted to six tins a day, each tin precariously perched on a rickety bicycle that can make the long trip only once a day. Jeri thus becomes a prisoner to environmental and economic forces beyond his control. The life he lives becomes a vicious trap, a cruel game in which he is forced to borrow a huge sum of money from Mr Brown (more than he could earn in a year), then go on to mortgage his paltry patrimony of land to a mere bicycle repairer to whom he is also a debtor. To make an already miserable life even more punishing, he turns to all sorts of menial jobs in a pathetically unsuccessful attempt to make ends meet — a move that brings him neither relief nor succour. He tells Mica in a voice full of pathos:

> You ought to have known I have no money. . . . Or would you want me to see myself? I have no land, no bicycle, no valuable property. (p. 188)

The crux of the matter centres on the subtle method by which Munonye presents his central theme: that of parental responsibility for children. At the beginning, he subtly makes the novel read like a paean, a tribute to every struggling parent who works hard so that each child will grow up, in Igbo parlance, 'to be greater than his father'. But the author's subtlety soon deepens into irony. In one voice, Munonye urges us to admire Jeri, the oil man; Jeri, the doting father; Jeri, the responsible husband; Jeri, the responsible and ambitious parent for whom no labour is undignified so long as the job helps to keep his six children in school. But at the same time, in another voice, he urges us to examine the situation critically, forcing us to wonder what sort of exaggerated sense of responsibility or parental love can so blind a man to his own limitations or block his ears against the sane advice of well-meaning friends and relatives and the warnings of his own inner voice, that he will ruin his health and mortgage all his lands for the welfare of the children he purports to be fighting for. From this ironic posture, the novel emerges as the greatest indictment in the literature of the Igbo people against unbridled love for and devotion to the welfare of one's children. There is a touch of Molière in Munonye's posture: even a great virtue if practised immoderately will give rise to absurdities and, in Jeri's case, to tragedy. Munonye has subtly hidden the central meaning of the novel in Mica's school motto which reads: *Da nobis recta sapere*, which is Latin for 'give us the right discernment'. For those who might have missed the Latin tag, Munonye comes directly to the point in the following passage which states the central theme of the novel. The narrative voice is the author's:

> But should this (the tragic end of Jeri) not be a lesson for all the living and sane? Was it fair that a man should practically destroy himself in the interest of his offspring — in his efforts to bring up his children? Must child-rearing mean self-effacement? (p. 237)

It is a rhetorical question. A man or a woman should not die for the sake of his or her children when there are sensible alternatives. Love for children, a good and admirable thing in itself, becomes self-destructive when untempered by reason and a sane appraisal of the situation, it leads to the death of the parents, as in Jeri's case.

The form of *Oil Man of Obange* shows a great advance in Munonye's narrative technique. The novel is held together and organized around certain rhythms and motifs that act as centripetal forces, making for cohesion in the various elements of the novel. First, there is the rhythm of falls and failures on Jeri's part, a rhythm that provides an important thematic concern, revealing the slippery path down which Jeri inexorably slides to tragedy. Munonye's artistic arrangement of these falls and failures is an advance both on his artistic insight and on his novelistic technique. He arranges each fall so that it appears more grievous than the preceding one, assuming a deeper dimension in Jeri's perilous march towards tragedy. To 'fall' has many semantic implications and Munonye's exploitation of each of these is a *tour de force* of his artistic intuition. To 'fall' means, in one sense, to drop from a higher place to a lower, to become less in rank, estimation or importance. When Jeri first turns oil man, scornful neighbours cannot understand why he should abandon the noble art of farming for the despicable profession of trading in oil. This fall from esteem hits rock-bottom when he also abandons his ancestral homeland to his enemies and moves to a completely new site: 'many said he was a coward. Onugo, his sister, had never stopped calling him a fool' (p. 5). To fall also means to collapse, to go to pieces. Jeri literally 'goes to pieces' each time he falls from his bicycle. It all begins harmlessly: the first fall in front of Marcellina, his wife, is an object of amusement and laughter for both. Jeri is carrying empty tins and he neither loses his oil nor is injured. The author records this fall thus:

The first one had occurred barely a week after he started the oil trade. It took place at the approach to the house, with all the tins empty. Only Marcellina, apart from himself, had witnessed the accident . . . (p. 86)

The second fall causes more embarrassment since it is witnessed by outsiders. This time, 'very little oil was lost', according to the narrator, but nevertheless there is some loss:

In the second fall, he was just lucky. As he was ascending a hill, the impact was quite small; very little oil was lost, and there were many passers-by who came up spontaneously and helped him to raise the bicycle and the tins. (p. 87)

The third fall, according to the narrator, 'was definitely the worst'. Jeri literally goes to pieces, having his 'knee severely bruised and his arm . . . fractured'. The progressively increasing severity and gravity of each succeeding fall reveals itself in this third fall:

The third fall was definitely the worst. Like the first, it occurred at the approach to the house, but this time he was leaving for Otta with six full tins of oil on the bicycle. His knee was severely bruised and his arm was fractured, and he had had to lie in bed for over a week; besides that he lost more than two tins of oil. . . . What was so disturbing about this latest fall was the feeling of being abandoned far away from home, and near Ukeleke of all places. (p. 87)

The fourth and final fall actually ruins him, and breaks him financially as well as physically. When the brakes of his bicycle snap as he rolls down a steep hill, it speeds 'furiously down in rebellion and treachery, meaning to plunge him into the stream, or into death' (p. 126). After this fall, Jeri spends seven weeks at the bone-doctor's on account of his fractured right leg. He has also lost six full tins of oil and his bicycle.

Another meaning of the word 'fall' is to fail, to 'fall flat' or to fail to produce the intended result. This is seen in Jeri's failure to meet the most elementary demands of his growing family. After his fourth fall from the bicycle, he can neither feed his family nor pay his children's school fees. He also fails dismally in his efforts to buy himself another bicycle and reclaim the parcel of land he has mortgaged to Ogonabo the bicycle repairer. Thus, it is not too hard to discern the hand of the conscious artist in the arrangement of the rhythms of Jeri's falls from his bicycle, reflecting the rhythms of his failures as a farmer, as an oil man, as a provider for his family, and his unsuccessful efforts to engage in other trades like palm-kernel-cracking as stop-gap measures. The final implication of 'to fall' that has relevance to Jeri's plight and which Munonye exploits is 'to fall among thieves'. When Jeri falls among thieves at Ukeleke, his mind cracks and he ends up a colossal ruin.

Another motif around which the novel is organized is the theme of 'madness' or insanity. Munonye's conscious artistry again reveals itself in his handling of motivation and foreshadowing. Jeri's ultimate insanity has been foreshadowed from the very beginning of the novel through subtle hints that at first mean nothing, but later assume the dimensions of a motif by the sheer force of repetition. Very early in the novel, as Jeri seeks shelter in one of the homesteads in Ukeleke, one of the children points him out to his playmates as 'a mad man' (p. 10) and they all proceed to run away. Again, when Jeri decides to be an oil man instead of continuing with farming, his loquacious sister, Onugo, 'held that he was positively insane', according to the narrator, and she calls him this to his face:

> 'Insane one! You it was who surrendered our main family land to an enemy, somebody with male part like you. And now, as if that were not enough, you want to abandon the remaining land and take to the oil trade. Let me tell you what you perhaps know already: you are a madman!' (pp. 23–4)

Next, when the same Onugo discovers that Celia, one of Jeri's daughters, is also being sent to school (a thing unheard of in the early missionary days) and not being kept to the house to get used to family chores and routine, she accuses both Marcellina and Jeri of madness: 'You two are mad — let me tell you in case you do not know' (p. 28). Much later, when Jeri goes to borrow money from Onugo to enable him to send Mica to college, she ridicules him and 'when she had gone some distance she turned round and called him an insane being' (p. 194). Finally, when he actually goes mad, Munonye writes:

> His mind had cracked; and it was complete, though never violent in its manifestations. People said things. Some . . . held that it was all a result of his love of money; that Jeri loved money so much that having lost the few pounds in his bag, he had lost his senses too. Another view, again held by a very few, was that it was the enemy with whom the family had contested the title to land who had struck him mad, employing as the principal material for their occult art his well-known dread for Ukeleke.

The enemy, they said, had been alarmed at Jeri's growing success with his children; so they decided to rob him of his senses, which was far worse than ending his life immediately, and that before the seeds he had been sowing could germinate and begin to grow. (p. 236)

Another motif which also reveals Munonye's conscious artistry, is the rhythm of evil occurrences in Ukeleke — a rhythm that gives that town the dimension and stature of a character in its own right. It is something definitely new in Munonye and it advances the tragic theme of the novel, adding to its artistic merits. Ukeleke, the land of evil happenings, is a world that no one would wish for. It is a world of nightmare, pain, and confusion, of warped minds and perverted personalities. It is a hell that man has created here on earth, where the machinery of fate is set in motion for Jeri by wicked and evil hands in the form of highway robbers and cheats. Ukeleke is a moral wasteland in whose wilderness lurk human monsters who act as scavengers and beasts of prey. Ukeleke is a land where generosity is mistaken for villainy, where suspicion is rife, and where adults are purveyors of poison to innocent little children. Munonye writes:

Ukeleke, the land of strange people and strange happenings! It was there that an irate father shot at his own son with a gun; and another man, a hunter, bit his dog; and a masked man robbed his own brother, bringing him down from a bicycle with the hooked end of a bamboo stick. Strange things indeed! They made you snap your fingers and shrug your shoulders and exclaim: 'May the good earth forbid!' (p. 9)

It is in Ukeleke that an irate mother charges Jeri with trying to poison her children through his gift of groundnuts. Only the intervention of her husband saves the situation:

'Oil man, please, in your own interest, don't go about giving things to the children of this town. . . . Just last month, somebody came in here, into this very obi, and gave poisoned meat to Nnenna. She's dead now — yes, Nnenna is dead. Ukeleke is bad.' (p. 11)

And it is at Ukeleke that finally Jeri is destroyed. As his mind begins to crack, he never ceases to curse those wicked men from Ukeleke who ruined him, duped him, stole his money and his rented bicycle:

They were real savages and Ukeleke was their home. Evil men! And this tree to which human beings were thus impaled must be evil too. It must henceforth be called an evil tree. (p. 235)

Finally, one must not fail to draw attention to Munonye's use of irony in *Oil Man of Obange*. It is one of the devices that help to structure the novel and lend it form. That Jeri goes insane in the end is part of the novel's ironic design, for no one takes seriously Onugo's incessant nagging that Jeri is behaving like a mad man. It is ironic that the extraordinary success of Jeri's children at school proves his undoing since he cannot cope with the demands placed on his limited resources by their cleverness at school. It is ironic that a responsible and loving parent like Jeri should prefer to deny his own children proper food and shelter (note their leaky roof) in order to invest instead in a doubtful future for each of them. The result is that in Jeri, we have a parent with an unbalanced sense of priorities where his own welfare and that of his children are con-cerned. In order to provide for the long-term welfare of his chil-dren, Jeri irresponsibly neglects their immediate needs, to the point of watching them starve. In the end, there is a touch of tragic irony in the course of action taken by the hero: his most noble intentions drive him to the most ignoble ruin.

I have hinted earlier that Munonye subtly hides the theme of his novel in Mica's school motto, *Da nobis recta sapere*, which reminds us of the Biblical appeal to the Lord to give us the grace to relish what is right. Although Jeri is virtually breaking his back trying to provide for his children's future, Onugo, his sister, does not see it that way when she urges Marcellina, Jeri's wife, to advise her husband 'to stop all this foolishness and attend to his house-hold'. It is a piece of advice loaded with irony, for no parent is busier than Jeri in attending to the needs of his household. But Jeri lacks the grace and the wisdom to relish and discern what is right. There is a touch of ambiguity, even contradiction, in Onugo's advice to Jeri (who is already sinking under the weight of caring for six children) when she tells him: 'children are wealth, Jeri my brother. . . . Get as many of them as possible' (p. 193). To ask Jeri to remarry in order to saddle himself with more children is as well-intentioned as it is foolish. There is a final touch of irony in Onugo's way of helping Jeri. Onugo who goes to considerable expense to repair Jeri's leaky roof, gratis, 'for the sake of the chil-dren', adamantly refuses to lend him a penny to help him pay his children's school fees.

I would like to add some final observations. Oil, the symbol of wealth to which Jeri aspires, seems to provide, in its lubricity, the slippery source for many of Jeri's 'falls'. Even the name of the chief protagonist, Jeri, is a fitting symbol for the man, because the Biblical name — Jeremiah — which he bears, seems an appropriate signpost to the tragic ending. Jeremiah was the weeping prophet, renowned as a prophet of doom and pessimistic about the present, who foresaw a calamitous future.

In conclusion, one must observe that in *Oil Man of Obange*, Munonye has written a novel that might survive him. The canvas is small and compact, the style is lucid, even engaging; the action is emotionally charged and often gnaws at our hearts: the plot reveals proper foreshadowing and motivation. These are qualities which have eluded Munonye in most of his other novels. *Oil Man of Obange* marks a turning-point for the better, in Munonye's novelistic technique.

NOTES

1. Don Carter, 'John Munonye: *The Only Son'*, *African Literature Today*, 3, 1969, p. 54.
2. Charles Larson, *The Emergence of African Fiction*, Bloomington, Indiana, Indiana University Press, 1971 and Macmillan, London 1978.
3. John Munonye, *Oil Man of Obange*, London, Heinemann (AWS 94), 1971; Exeter, NH, Heinemann Inc. (All further page references in the text are to this edition.)

'Les Vies Africaines': A Series of Popular Literature

Alain Fresco

'Les Vies Africaines', a series created by the Nouvelles Editions Africaines, was established to publish individual authors who, under normal circumstances, would not have had the opportunity to see their work in print. From 1974 to 1978, five books have appeared: three autobiographies and two short novels. These are all very short works, ranging from 57 to 176 pages.

Who are these authors? Although biographical information is scant, a few facts are available. One was born in Mauritania, but has become a citizen of Senegal; two are Senegalese by birth; one is from the People's Republic of the Congo; and one is from Niger. The formal academic training of these writers has been very limited. None of them completed the *baccalauréat* degree, which normally opens the door to a university education. The highest grade completed by any of them was the *seconde*, equivalent to our eleventh grade. Thus, none of these writers received the literary training or the university education in Europe enjoyed by the generation of post-independence writers like Mongo Beti, Cheik Aliou Ndao, Halilou Sabbo Mahamadou or Mudimbé. Each of these new writers comes from a working-class background, with the exception of Nafissatou Diallo, whose family is middle class. She is a midwife and directs a clinic that treats pregnant women and their children. Seydou Traoré began as a houseboy and worked himself up to the position of *planton* or messenger in the colonial administration. Moussa Ly Sangaré was trained as a cabinet maker and carpenter. Pierre Biniakounou has held a variety of jobs — typist, customs official, *maître d'hôtel*. He is presently secretary to a hotel chain in Brazzaville.

The first thing that should be noted about this group of books is that they appear to be addressed, not to a European or expatriate readership, but to Africans, who will recognize situations that reflect their daily lives. The style of these works is one that can easily be understood by a semi-literate audience: simple, direct, often sentimental. It is sometimes choppy and lacks nuances; points are laboured and little is left to subtle suggestion. The authors generally choose a straightforward chronological structure. Exception must be made of one work, *Sourd-muet je demande la parole* by Moussa Ly Sangaré, whose diction, prose style, and composition all show a surprising degree of sophistication.

What was the purpose of the authors in writing these books? In the three autobiographies we find an explicit, personal reason given. Nafissatou Diallo tells us in her foreword that she is writing out of nostalgia for her childhood. During a meeting with the author of this article in 1977 in Dakar, she explained that she wrote *De Tilène au plateau* to acquaint her children with the two people who most deeply affected her development — her grandmother and her father. In more general terms, she wrote for the younger generation to preserve for them traditional values that are being eroded by the forces of westernization and modernity. Seydou Traoré likewise writes *25 ans d'escaliers ou la vie d'un planton* to preserve his experiences under colonial rule for his children and their generation. He feels that West Africa has changed so rapidly since independence that he must record a way of life that is already part of the past. His book gives a view of the daily life of a servant who lived in close proximity to important personages of his day and whose travels led him all over West Africa. Like Nafissatou Diallo, he claims to give no more than a purely personal account of his own experiences.

Moussa Ly Sangaré's book, *Sourd-muet je demande la parole*, can perhaps be seen as his way of exorcizing the despair arising from his illness and disability as well as his way of coming to terms with the conditions and events that have formed him.

The two short novels are also based on personally observed situations. *Chômeur à Brazzaville* by Pierre Biniakounou plunges the reader into the disintegrating world of Guillaume Mapouata and his family who are expelled as foreigners from the home they had made themselves in Bulamatadi. Back in their native Brazzaville, they are confronted with unemployment and an increasingly desperate living situation. In *Abboki ou l'appel de la Côte* by

Halilou Sabbo Mahamadou, a short introduction summarizes the severe problems caused by the flight from the countryside to the coastal cities — overcrowding, unemployment, and disease. It is important to note that in none of these books, autobiographies and novels alike, is the white man given much attention. This fact distinguishes this group of works from those of the pre-independence generation of writers, for whom the major conflict was between European and African, colonizer and colonized. These new writers are interested in problems that uniquely concern Africans. What, then, are their most striking themes?

The overriding concern of these authors seems to be the tension between tradition and modernity, the fast pace of westernization and the tremendous pressures which this places upon traditional ways. The modern African city is the arena of this conflict and itself becomes a dominant image for the plight of the individuals caught in this society in transition. The author of *Sourd-muet* evokes the disintegration and dilapidation of the 'popular' quarter of Dakar:[1]

> Tilène was a hotchpotch of boards, bricks, and straw. Dilapidated shanties and straw huts stood side by side, masked on their periphery by houses built of cement.[2]

The quarter is bordered by an open sewage canal along which children play. One character in *Abboki* feels fortunate to be able to share a one-room store as sleeping quarters with his fourteen friends. In these cities, many people are without homes, so they take refuge around mosques and in the commercial districts. The despair of the *sans-logis*, the homeless, who have nowhere left to turn but the poor-house, is portrayed near the end of *Chômeur à Brazzaville*:

> In the corner a man of about sixty, dressed in nothing more than a piece of burlap, was coughing, groaning, and vomiting. A few steps away from him, a woman moaned as she talked in her sleep, and cried aloud as if invisible monsters were trying to strangle her.[3]

This material wretchedness takes its toll on the individuals who are forced by circumstances to live in it. Often the struggle for survival has hardened them to the suffering of others. One character in *Abboki* who has just left his village is bewildered by the cynicism of the city police. He and his friends are detained and then ignored by the police until someone advises them to bribe the officers. This is only the first step which will open the eyes of these peasants to the harsh realities of city life. A veteran traveller warns them that the promises of independence have not been kept. The fact that blacks are in power today is no guarantee that the corruption and abuse of colonial days are over. In the world of the city, money opens all doors and is considered to solve all problems. The city dwellers look down on the new arrivals from the countryside. They resent them because they will compete for the jobs which are already so scarce.

The city can be viewed as an image of moral as well as material decay and misery. Ahmadou, the simple young man from the bush, soon becomes accustomed to the ways of the city and in the process loses his innocence. After his landlord cheats him of his money, he moves to an unsavoury part of town and becomes involved in gambling and black marketeering. He soon forgets his plan to return to his village and instead spends all his money on nightclubs and drinking.

Over and against the problems clustering around the theme of the modern city — the physical destitution, the homelessness, the alienation bred by the dog-eat-dog existence — there stands in all these books the positive element of human relationships which comfort and sustain the individual. There is a solidarity between Moussa Sangaré's mother and the other women who live in the compound, for instance. They know that they can turn to her for advice and even for financial assistance, though her own situation is precarious. In *Abboki*, when one-legged Ahmadou finally does return to his village, his friends and relatives come from the surrounding villages with gifts to show their welcome. In another instance, the village unites to save from humiliation and brutalization three of its members who cannot pay their taxes. Resources are pooled to meet the sum. By supporting one another morally and financially, the village creates a collective bond that enables its members to surmount the crisis.

The family can also be a source of solidarity and support. Let us briefly compare the portrayal of the family in two of the works. In *De Tilène au plateau*, the cohesion of the family is unaffected by the move from Tilène and its dispersion into different locations. Close ties are preserved in spite of the fact that the extended family no longer lives under one roof. Home provides not only bonds of deep affection, but also the moral guidance which permits Nafissatou to meet the challenges of growing up in a modern world.

By contrast, the move undergone by Guillaume Mapouata and his family in *Chômeur à Brazzaville* is presented as the crushing of the family unit by economic and political forces which they cannot control or even fully understand. The progressive deterioration of the family's circumstances is reflected in the quality of their housing. The house in Bulamatadi, which they are forced to leave, is simple but adequate. In Brazzaville, on the other hand, Guillaume, his wife, and their nine children must live in a two-room hut whose straw roof and dilapidated walls eventually crumble after severe rains. The family is reduced to seeking shelter in the public poor-house whose horrifying conditions were described earlier. None of these trials, however, vitiate the bonds of affection which link the family members.

In other works, fragmentation of these bonds does occur. Seydou Traoré describes the effect of his long absence on his relationship with his family. When, after six years, he returns to his village, he realizes that a change has taken place within himself:

> I remained a stranger, as if I were different. I told myself, 'These are your people, your relatives. See how they love you,' but I looked wonderingly at the crackling firewood, at the mats, and my mind turned to light switches.[4]

He feels alienated from these people to whom he can no longer relate and he longs for the comforts of the city. His next visit occurs twenty-two years later. He has not kept in touch with his half-brothers and they had thought he was dead. Alienation can also occur between family members who live together. In *Sourd-muet* we see such distance between Moussa and his mother when, exhausted by her work and discouraged by the difficulty of making ends meet, she withdraws into herself and shuts out her son.

Chômeur à Brazzaville, too, shows how absence and the stresses of poverty can vitiate the ties between blood relatives. When Guillaume returns to Brazzaville, his sister resents that he has not kept in touch while things were going well for him in Bulamatadi. This must partly account for what happens when, one day, he asks her to return the earnings which he had entrusted to her for safe-keeping. She lies to him that she has had to use the money but, actually, she has used the money to buy her son a bicycle so that he can get to school on time. On the one hand, her relationship with her brother has weakened; and on the other hand, she is deeply concerned that her son shall get the education to provide him with a way out of their life of poverty. Thus, she countenances a betrayal of Guillaume's trust.

This group of works offers various resolutions to the conflict between tradition and modernity. *Chômeur à Brazzaville* ends on a note of despair. At the end, Guillaume seeks out a friend who works at the morgue to find out whether anyone who has died may have left a job vacant. A more hopeful perspective is expressed in *De Tilène au plateau*, where Nafissatou manages to resolve the conflict between tradition and modernity in her own life. In her marriage, she departs from convention by choosing the man she will marry, but she follows tradition when she accepts the notion that he will be the head of the family. It is the spirit of the marriage that is new, not its form. By becoming a midwife, she affirms a role traditionally associated with women, but she brings to bear on it her knowledge of modern medical techniques. It is an insight she has learned from her father, that for traditional values to survive they must be integrated into the fabric of modern life.

A similar pattern of resolution occurs in *Abboki*, which concludes that happiness can only be found on one's own soil. It is through their collective efforts that the villagers are able to overcome the problems facing their community. They learn modern agricultural methods and ways to market their crops, realizing that by pooling their resources they can have a greater measure of control over their lives and protect the individual through the support of the group. The village becomes a place where modern values and traditional values come together.

On the whole, then, these books do not possess the literary merits of works produced by former generations of francophone African writers. They have another function. They are important because they depict a society in transition. They constitute a sociological document that reflects the life and concerns of the people of post-independence Africa.

NOTES

1. Since none of these books has been translated, the quotes in this article are my translations.
2. Moussa Ly Sangaré, *Sourd-muet je demande la parole*, Dakar, Les Nouvelles Editions Africaines, 1978, p. 49.
3. Pierre Biniakounou, *Chômeur à Brazzaville*, Dakar, Les Nouvelles Editions Africaines, 1977, p. 75.
4. Seydou Traoré, *25 ans d'escaliers ou la vie d'un planton*, Dakar, Les Nouvelles Editions Africaines, 1975, p. 49.

BIBLIOGRAPHY

Pierre Biniakounou, *Chômeur à Brazzaville*, Dakar, Les Nouvelles Editions Africaines, 1978.

Nafissatou Diallo, *De Tilène au plateau: Une Enfance dakaroise*, Dakar, Les Nouvelles Editions Africaines, 1975.

Halilou Sabbo Mahamadou, *Abboki ou l'appel de la Côte*, Dakar, Les Nouvelles Editions Africaines, 1978.

Moussa Ly Sangaré, *Sourd-muet je demande la parole*, Dakar, Les Nouvelles Editions Africaines, 1978.

Seydou Traoré, *25 ans d'escalier ou la vie d'un planton*, Dakar, Les Nouvelles Editions Africaines, 1975.

Reviews

N. D. Williams, *Ikael Torass*, Havana, Casa de la Americas, 1976, 501pp.

N. D. Williams, the author of *Ikael Torass*, was born in the Republic of Guyana. He taught briefly in the University of the West Indies. Williams has published several short stories which have earned him gold medals in the Jamaica Festival (Literary) Competition. *Ikael Torass* is Williams's first full-length novel and won the prize for the novel in the 'Casa de las Americas' competition of 1976.

Ikael Torass is a novel in the picaresque tradition — a going-away, a journey into the unknown. The protagonist, Michael Abensetts, starts out on a journey of escape and rejection which turns out to be a miniature *Pilgrim's Progress* as Michael's journey, when viewed in proper perspective, is more important spiritually than physically. Physically he travels only from his small Caribbean island to Jamaica but, psychologically, Michael travels through many significant social experiences and situations.

The first part of *Ikael Torass* is entitled 'The Departurists'. Michael is departing from his island not so much to 'further his studies' as to escape from his father and the new post-independence bourgeoisie to which he belongs by accident of birth and for which he harbours only resentment and contempt.

The novel opens with Michael's journey to the airport. Gradually, through his personal reflections, a picture of his background emerges — his father, Minister of Interior, pseudo-intellectual, a 'man of the people', is both corrupt and false. We also have a picture of Michael's childhood — being brought up by a desiccated spinster aunt who taught music to middle-class daughters. Michael shows his early resentment of class by his determination:

> to lure one of those music pupils to my room and . . . rape her till she
> gave up the whole thing, turned nymphomaniacal with urges and left
> home to sing raucous calypsos in nightclubs. (p. 38)

But easy as it seems to plan this rape of bourgeois society, it is not as
simple in realization:

> it became so frustrating that had I a crowbar I would have clouted her
> twice on the head and walked out instead of trying to pry apart her
> heavy legs . . . Skully Wilson didn't have half that trouble with his
> women. (p. 39)

Skully Wilson, one of the main characters of this work, is representative of the masses — the dispossessed. Skully Wilson shows a
vitality that is denied Michael and his kind. This contrast is portrayed on a macroscopic scale in the two rival schools, Montrose
and St Francis. St Francis always lost to Montrose. Transplanted to
St Francis, Skully failed; he came in a loser, booted down the social
slide by the brutality of his frustrated father and the insensitivity
and lack of sympathy of an equally frustrated teacher, who resented
Skully as a reflection of his own shortcomings.

Other characters who significantly participate in the unfolding
of Michael's island background are Anna, the effeminate library
assistant, whose father was rumoured to be a visiting officer on a
British warship, and Mrs Valentine, the librarian:

> She was the nearest our island came to boasting of *landed aristocracy*,
> with a line you could trace through her light complexion to someone
> English, vastly propertied and rampant among the slave women. (p. 28)

Mrs Valentine is one of the society women of the island and her
conversation with Anna brings out their narrow preoccupations.
For Michael, their interest is completely alien even to him who
'belonged':

> our island might be small but there are times when you stand next to
> some people and you can't help overhearing what they are saying and
> you feel that they belong to a completely different world which had to
> be somewhere far out there. (p. 29)

This cultural preoccupation between the mulattos is encountered
again later on in Michael's meeting with the 'octaroons' in the
second part of the novel. It is not just a coincidental mention but
rather a critical exposure of a racial attitude in the West Indies in

general — a superiority claimed by these people of mixed race which in turns sparks off in others a burning desire to lighten the race and sometimes induces black people to bleach their hair blond in an effort to copy their blond and blue-eyed ideal — a manifestation of a deep-rooted complex born of complete subjection and humiliation over the years.

If we are to accept young Michael's judgement, his island is indeed in a sad state. The new ruling class is so out of tune with the realities of their situation that one wonders what future lies ahead of their island. The sons go away to one or other developed country to 'further their studies' and come back in a year unrecognizably changed in manner and irresponsibly critical of all their heritage stands for.

The fathers too are no better. Michael's father provokes in his son a strong anti-establishment feeling and one cannot but sympathize with such a reaction in a young man who is faced with stories of his father's philandering, and other stories like the nauseating one of the Cabinet minister who, after being blackmailed by his fellow ministers, 'allows his wife to be pleasured' to satisfy the whims of an American investor:

> And so that came to pass as did many other happenings too revolting for any intelligent person to pursue further, lest it turned out to be true. (p. 61)

Michael, fittingly enough, leaves home after a traumatic experience. He has let down his school friend Skully Wilson in his greatest hour of need and, as it were, put the final nail in the coffin that has been so consistently fashioned in Skully's life by people like Mr Robotham, their teacher and by Skully's own father.

Michael misses his plane and is thrown into the company of two fellow-voyagers in distress: Xavier Nasciminento and Teleta, through whom the author opens another window on the West Indian world. Nasciminento is a present-day buccaneer of the Guyanese backwoods, whose presence in the novel opens spicy vignettes to the reader; at the end of the plane-ride he disappears from view for good like the bright butterfly that he is. Teleta, the Indian girl, however, represents a more constant factor in the scheme of things. She is representative of the Indian population in the West Indies. Teleta and her elder brother are rebels who have decided to break away from an attitude which is neatly summed up by her:

> ... We used to live in an area with black people. But in the night
> when we finished playing, he [their father] used to question Sonson
> and me, ask us about the neighbours how they live and what they
> do ... And then he used to say some terrible things about black peo-
> ple — yet he never stopped us from playing. Until the riots, some-
> body threaten Pa, but that was all. But suddenly he didn't want us
> talking to the neighbours and I mustn't go out with black boys ... he
> didn't want no black man intefering with his daughter. (p. 120)

Yet he too was harbouring incestuous thoughts about his daughter,
as was his brother. The wealthier Indians try to form themselves
into an aristocracy, a perpetuation of the 'old raj', but as Teleta says:

> At least an aristocracy can claim to be intelligent and educated. All
> these people have is money and a bag of borrowed manners ... they
> have nothing but contempt for other people ... It's as though they're
> from another world — the television world ... (p. 161)

These people in reality have nothing but an 'image' which they
have created for themselves.

Indeed, most of the characters of this world have an 'image' to
preserve — it is, as a popular Jamaican song puts it, a 'synthetic
world': 'P.C.' and his 'tankside', Johnstone, the young assistant
lecturer carefully planning his way up the social ladder; Albertine
the female lecturer carefully guarding her independence behind a
show of outer hardness — the hard polished shell of a tortoise that
conceals the soft vulnerable parts. We are not totally surprised (or
are we?) when Albertine finally cracks. Albertine is a revolutionary, a rebel in her own way which she symbolizes by her
passion for her visit to Haiti and her dressing in African gowns.
But inside, Albertine is lost and groping in a disoriented world
and when she has to face her real situation, her inner frustration
is poignantly compressed into her simple 'I am so afraid' (p.
345). What is Albertine afraid of? Obviously no physical danger,
but a lack of a sense of direction, for despite all her seeming
independence and 'capableness' she is like a child groping in the
dark — lost in the limbo of a 'colonial imperfect'. As one of the
characters in the novel puts it:

> there is no gulf between us, Michael, that's the illusion of our social
> architects: it's the horrible void within us that's real, left entirely on our
> own. (p. 215)

Albertine's frustrations, her class frustrations, are revealed in the almost cathartic love-making that follows:

> ... There were no soft gentle first caresses, just hungry sloppy kisses then a truly frightening embrace, a desperate clinging as though we were caught in the middle of rapids rushing to the brink, the canoe overturned: we could do nothing but clasp each other and wait for the sudden dip, the empty spinning dive over the edge ... We went into sex with clawing screaming limbs saying no to death's brink and swimming back upstream with all we had for a second chance at life. (p. 346)

In fact, Michael Abensetts and Albertine Latiboudiere have much in common. Both come from the new bourgeoisie, the former by birth — a 'colonial imperfect' trapped into his situation by the accident of birth — and the latter by both birth and achievement. Names have a significant part to play in the portrayal: it is the Latiboudieres, Abensetts, Robothams and Haughtons against the Wilsons, Ims, Jubbas and Sybils.

Im, Jubba and Sybil are in fact Michael's introduction to the other side of Jamaican or rather West Indian society. His meeting with Jubba is an almost psychic experience:

> I felt a strange coolness come over me, as if my body was being lowered into a pool ... it was as if all the organs, the tissues, all the wires that kept my body functioning had suddenly stopped ... (p. 274)

Jubba takes Michael to a part of the city that even words like 'ghetto' or 'shanty town' cannot adequately describe:

> the whole area looked more like a vast abandoned rubbish yard; the people part of the daily truck dumpings that accumulated over the years.

Jubba gradually emerges as a person like any other who lives and loves and possesses the strength and weakness of a normal human being, beneath his 'image' of the hairy-chested, tough, 'cool rider'.

The marks on Jubba's back and his story of how he got them, tell a chilling tale of police brutality, a story which is confirmed by T-man and his group. But these happenings are not of much interest to the 'other side' of the island society. These wretched people never had a chance and the others could not care less. The 'haves' are like Albertine who had:

this disconcerting tendency to cruise through the choppy waters of life not bothered seriously by anything. The buffet, the Roman orgy, the theatre all simply happened; you washed up the next day and said a prayer to God and the police force. [Albertine] had to be impossibly callous or blinkered; there were control knobs set to automatic where her heart, her mind or her conscience should be. (pp. 389–90)

Im, the Christ, finally draws Michael into the fold of the Rastafari: a people so wretched and oppressed that 'they have reached a point where the only thing left for them to do was to sing praises to His Imperial Majesty Haile Selassie, and hope for freedom one day from Babylonian oppression. . . . ' Im fittingly baptizes Michael, Ikael. After his baptism there is no turning back. After leaving Albertine's flat:

I aimed to where I thought the highest hill stopped short to touching the sky, and with all the fearful power I had never used before I screamed, IKAEL! IKAEL! TORASS! (p. 428)

To 'rass' with 'Michael' and all it had stood for! This is an interesting pun as Michael uses the word 'rass' in such a way that it could mean the Ethiopian 'ras' — a term of high respect and identification with Africa — or it could mean the more earthy West Indian use of the word 'rass'.

Part III of *Ikael Torass* is centred on Michael's brief stay with the Rastafarians: Ras Alphonsus, Sybil, Jah Mighty, and Vivienne who, though dead, exerts a very strong presence. This is the consummation of Michael's or, rather, Ikael's adventures. These island people have lost their roots:

Black man loses him way. Cause four hundred years rob 'im of spiritual consciousness, make him lust for the flesh and for material things. (p. 471)

But they are groping back to find spiritual roots — back to Africa symbolized by Ethiopia; they have directed their religious energy into deifying Haile Selassie who for them symbolizes the Africa they have lost and long for. In their interpretation of the Bible these Rastafarians see themselves as the true children of Israel and Haile Selassie as the promised leader who has been sent by divine wisdom to free the children of Jah (God) from bondage in Babylon (the affluent society).

Also in this last chapter of the novel we again meet the 'Departurist', Teleta, who has throughout been an irrepressible spirit but is now in a hospital psychiatric ward under observation. Michael, after spending a session at the university without doing any academic work, prepares to go home on a boat as does Teleta; not eager students rushing home, but rather traumatized individuals creeping reluctantly back to their rejected past. Has Michael made any progress? Has he cast off the guilt of his society? In a way he is still unresolved: probably another case of someone who might have 'developed into something'. His future is unsure but certainly he has not rid himself of his social chains. He is confused, not resolved. Society has triumphed once again.

Ikael Torass is a highly readable work which takes a hard relevant look at West Indian society. Williams says of two of his characters:

> they might have been practitioners of a sort with scalpels for intellects; they worked on other people to remove terrible flaws the way a dentist removes a decaying molar; only they held up the offending foible high to the light and gloated. (p. 334)

This statement could be essentially a summary of his own attitude to his society in *Ikael Torass*; only he does not gloat, but he certainly holds up the offending social foibles to the light.

Ikael Torass in many ways could be interpreted as a critique of the new middle-class African society. There is a class identification rather than a regional character phenomenon. Despite the physical distance between the West Indies and Africa, one easily identifies characteristics of the 'colonial imperfect' bred of the same system. In fact the world of island intellectuals depicted in *Ikael Torass* is strongly reminiscent of its parallel in Wole Soyinka's *The Interpreters*. It is the same world of borrowed manners and inconsistent postures. Also, certain aspects of the conflict between traditional values echo Chinua Achebe's *No Longer At Ease*. A one-to-one correlation of attitudes and situations cannot be too easily identified but the cross-currents are strongly evident, indissolubly linking two peoples with one past.

Francis B. Rosenior

Bode Sowande, *Farewell to Babylon*, Longman Drumbeat, 1979, 179 pp.

The volume *Farewell to Babylon*, includes three of the plays of the Nigerian Bode Sowande, who is certainly one of the most promising of the new generation of African dramatists. It also lends support to the view that social and political comment is becoming the dominant preoccupation of contemporary African drama. The first play, *The Night Before*, brings together a group of recent university graduates for their usual palm-wine-drinking ritual on the eve of their graduation ceremony. It is clear that the ritual on this occasion is going to act as an eye-opener, revealing clearly to the young graduates the complacency and ineffectiveness of the university as an agent of change, the bleakness of their own prospects for the future, and the general decadence of their society. The Babylon of the title carries the same connotations here which it has come to hold in protest songs and literature: it represents an oppressive, inhuman, unfair and totally corrupt system which sensitive minds are convinced must be destroyed.

The effect of the system is poignantly demonstrated in the case of Moro the articulate student who, like Soyinka's Sekoni, goes mad with frustration and disillusionment. This incident in the past has a profound effect on many of the recent graduates in the present, and also colours their outlook for the future. Throughout the play there is an insistence on society's corruption, stupidity, nepotism and incompetence. There is also a realization among the young graduates that every minute of this particular night matters. In this connection, the reader notes the importance of the symbolism of nakedness which is also linked with the idea of rebirth. For this is a night during which all the characters are symbolically stripped naked and forced to face the truth not only about their society, but also about themselves. They must come to terms with the roles they have all played in the past, but they must also prepare themselves for the future; hence the idea of rebirth. The symbol of building is also pervasive in the play. In a sense, these new graduates are all future builders of their society, but the significance of the symbol is inverted, for the young people are not permitted to build. One young engineer, for instance, who makes grandiose plans for a new public highway is told by a corrupt and unprogressive boss to merely 'touch up' an existing footpath. Similarly, the idea of rebirth, far from signifying hope, means disillusionment for most of them. Thus Dabira discovers that his girlfriend has been secretly in love with another friend, and symbolically burns his graduation gown. In the light of this the Vice-chancellor's graduation speech, with its fulsome platitudes, takes on grimly ironic significance:

> You must face life with the vigour of the reborn. You are the privileged ones. You are the chosen few. Go out and minister unto your nation, the virile and tender plant of today, the strong and mighty baobab of tomorrow. Turn the old hut into a skyscraper, the lake into a dam. Build a straight road from a footpath and lead mankind to progress, because progress is the watchword of today. (pp. 46–7)

Though Sowande is aware of the idealism of his young graduates, he is not blind to their defects. As undergraduates their conversation about politics consists of jargon, slogans and meaningless catch-phrases. Their election campaign is disorganized, and one potential leader, Moniran, is confused about his objectives and consequently ineffective. They are generally presented as idealistic and well-meaning but ill-informed and impractical.

There are varying degrees of sensitivity among the new graduates. The least sensitive is Nibidi who refuses to face up to the serious implications of this last night before their graduation day, seeing the acquisition of a university degree only in terms of the social prestige and material aggrandizement that it will bring. He is determined to make his way in this corrupt contemporary society and acquire all the artefacts that are the marks of success. In a play which lays so much stress on the importance of the past and its relationship with the present and future, Nibidi is determined to forget the past, for the past can be inconvenient. One flashback to his student days shows him in an altogether degraded situation, where his failure to communicate because he has adopted an alien and pretentious speech pattern is disastrous. Some may see him as a realist; others merely as an opportunist. Another character, Moniran, shows his sensitivity by not wishing to get involved in Nibidi's rat-race and acknowledging the importance of the past. But he is intellectually timid. Onita, the brilliant student who gets a first-class honours degree, is the most idealistic and the most sensitive. He shows a capacity for feeling, and is fully aware of his country's predicament and unwilling to compromise his principles. He, more than anyone else, is aware of the pressures of the past on the present. The only ray of hope the play holds out resides in the union of Onita and Ibilola; it is in this that Onita finds his rebirth.

Farewell to Babylon is a sequel to The Night Before. In this play, the revolution which was foreshadowed in the earlier one becomes an actual fact, as sensitive minds mobilize their forces to overthrow a dictatorial regime and create an alternative society. Two leading characters in the earlier play recur in this one, and it is a tribute to Sowande's power of characterization that their development is quite consistent with what might have been expected. Thus the brilliant, sensitive and idealistic Onita has matured into a doctor of philosophy who, refusing to compromise his principles and endorse an inhuman system, has resigned from his university position and now lives entirely by his books. Everyone, including the crude muscle-man and Commissioner of Counter-Insurgency Kaago, is eventually impressed by Onita's sincerity and honesty. Nor are we surprised to find that the intellectually timid Moniran has apparently compromised himself and now works for the regime as head of state security. He did not have enough moral courage to dissociate himself completely from the system at the start of his career, so he readily acquiesced and has worked his way gradually up the ladder to become head of state security, the most important arm in the regime's network of repression. But Moniran has retained sufficient sensitivity to be still disgusted with the system; unknown to most people, he is working secretly for its overthrow, and he eventually succeeds in his design. Both Moniran and Onita have the same end in view, the difference between them is only one of means. The honest Onita is prepared to take his stand courageously and unequivocally against corruption and tyranny, while Moniran prefers to undermine the system from within.

Indeed the play throws into sharp relief the problem of the African intellectual in an oppressive and inhuman society. He could, like the insensitive Nibidi of The Night Before, throw in his lot completely with the system; or he could, like Moniran, pretend to co-operate with the system while undermining it or attempting to reform it from within. In this case his motives are likely to be misunderstood, as Moniran's are by Onita who accuses him of having lost the idealism of their student days. But even if he openly declares his hostility to a system which he nevertheless seems powerless to reform, he could so easily appear to the insensitive to be opting out and under-utilizing talents which could otherwise bring some benefit to his countrymen. This is exactly how Cookie, the homicidal band-leader, sees Onita. In the end, it seems that only Moniran's method offers any hope of success.

The play is mostly concerned with the relationship between the former friends Moniran and Onita, who are now apparently on opposite sides, and the revolt of the farmers which acts as the springboard to successful revolution. As head of state security, it is the duty of Moniran to interrogate Onita who is suspected of instigating the revolt. This enables Sowande to expose the terrible realities of life in dictatorial African regimes: the platitudinous ideologies which merely provide a cover for oppression; the sycophants like Majidun who grow prosperous out of their exploitation of the people's misery; the inhumanities of detention without trial and the brutalization of the individual that can result from such detention. The head of state, the Field-Marshal who is responsible for such mindless brutality, makes only one appearance in the play, but his sinister influence is felt throughout. His grotesque antics suggest that Sowande modelled him on Uganda's Amin.

The third play, *A Sanctus for Women* is based on a Yoruba folk-tale. When Olurombi who has been reduced to poverty, offers her only daughter to the service of a god in return for material prosperity, she does not realize the full implications of the oath — that the god will later claim the life of her daughter. The author informs us that the story is still used by the Yoruba as one of the warnings against spiritual immaturity under the threat of aggressive materialism. However, his play exemplifies the difficulty of transforming the folk-tale into a realistic drama carrying conviction. The folk-tale, with its simplification of character and its insistence on rigid moral opposites, creates a different atmosphere from the drama which thrives precisely on human complexity. It is difficult to see in Olurombi a spiritually immature woman who condemns herself by entering into a bond in order to achieve material prosperity, and who should therefore serve as a lesson to posterity. What the play powerfully demonstrates is a woman who is reduced to poverty by the schemes of the wicked and the indifference of her society and who agrees to the pact because she has no alternative. If there is any lesson to be learnt from this play it is about the harshness and complacency of a society that connives with the wicked to reduce the good to misery.

Sowande's dramatic technique in all three plays suggests that he belongs to the mainstream of modern drama as a whole and African drama in particular. He demonstrates a very sound knowledge of modern theatrical techniques. All three plays require very skilful and imaginative use of lighting. There is no break in the action and therefore no time for scenery to be changed. All the required scenery is therefore on the stage simultaneously, the producer merely focusing the lights on the relevant set. The use of lighting has to be all the more skilful since, in the first two plays especially, there are several unobtrusive excursions into the past. For instance, in *The Night Before* there is a flashback to the enactment of Moro's experiences as a student and another to the student elections. In *Farewell to Babylon* there is an equally unobtrusive flashback to Onita's encounter with the young female student. However, the change of scene does not involve new actors; the same actors merely switch roles automatically.

Occasionally Sowande contrives to have two or more situations going on simultaneously. In *Farewell to Babylon*, for instance, Moniran is discovered on his own in a prison scene, but at the same time the lights are focused on the Field-Marshal and one of his henchmen in another scene, while the scene in the prison cell with Onita, Yulli and Cookie continues. The three different scenes are indicated by spotlight, but the action in two of them is mimed while conversation and singing go on in the cell scene. Sowande's stage directions suggest simple sets with suggestive backdrops. All the plays invite audience participation. The characters in *The Night Before* try to involve the audience by addressing them directly, and in *Farewell to Babylon* the audience is expected to participate in the singing of 'We shall Overcome'.

All three plays unmistakably convey an African atmosphere. Very skilful use is made of singing, dancing, drumming and miming and this helps to reinforce the ritualistic aura. Indeed, *A Sanctus for Women* thrives on the re-enactment of a ritual, while central actions of *The Night Before* and *Farewell to Babylon* are presented in the form of ritual. *Farewell to Babylon* even includes a pantomime re-enacting a folk-tale about the elephant and the tortoise. And the relevance of the pantomime is obvious since the relationship between the 'King' elephant and the tortoise is exactly the same as that between dictatorial African leaders and their people.

Perhaps it is on his manipulation of the language that Sowande could be faulted. His rural characters do not always carry conviction when they use the English language. Would a character like Olurombi, who operates entirely within rural traditional society, ever refer to 'a vague sense of optimism' or say: 'There is a monologue that a poor man always engages in. It is his sense of consciousness'? And Korii, another villager, talks of the 'anaemic eclipse of vision'. This is not even the language of English conversation. Of course, we all know that in real life Sowande's characters would have used Yoruba, but then the rendering of it in English should reflect their social situation.

These, however, are small faults. Sowande's exploration of themes and deployment of techniques surely make him one of the most exciting African dramatists writing at the moment.

Eustace Palmer

Donald Burness, *Fire: Six Writers from Angola, Mozambique and Cape Verde*, Washington DC, Three Continents Press, 1977, 144pp.

In Third World countries, the attainment of independence from the colonial master is usually followed by a rash of literary output. The shackled mind pours out its venom against the oppressor, zealously welcomes the opportunity, rarely known in the past, to explore new grounds of imagination and art, and presents to the world with pride notions and forms that have long been imprisoned. The phenomenon of internal literary activity is usually matched by the external, sudden interest in the newly liberated land. Critics descend upon the virgin land like vultures, devouring everything in sight, not out of a genuine desire to educate the public about their prey, but largely through the very human wish to make a name; for after all the niche of being pioneers and discoverers has always been revered by humanity.

Now, it is common knowledge that Portugal until recent times has been a harsh master on the African continent, obstinately and desperately clinging to her acquisitions, rich sources of human and material instruments. Britain withdrew to her royal island. France also returned to her beloved *métropole*. It is true that those two departures have sometimes seemed dubious, especially as the Commonwealth and the Common Market, as well as *Coopération* (the French word has always had a special ring, a peculiar connotation to it) have continued to wax stronger despite the criticism against neo-colonialism by 'civilized' children of the ex-colonies. But the fact is, Britain and France left, while Portugal stayed. The final departure of the latter came dramatically and the shocked world almost forgot the suffering masses of the liberated lands in the excitement and sensationalism of the occasion. No wonder, for Portugal, it must be said, has never been a 'normal' nation.

Just as she proved different in her colonial system, so has she acted extraordinarily in the realm of literature. First, contrary to my general remarks in the opening paragraph above, a well-established literature has existed in Angola, Mozambique and Cape Verde, even while the Portuguese were clamping down on everyone and everything in sight. Moreover, despite the emergence of the new nations, there has not been the literary 'gold rush' that one would have expected. This dearth of publication is not however symptomatic of a lack of interest in Luso-African Studies. Rather, it is, to this critic's mind, indicative of an authentic desire on the part of many a scholar to thoroughly digest the material available before analysing it. It may also be due to the fact that the vehicle of communication in the area concerned is not accessible to many students of African literature.

Donald Burness is one of those scholars fortunate enough to know the Portuguese language and to be sincerely committed to the interpretation and dissemination of Lusophone African literature. His book, *Fire: Six Writers from Angola, Mozambique, and Cape Verde* (Washington, DC, Three Continents Press, 1977), clearly reveals those qualities that exceed the superficial attitude of the white liberal observing black literature as a sort of exotic pastime. In a short but well-documented introduction, Burness addresses himself to the subject of Portuguese colonialism and the particular situation of Lusophone African writers who lack the international recognition enjoyed by their French-speaking and English-speaking brothers. 'The Lusophone writer, 'states the critic, 'is an anomaly in Africa.' An anomaly, not only because of the obscurity to which he has been condemned, but also because the colonialist racist domination of which he has been a victim differs from that undergone by the Francophone and Anglophone writers. Indeed, much of the reader's interest in reading Burness's work stems from such statements as: 'As a result of the large *mestiço* population in Lusophone Africa, a unique situation was created and this situation is reflected in the literature.' The surprises pile up rather quickly: racist tendencies of whites in a Portuguese-African community were minimal or far less than one would imagine; due to the authenticity and commitment of their writings for the black cause, certain white writers are often mistaken for black, and no less a luminary than Léopold Sédar Senghor has made such a mistake; white Portuguese artists have moved permanently to Africa and now constitute an integral part of 'African literary voices'.

As further introduction to his critical work, Burness makes a distinction between the situation in Cape Verde on the one hand, and Angola and Mozambique on the other. In the former, 'an altogether unique culture', over two-thirds of the population are *mestiço* and real bilingualism (Portuguese and Crioulo) exists. In fact, a unique Crioulo culture has developed on those islands and there is a noticeable absence of sentiments of negritude. The opposite is seen in the writers of Angola and Mozambique. Burness is quick to point out, however, that all three ex-colonies have a common socio-politico-cultural posture that rejects Portuguese domination.

The cultural synthesis affirmed in the literature under consideration is fully substantiated by the critic's choice of writers, a mixture of two blacks, one white and three *mestiços*. The first artist, J. Luandino Vieira, is white and already in the introduction, Burness has quoted an essential statement by him: 'Certainly a white man can be an African writer.' The critic immediately supports that by giving us a short biographical note. Vieira, whose poor family had emigrated to Angola, spent his childhood in *musseques* (a kind of ghetto) and grew up to become an active worker in the Popular Movement for the Liberation of Angola. Vieira's novels and stories describe life in the Angolan *musseque*, depicting the pauper's sufferings and human nature. Burness studies several works and deduces that Vieira has largely contributed to the birth of a modern Angolan literature: use of 'language as a dynamic means of perception'; invention of words; a realistic look at childhood and a love for *'nossa terra de Luanda'* (our land of Luanda).

The second writer studied is the Angolan president, Agostinho Neto, a black who has written militant poetry. As Burness mentions, Neto's importance is underscored by his choice of the hard life inside Angola during the years of the struggle for independence, instead of a sweet sojourn of exile in some European haven. Neto's poetry goes hand-in-hand with his political life and his literary output is a projection of his fight for national liberation. The earlier poems, full of descriptions of victims, we are told, are dominated by the image of night. The 1960s poems are especially verses of combat. Burness traces the evolution of the Angolan nationalist struggle through Neto's poetry. The verdict: the poet-president is fully committed. Individual love hardly exists for Neto as a theme. For love is a luxury. Neto writes about his love for his people, of his land and of liberty. And he writes primarily for his people.

Next comes the essay on Geraldo Bessa Victor, a mulatto, whose poems, apolitical in contrast to his compatriot Neto's, express a 'gentle negritude' built upon a belief in the value of African culture and in a future world of brotherhood among all men. Burness states: '[Victor] does not shout; he does not cry out — rather he sings sad songs of human folly and canticles of joy.' The images are: children, white and black, playing together, devoid of the inhibitions and hatred of adults; cultural harmony destroyed by the intrusion of adults into the child's world; man and woman in love, celebrating life; the vagabond poet singing of love to deaf ears. Victor, acknowledged as 'a modern master of the Portuguese language', uses rhyme very effectively and also exhibits his mastery in the short story. Here, the centrepiece is the suburbs of Luanda where African culture has been sadly lost, where blacks hate each other and revere the *mestiço*, where illegitimate children of mulatto fathers abound. Burness, in his analysis, uses Frantz Fanon to explain the cultural schizophrenia of some of Victor's characters and also calls our attention to the influence of Portuguese society on the writer (the element of *saudade*, the yearning after something seemingly unattainable).

The fourth writer examined is Mario Antonio, another Angolan mulatto whose literary output has evolved from early poetry about the people of Luanda to a later imagery of abstracts suggesting 'endless labyrinthine corridors'. Antonio's work is fraught with an underlying melancholy: love is transitory; then there is the poet's alienation from his African roots, and his flight to Europe into which he is not completely integrated. Burness emphasizes the African aspect of the man's writings and examines a short-story collection (*Mahezu*, 1966) that reflects African wisdom. What sets Antonio apart from the others in the text is that, in his case, *mestiço* is not a happy resolution of two cultures, but an alienation from both. Indeed, it is worth mentioning that the writer under consideration has the least claim to being included in Burness's very useful study.

Baltasar Lopes of the Cape Verde Islands is the fifth writer. The paradox of the Cape Verdean Islands lies in the combination of a very inhospitable geographical setting with an ideal social existence. Manuel Ferreira, quoted by Burness and contributor of an excellent Afterword to the text, calls the islands 'the most perfect example of racial harmony that the world has yet known'. Lopes, a mulatto, represents that unique element, the blending of Euro-African cultures into something original and culturally viable, exceeding the restrictive scope of racial codification. Lopes is a short-story writer and a poet, who captures the mystery of the sea, depicting the continuity of life, celebrating the image of the mother and, especially in his stories, analysing the psychological anguish and agonies of lonely women and children.

According to Burness, the short stories penned by Lopes are a microcosm of the world portrayed by the author in his only novel, *Chiquinho*, which the critic studies at length. That Crioulo world 'in which belief in orthodox Catholicism and stories of witchcraft are harmoniously blended' reminds us of the Haitian society where Voodoo and Catholicism form part of the peasant syncretism. *Chiquinho* is a novel of suffering and deprivation in Cape Verde, of emigration of the hero overseas and a return home marked by alienation and inadaptability, of dreams of America, symbol of prosperity and unspecified potentialities. The novel is 'the tragedy of a land continually ravaged by starvation', a long *morna*, that is, a tearful song expressing man's illusion and disillusion. Burness points out several autobiographical elements in Lopes's novel, particularly the 'lifelong commitment to literature and social progress'. It is however not clear where, exactly, the critic's verification of that 'progressive' element comes from in reading the novel. Perhaps the most revealing statement of his study on Lopes concerns the women of the stories compared to the man of *Chiquinho*: while the latter have the opportunity to escape, to seek freedom far from home, the women appear to be in a cul-de-sac, imprisoned as they are in their destiny of desolation.

The final study is on Luis Bernardo Honwana, a black Mozambican prose-writer who has published only one collection of short stories (translated into English as *We Killed Mangy-Dog*). Here is Burness's comment on the writer: 'He never raises his voice to scold. In fact, he seldom speaks directly of the fears, the isolation, the repressed hatred and the frustrations that his people face.' In spite of the soft tone, however, the stories vividly depict the sordid realities of colonial life: economic exploitation, racism with its attendant barbarity and inhumanity. The title story, about a dog, is rightly analysed by Burness as the portrayal of the social life of the colony: the cowardliness of the whites bent on destroying the blacks to prove their strength and superiority, and the often forced complicity of blacks in the dehumanizing process.

Burness's final statement on Honwana is rather controversial, commending as it does the writer's sympathy for old men and women who have endured, 'and made it possible for a later generation to change the direction of society in Mozambique'. Such support for what the critic terms 'understated social protest' will no doubt arouse the ire of many a revolutionary in whose opinion the older generation was often too passive before the monstrous master. The forced smile visible on the faces of Honwana's old folk does hide their deep suffering; but it could also be a symbol of their complicity with the oppressor. We must mention that images of such old men exist elsewhere in black literature and that the black writer, even while understanding the plight of such individuals, does not always condone their action. A poignant example is the celebrated poem of Aimé Césaire, *Cahier d'un retour au pays natal*: with the birth of a new day, with the arrival of the new revolution among the black race, the poet himself newly returned after his psychological alienation from the roots, shouts his happiness at the death of his grandfather, symbol of the old negritude (that is, the former, colonized, 'chosified' existence of the negro in the colony). Césaire mentions the contrast between his viewpoint and that of the colonizer, in whose eyes the grandfather is 'a good negro, a real good negro'. The essential point is, that to the African mind, a man smiling at the white man who dehumanizes him cannot be glorified for his act.

Indeed, that is part of the criticism that we find imperative to make about *Fire*. Due to his deeply felt attachment to the literature under discussion, the critic at times seems to gloss over certain areas where negative elements exist. Criticism turns into complicity, analysis gives way to adulation. Fortunately, Burness mostly maintains an even keel. While still on the point of criticism gone astray, let us address ourselves to a couple of other examples taken from the text. The first concerns the work of Baltasar Lopes whose novel, *Chiquinho*, is discussed at length by Burness. It is our belief that the critic attaches too much of an optimistic outlook to that work. If it is true that tragedy does not reign supreme, that all hope is not lost, it is no less true that Lopes does not really offer any concrete way out to his characters. Does emigrating to America constitute social progress? Is there hope in this seemingly endless circular motion? Burness mentions the element of tragedy but then tries to remove emphasis from it.

The other objection concerns the essay on Bessa Victor, that great Angolan writer influenced by the Portuguese *saudade*. Here again, the critic appears to over-emphasize the optimistic aspects. The *saudade* yearning for a seemingly unattainable objective is in itself often symptomatic of deep pessimism, of hidden frustrations, of a basically tragic posture. The themes of Victor's stories reveal that less-than-optimistic outlook. Racism, forced illicit love, schizophrenia, are hardly topics to warm anyone's heart. And a brief study of the eight poems of Victor's translated by Burness (pp. 108–25) helps to prove that point further. In 'That old mulemba', the poet laments the destruction of an old tree that used to provide him as a child with shade. But the tree is more than that: it symbolizes refuge, consolation, companionship:

> Once as a boy
> I tugged at the mustaches of my old grandfather;
> he gave a slap,
> so that my black face turned red.
> So, for many years, day after day,
> I used to pull the branches of the old mulemba,
> out of them I made a swing to play. (*Fire*, p. 111)

So, the poem's theme is childhood solitude and suffering, followed by adult disillusion. The child was happy once, but that did not last. And it is significant that the momentary joy was furnished, not by a human being — the grandfather slapped his face — but by a tree: 'I alone know what makes me suffer.'

Another poem, 'I am again a child', portrays the child. Once more, there is the underlying sadness, the fear — 'the formal dance was a forbidden dream'. An escape is brought about by a mysterious transfiguration:

> I am again a child;
> Seen again my child's smock;
> but now without fear of the night
> neither of men nor of anything. (*Fire*, p. 115)

The child is free of all restrictions and laws. He is not yet a part of the society with its traditions. He plays his music merrily along the streets, filling people's souls with joy. However, as in the former poem, the instant does not last. It is all a dream — that is an adult projecting his view back into the long-lost past — and when he wakes up, he will return to the world of reality. For the adult, it is already a world of illusion or, rather, of disillusion.

Manuel Ferreira's Afterword, as we have stated, is an excellent addition to the very good work already done by Donald Burness.

Professor of African Literature at the University of Lisbon, Ferreira, in less than ten pages, fully convinces the reader about the uniqueness of African literature in Portuguese, of its 'profound national and nationalistic stamp', and its freedom from ambiguity. What the essay adds to the text is, first, a broadening of scope, a comparative effort to substantiate the viability of that literature as black: Lusophone African and Afro-American/Antillean; Cape Verdean/Brazilian; Angolan/Mozambican. Further — and it is of immense importance — Ferreira examines the absence of a literature in Afro-Portuguese, 'no longer the standard Portuguese language but a language marked by ruptures and restructuring'. His conclusion: there is hope for the birth of such a literature.

Meanwhile, Portuguese-African literature is managing to reach the masses through its strong national and nationalistic basis. As Burness has shown, the poetry of Neto, for example, is well-known to people on the streets of Luanda. A poetry sung by commoners; verses whistled with relish by soldiers: 'In Neto's words, the dreams of Angola are expressed.'

Part of those dreams, not different from those of the Mozambicans and from the dream-become-reality of the Cape Verdeans, is the desire for a society not based on race or colour but on social and cultural unity. That, no doubt, is one of the points of contact between a Neto, an Antonio, a Victor, a Vieira, and a Césaire, a Roumain, a Guillen, a Hughes. In a lot of ways, 'everything on earth is darkness' (Neto, in *Fire*, p. 22). Memories of slavery continue:

> And I saw
> And I saw rows of slaves in the bush
> And I saw black men crying in the holds of slave ships. (Antonio, *Fire*, p. 59)

But, already, in spite of those signs of negation and the resilience and inventiveness of purveyors of evil, glimpses of harmony exist. Love of children:

> Neither black children nor white children,
> but children
> Neither canticles of the slave nor songs of the master
> but only hymns
> of love. (Victor, *Fire*, p. 39)

The message of the black poet rings out clear:

The black poet brings to the world a message of love and brotherhood.
(Victor, *Fire*, p. 119)

Harmony between black and white, between Africa and Europe:

> my poet's soul
> — a hybrid soul, luso-tropical
> discerns signs of Africa
> in the gesture of the white child
> and visions of Europe
> in the look of the black child. (Victor, *Fire*, p. 117)

Unfortunately, as of now, the African's 'visions of Europe' outstrip by far the 'signs of Africa in the gesture of the white child'.

Femi Ojo-Ade

D. I. Nwoga, ed., *Literature and Modern West African Culture*,
Benin City, Ethiope Publishing Corporation, 1978, 148pp.

Collating and editing collections of critical essays is usually a painstaking task. It demands sharp critical acumen, unqualified editorial skills, and a rigorous, sustained effort. In short, it is not a leisurely arm-chair affair, and certainly not a task for the amateur. Only the able and the hardworking professional can bring such a task to successful fruition.

The editor of the above book of essays, *Literature and Modern West African Culture* has quite frankly done a qualified editorial job. The book has serious shortcomings, not in its physical format but in its content. In general, some of the essays are thin in ideas, a rehearsal of old and familiar issues, and a few are ill-conceived and poorly executed. If the editor had been more discriminating and tough-minded in his selection, in other words, if he had made excellence his primary and indispensable criterion, he would have deleted some of the essays published here. While not all the essays in this book are mediocre, the mediocre, especially those included for reasons other than their literary qualities, outnumber the competent.

Specifically, *Literature and Modern West African Culture* is composed of ten essays written for the most part by established Africanists such as E. N. Obiechina, Kolawole Ogungbesan, D. I. Nwoga and R. N. Egudu. These essays are coherently grouped into the following four related parts: Part I, the writer and commitment; Part II, the traditional literary artist and his society; Part III, the writer and the West African past; and Part IV, the writer and the West African present. It must be stressed here that although the various critics explore different and unique aspects of the literature and culture, and at times arrive at conflicting conclusions, they do share the belief that West African literature is a vital human activity that reflects, explores and shapes West African culture and values and that the diachronic (interdisciplinary) rather than the conventional synchronic approach is more responsive to a study of the literature.

The question of African writers' ideological commitment has been one of the recurring, controversial issues in the criticism of African literature. Appropriately, two articles in this book, 'The Modern Writer and Commitment' by Kolawole Ogungbesan, and 'From Commitment to Essence' by Kalu Uka, vigorously (and in the case of Kalu viscerally) address this thorny issue. Of the two essays, Kolawole's is more incisive and informed. Although some of his ideas, especially the dialectical relationship between art and society and between the writer and socio-political ideologies, are familiar ones, he restates them with persuasive competence and conviction. His discussion of the role of the artist and of the politician is both refreshing and illuminating. Echoing J. P. Clark, he states:

> If he [the writer] feels more committed to politics, he should go into politics or write political tracts. As a writer, he must write as best he can, dedicate himself to 'a writer's morality', which includes holding allegiance to individual human beings instead of race or cause. (p. 18)

On the other hand, Kalu, a Marxist critic, views the role of the African writer quite differently. Eclectically citing several 'politically committed' contemporary Russian and western writers to buttress his position, he proposes that African writers should play the roles of legislators, prophets of the future, monitors of values and propagandists. He states:

> If the writer must be committed and we must all agree he ought to be, he must fit into some kind of practical programme for action. Because he is an intellectual and a writer . . . but is committed to truth as he sees it, he must so shape his action that his own integrity is preserved at the same time that he influences policy. He must confront those in power with

criteria by which their actions as government must be judged. (pp. 21–2)

Attractive as Kalu's Marxist view of the writer and the socio-political ideologies the writer should champion might appear, it has serious and damaging limitations. He seems uninformed about the proper role of the writer — which is to explore, define, and render in significant form vital human experiences. The writer's aim is not to legislate or prescribe national policy, but to bring us an added sense and perception of life; to widen and sharpen our contacts with vital human experiences. Furthermore, to pro-gramme writers, and to legislate for them what views they should champion, as Kalu insists, is, as I have stated elsewhere,[1] to encourage a rigid, stereotyped mode of perception and same-ness in articulation — culminating in the tyranny of uniformity and the consequent castration of the literature. The simple truth that seems to elude Kalu and those who share his skewed views is that fickle ideological tracts do not constitute great and com-pelling literature. Along with Kalu's heretical misconception of the role of the creative writer and the function of literature (which in his view should be used as an instrument for defining and modulating national policies), the whole essay is fraught with fallacies, contradictions, incoherence and mawkishness.

Of the non-theoretical essays, 'Perception of Colonialism in West African Literature', in which the main focus is on Yambo Ouologuem's controversial novel, *Bound to Violence*, is the most impressive. Obiechina's ideas are well thought out and elegantly presented. I must hasten to add here that this is the most insightful analysis of the novel I have read so far. Here, Obiechina does not only go beyond the usual Achebe-like stereotyped, uninformed response to the novel (see Achebe 'Thoughts on the African Novel' in *Morning Yet on Creation Day*, London, Heinemann, 1975, pp. 49–54), he deals with the novel on its own terms as a significant artistic-historical document. While demonstrating the uniqueness of the novel (both in content and style) in the corpus of African literature, he convincingly establishes the fact that such novels of 'self apprehension' have a place in modern West African literature. 'Escape to romantic fantasy is no way for a continent to grow up by coming to terms with the past of its history,' he perceptively states.

There are two other essays in this book that are insightful: 'Litera-ture as History: Crisis, Violence and Strategies of Commitment in Nigerian Writing', by Samuel Asein, and 'Religion in Modern West

African Poetry' by Donatus I. Nwoga. On the other hand, 'Igbo Traditional Poetry and Family Relationships' by R. N. Egudu is for the most part a superficial ethnological evaluation of Igbo poetry. Although Igbo traditional poetry reflects the social-philosophical and moral values of the Igbo people, it is essentially a work of art — work in which the artist is concerned not only with the content of the art but also, and more importantly, with how the content is shaped into a living artistic whole. To disregard the formal literary elements of the poetry, as does Egudu in his stagey evaluation, is to undermine the living artistic vitality of Igbo traditional poetry. Igbo traditional poetry should be studied as a living organism rather than a museum piece of extinct civilization.

All in all, *Literature and Modern West African Culture* contains valuable and insightful essays on West African literature and culture. However, these are too few and far between to make the book an important contribution to the study and appreciation of West African literature and culture.

Solomon Iyasere

NOTES

1. In 'Modern African Literature: The Question of Ideological Commitment', *West African Journal of Modern Languages*, 2, (1976).

J. Voorhoeve, ed., *Trefossa*, Paramaribo, Bureau Volkslectuur, 1977.

Trefossa, the pseudonym of the Surinamese poet, Hennie de Ziel, was undoubtedly one of the greatest Creole poets. He is practically unknown outside the geographical confines of Surinam and sadly, remembered by only a few people in the former colonial territory, the Netherlands. Few Dutch scholars of literature, let alone poets, are aware of the fact that Trefossa spent a considerable portion of his life in Holland and is actually buried in the city of Haarlem. One of the persons largely responsible for the propagation of Surinamese Creole literature and language in Holland, Professor J. Voorhoeve, was intimately acquainted with Trefossa for many years. In fact, Voorhoeve was what one might call symbiotically involved with Surinamese Creoles and Creole literature for the last twenty years. This posthumous anthology was intended as a eulogy to a poet and friend. It was Trefossa who indicated the vast linguistic possibilities locked up within Sranan Tongo in the mid-1940s. He, with Papa Koenders,[1] helped to reject the 'nigger tongue' aura which formerly surrounded the Surinamese Creole language. The efforts of poets like Trefossa and essayists of the stature of Koenders pre-empted movements such as *Wie Eegie Sani*[1] (Our Own Things) among the younger generation in Amsterdam in the early 1950s.

This posthumous homage is far more extensive than the two pages dedicated to Trefossa in *Creole Drum* (1975). There is an introduction by the creologist, Professor Voorhoeve, followed by a discussion by Ronnie Klimsop, a man who knew Trefossa very well. Towards the end, there are one or two analytical passages by Voorhoeve and the Surinamese author, Albert Helman — a very knowledgeable cast indeed. Unfortunately, some of the shortcomings of this anthology, as it is so modestly called, may reside precisely in this division of labour. It is certainly responsible for the rather disjointed impression this publication makes on the reader.

Trefossa was remarkable in more than one respect. He, for instance, kept a diary in a society which was largely preliterate. This in itself might give rise to the hope that more of the man would be revealed. Klimsop, who acknowledges an emotional and intellectual debt to Trefossa, does the student of Surinamese Creole literature a disservice by either censoring or withholding information at times. One suspects, nay knows for certain, that this has been done to protect living descendants and out of shame and embarrassment. For example, in Trefossa's diary of 19 January 1936, one reads (Voorhoeve, J., ed., 1977):[2]

> For especially these days, I was besieged by a strong urge to go and work in order to earn money, because I can no longer bear to witness the poverty mother finds herself in. (p. 26)

One would have liked to know more about Trefossa's personal relationship with his mother, his family circumstances, and the effect all this had or might have had on the poet. Instead, one is left completely in the dark. The reader is presented with what I would like to call a biographical laundry list, in which one finds out how much Trefossa earned as a student nurse, a teacher, a head-master. This may very well be of interest to the educated in an independent

Surinam, but contributes nothing to an understanding of Trefossa, the man and poet.

One learns further, that the poet underwent a rather strict Christian education. According to Klimsop, the series of Christmas poems towards the end of Trefossa's life, are directly traceable to these early Christian influences. The poet had a great admiration for his grandfather. He comes over as a withdrawn child who was fond of books in a society which did not cater for such luxuries if one was black. He was a sensitive youngster and teacher who was deeply involved in his work. At times, an almost ethereal quality and lyricism is evident in his diary. He himself writes 'I would like to be like a good and well-written and beautiful book in the community which could be of use to people' (p. 21).[3]

The well-known poem 'Bro' (Repose), is contained in his notes of 3 January 1933. That Trefossa was an exceptional personality within the Surinamese context is further illustrated by one of his ex-teachers, Mr Lauriers:

> I got to know Hennie de Ziel in 1932 . . . Hennie was one of my pupils (sixth class). I was struck by his polish and friendliness. . . . He loved making speeches. . . . He was a very sensitive young man who cared a lot for honest friendship'. (pp. 23–4)[4]

Trefossa worked variously as a male nurse, librarian and teacher. He was forced by ill-health and, according to Klimsop, the moral decay and decadence in Surinam, to return to Holland for good. While in Holland, he was encouraged by Professor Voorhoeve to work on the diaries of the bush negro prophet Johannes King and to prepare it for publication.

Trefossa's remarks on the Surinamese language and literature are very illuminating when seen in the proper historical context. In a personal conversation with Klimsop he maintained:

> We transplant our personal uncertainties about the Dutch language onto our pupils without realizing it. The painful thing is that we do not know or do not wish to know that we are uncertain in our attitude towards the Dutch language. We handle the language differently from the thoroughbred Dutchman, and that, to my mind, is the most natural thing in the world. But we must be prepared to face the consequences of all this. (pp. 33–4)[5]

The poet gives a detailed and interesting account of language and culture within the sociological framework of Surinam. It is an eloquent plea for the use of their own (Creole) language, although Trefossa was the last person to deny the value of Dutch as a language. In a sense, his plea was also a political one, for the question of language in a colonial or post-colonial situation is fundamental in a country trying to carve out its own cultural identity. Of Sranan Tongo he wrote:

> It is deeply immoral to neglect or kill a cultural phenomenon (a language) born out of interchange and historical circumstances of the entire society. Under no circumstances whatsoever should one do so, even if it means that we would add a few problems to our existence. (p. 37)[6]

Trefossa's poems can, in my opinion, generally be divided into (1) poems of reflection, the earlier 'Bro' (Repose); (2) poems of national and historic interest, 'Joli coeur' and 'Refensi'; (3) political poems, 'Nanga wan ai'; (4) poems of exile, 'Kopenhagen' and 'Mi go — M'e kon'; (5) lyrical poems, 'Yu ay'; (6) poems concerning the act of creativity, 'Wan troe poewema' and 'Santa'; and (7), what I would like to call his Christological poems, 'Hoemor in èksèlsis', 'Pin-pin Jesus' and 'Josef ori-tjar Maria'. To Trefossa, a 'true poem was a struggle unto death'. Rightly does Voorhoeve comment in his foreword that the act of creativity was literally a process of re-creation. His struggle to write in Creole (Sranan Tongo) was also a blow against the Dutch colonial policy. This theme of a deadly struggle is reiterated in the poem 'Santa':

> No one
> shall know my sadness
> if this unwritten scrap
> shall wait in vain
> because I did not delve far enough
> to fill my pen
> with the black
> of my deep blood. (p. 46)[7]

The creative act was, in the case of Trefossa, an historical and a political act. He reminds one of the South African poet, James Matthews, for whom the creative act was even more of a political act (Matthews, J. and Thomas, G., 1972):

> It is said
> that poets write of beauty

of form, of flowers and of love
but the words I write
are of pain and rage. (p. 1)

The Afro-American poet and dramatist, Le Roi Jones (Baraka)
speaks of 'poems that kill'.

Of the poems of exile as I call them, the two most cited are, 'Mi go
— M'e kon' and 'Kopenhagen'. Voorhoeve has given an extensive
analysis of the latter poem in a publication called *Trotji* (1957). The
central theme in 'Kopenhagen' is about a mermaid and in particular, the statue of the mermaid in the harbour of Copenhagen. The
subtle way in which the poet uses the Danish mermaid to highlight
a peculiarly Surinamese cultural situation is one of the striking
features of this poem. Trefossa starts off with the image of the
mermaid in a western milieu and then proceeds to establish a
Surinamese context. He knows the mermaid but is surprised to find
her in Europe. Surinam also has such a symbol, yet there are
significant cultural differences. After the initial shock, the poet
informs his readers that the Surinamese mermaid has a golden
comb on its head. The deception is unmasked. The authentic mermaid is still in Surinam. Thus a well-known European landmark
affords the poet a chance to delve into his Surinamese background.
It also reveals his loneliness and longing for home.

The second poem, 'Mi go — M'e kon', deals even more explicitly
with the trauma of exile. Trefossa describes a Creole who is a
product of cultural ambivalence, ensconced between his Dutch-
ness as a result of colonialism on the one hand, and his Surinam-
eseness on the other. This duality is amusingly reflected in the
image of the different types of food eaten by the Dutch and the
Surinamese, that is potatoes as opposed to boyo (Voorhoeve, J., and
Lichtveld, U., eds., 1975):[8]

Sister Mina potatoes are so nice
But your boyo has no peer. (p. 205)

In 'Nanga wàn ai', Trefossa strongly fulminates against the hypo-
crites who deceive people but enrich themselves:

with one eye they look
as if they're doing good work,
with the other eye
they carry on their underhand business . . . (p. 80)[9]

He can write lyrically as in 'Yu ay' (Voorhoeve, J., and Lichtveld, U., eds., 1975):[10]

> Thy hair frames thy face
> so festively,
> like when the dry season is about to dawn. (p. 207)

And threateningly in 'Wan enkri gado-momenti' (Voorhoeve, J. and Lichtveld, U., eds., 1975):[11]

> Woe unto me
> when I don't succeed
> to penetrate
> time's hide. (p. 203)

Towards the end of his life, Trefossa wrote a sequence of Christological poems. Voorhoeve maintains in his foreword that the poet had at last found the right form (presumably, inner harmony and the right combination of harmony and theme). Helman, the Surinamese novelist, gives a very penetrating analysis of at least one of these poems, namely, 'Hoemor in èksèlsis'. He shows how Trefossa resorts to the typical sonnet form of the western European tradition, detecting parallels between Trefossa's poem and Schiller's epic poems. At the same time, he points out how specifically Surinamese the poem is in parts. Trefossa wrote a humorous poem. Yet his humour is neither bitingly sarcastic nor vehemently anti-clerical as in the case of the French Antillean negritude poets during the 1930s. It is the laughter of someone who is free from ideological restraints and arises out of what Helman calls, 'freedom and self-liberation'.

There are, however, several questions which arise in reading through these religious poems. Since Trefossa was, in my opinion, a poet of no mean ability, I would like to formulate my doubts in a series of questions. (1) Are these religious poems a logical outpouring of the inner harmony and creativity suggested by Voorhoeve? Or is it the poet's increasing awareness of approaching death — an acceptance of the inevitable? (2) One notices the frequent use of the word *pikin, manpikin* in relation to *Maria*. Are we dealing with a form of regression — the man become child at the end? Is the accent on *manpikin* — *Maria* so accidental? (3) Does one detect a childlike mother binding? Possibly, Trefossa's reference to his mother in his diary is not entirely innocuous. Should the *Engeline* in *Auffahr-*

tikon not be looked upon as an extension of the *pikin* — *Maria* relationship? It is noticeable that there is no reference whatsoever to Trefossa's father.

Trefossa was a great poet and will hopefully one day be known to other teachers of African, Afro-Caribbean and Afro-American literature. I can find no more fitting tribute to this Surinamese Creole poet than the following lines from his poem 'Gronmama':

I am not myself
as long as my roots
don't penetrate, don't shoot,
earth mother of mine
into your heart. (p. 50)[12]

V. A. February

NOTES

1. For further information on Koenders and *Wie Eegie Sani*, consult the English translations of V. A. February in *Creole Drum*, Voorhoeve, J., and Lichtveld, U., eds., Yale, 1975.
2. All further page references are to this edition. Original quote in Dutch: 'Want juist dezer dagen kwam geweldige drang in me op om te werken en geld te verdienen, omdat ik niet langer kan aanzien de armoede en ellende waarin moeder verkeert.'
3. Original Dutch quote: 'Ik wil in de samenleving zijn als een goed en mooi geschreven boek, waaraan mensen iets hebben.'
4. Original quote: 'Ik heb Hennie de Ziel leren kennen in 1932 . . . Hennie behoorde toen tot èèn van mijn leerlingen (6e klas). Hij viel op door door zijn beschaafdheid en vriendelijkheid . . . Hij hield veel van speechen . . . Hij was een uiterst gevoelige jongeman die onnoemelijk veel gaf om "goede" vriendschap.'
5. Original Dutch quote: 'Onze onzekerheid m.b.t. het Nederlands brengen wij op onze leerlingen over zonder het zelf te beseffen. Het pijnlijke is dat velen van ons niet weten of niet willen weten, dat we in onze houding t.o.v. het Nederlands onzeker zijn. Wij hanteren die taal anders dan de geboren Nederlander en dat is volgens mij de meest natuurlijke zaak van de wereld, maar wij moeten bereid gevonden worden om konsekwenties hieraan te verbinden.'
6. Original Dutch quote: 'Het is diep immoreel om een cultuurverschijnsel(een taal) geboren uit wisselwerking en geschiedenis van de gehele gemeenschap, te verwaarlozen of te doden. Om geen enkele reden zou men dat mogen doen, dus ook niet omdat het aan onze problemen nog enkele zou toevoegen.'

7. Original Creole poem:
   no wan sma
   sa sab mi sari,
   te na krin papira disi
   sa wakt f' soso
   foe di m' doekroen fara nofo
   foe foeroe mi pen
   nanga na braka
   foe mi dipi broedoe.
8. Original lines in the poem 'Mi go — M'e kon':
   -s'sa Mina, ptata bun,
   -ma boyo fu yu kir-kiri . . .
9. Original lines in the poem 'Nanga wàn ai':
   nanga wàn ai d'e loekoe
   lek d'e doe den wroko boemoe,
   nanga a trawan d'e nogosi
   wan kron-kron nogosi,
   foe lai den botri.
10. Original lines in the poem 'Yu ay':
    Edewiwiri lontu yu fesi
    so prisiri,
    lek te dreyten e kon.
11. Original lines in the poem 'Wan enkri gado-momenti . . . '
    elu fu mi!
    ef mi no doro
    fu boro
    buba fu ten
12. Original lines in the Creole poem 'Gronmama':
    mi a no mi
    solanga mi loetoe
    n'e saka, n'e soetoe
    mi gronmama, te na joe ati.
Note: all translations are by V. A. February.

BIBLIOGRAPHY

1. Matthews, J. and Thomas, G., *Cry Rage*, Johannesburg, Ravan Press, 1972.
2. Voorhoeve, J., ed., *puëma fu Trefossa — Trotji*, Amsterdam Noord-Hollandsche Uitgevers-Maatschappij, 1957.
3. Voorhoeve, J. and Lichtveld, U., eds., *Creole Drum*. English Translations by V. A. February, New Haven, Yale University Press, 1975.
4. Voorhoeve, J., ed., *Trefossa*, Paramaribo, Surinam, Bureau Volkslectuur, 1977.

I. N. C. Aniebo, *The Journey Within*, London, Heinemann (AWS
206), 1978, 242pp.

One of Aniebo's major concerns as a writer is the exploration of the
meaning of human existence. The theme runs through many of his
short stories and his other novel *The Anonymity of Sacrifice* (London, Heinemann, AWS 148, 1974).

In *The Journey Within* he uses the marital experiences of two
Igbo couples, Christian and Janet, Nelson and Ejiaka in dealing
with the theme. Christian and Janet have been married in the
Christian church while Nelson and Ejiaka have contracted the
traditional Igbo marriage. Aniebo contrasts the two types of marriage in terms of their relevance to the African's search for self-
fulfilment in life. The former works against the interests of the
African while the latter helps him to cope with the pressures of
everyday existence. Christian and Janet have never lived happily as
a couple; consequently, Christian is so shattered as a person that
'he did not know what he was doing when he ran out naked and
was struck by a car' (p. xiii) and Janet is portrayed as being so
helpless in life that she even falls into the hands of rapists. On the
contrary, Nelson and Ejiaka are relatively happy, probably because
Nelson gets a second wife and Ejiaka, after initially protesting
against it, has to accept her new status. Aniebo is a cultural
nationalist who furiously rebels against western values.

This attitude is reflected in his narrative technique. The story
starts with the prologue 'End/Begin', which announces the marital
problems of Okechukwu and elucidates the nature of Christian's
death. The rest of the narrative is an extended flashback (with other
flashbacks incorporated into it) centring on the early childhood
days of Okechukwu and the marital experiences of Christian and
Janet, Nelson and Ejiaka. The short prologue therefore encompas-
ses events which chronologically have taken place several years
before. By serving both as the end of the narrative and its beginning, it has the effect of portraying life as a repetitive pattern of
human follies, in which mortals grope endlessly for values that
could give meaning to existence through satisfying relationships
in marriage.

The quest for these values is structured around events taking
place in urban and rural environments. Urban life derives its force

from values imported from the West, while rural life is rooted in those of African civilization. The author presents the urban setting of the novel with great impatience: he does not allow the characters to live their lives. In other words, he obtrusively condemns western civilization; he does not fully use dialogue and description to reveal the attitudes of his characters to external reality, a technique that the inner logic of the novel calls for. On the other hand, he feels quite at home in depicting the rural setting of the work: dialogue and description are generally woven into the fabric of the narrative, and the interior monologue is carefully manipulated here. The *ogbanje* scene is remarkable; the author uses various strategies to make it come to life and to suggest that it is a viable counterpart to European systems of religious beliefs.

Aniebo's world-view borders on the absurd and often makes one think of Camus. He seems to be saying that the internal patterns of man remain the same in spite of changes in his environment. The quest for happiness is a constant phenomenon of life. The task will be easier for the African if he models his behaviour on values emanating from African social institutions.

Aniebo does not, however, blend the various elements of the novel (the theme of marriage, reflections on life, dialogue, description, and the moving train) to bring out this world-view. His dialogue is particularly monotonous and boring, for it is not generally related to characterization and the development of plot.

This weakness does not, however, obscure his strength; his keen sense of observation; and his use of language to reflect the African setting of his fictional world.

Chukwudi T. Maduka

Cumulative Index of Volumes 1–12

Carol Bundy

All figures in **bold** refer to issue number.
All figures in roman refer to pages in that issue.
Index entries for individual authors are arranged with general references alongside individual's name, then sub-headings grouped as follows:

(i) articles in ALT by/about the individual
(ii) book reviews in ALT by the individual
(iii) other topics/references
(iv) works by the individual.

Lightning Source UK Ltd.
Milton Keynes UK
UKHW021958281122
413003UK00012B/719